Related Books of Interest

Mobile Strategy
How Your Company Can Win by Embracing Mobile Technologies

By Dirk Nicol

ISBN-10: 0-13-309491-X
ISBN-13: 978-0-13-309491-6

Mobile Strategy gives IT leaders the ability to transform their business by offering all the guidance they need to navigate this complex landscape, leverage its opportunities, and protect their investments along the way. IBM's Dirk Nicol clearly explains key trends and issues across the entire mobile project lifecycle. He offers insights critical to evaluating mobile technologies, supporting BYOD, and integrating mobile, cloud, social, and big data. Throughout, you'll find proven best practices based on real-world case studies from his extensive experience with IBM's enterprise customers.

Modern Web Development with IBM WebSphere
Developing, Deploying, and Managing Mobile and Multi-Platform Apps

By Kyle Brown, Roland Barcia, Karl Bishop, Matthew Perrins

ISBN-10: 0-13-306703-3
ISBN-13: 978-0-13-306703-3

This guide presents a coherent strategy for building modern mobile/web applications that are fast, responsive, interactive, reusable, maintainable, extensible, and a pleasure to use.

Using well-crafted examples, the authors introduce best practices for MobileFirst development, helping you create apps that work superbly on mobile devices and add features on conventional browsers. Throughout, you'll learn better ways to deliver Web 2.0 apps with HTML/JavaScript front ends, RESTful Web Services, and persistent data. Proven by IBM and its customers, the approach covered in this book leads to more successful mobile/web applications—and more effective development teams.

W9-DIF-426

Related Books of Interest

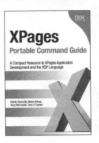

Mastering XPages
IBM's Best-Selling Guide to XPages Development—Now Updated and Expanded for Lotus Notes/ Domino 9.0.1

By Martin Donnelly, Mark Wallace, Tony McGuckin

ISBN-10: 0-13-337337-1
ISBN-13: 978-0-13-337337-0

Three key members of the IBM XPages team have brought together comprehensive knowledge for delivering outstanding solutions. They have added several hundred pages of new content, including four new chapters. Drawing on their unsurpassed experience, they present new tips, samples, and best practices reflecting the platform's growing maturity. Writing for both XPages newcomers and experts, they cover the entire project lifecycle, including problem debugging, performance optimization, and application scalability.

XPages Portable Command Guide
A Practical Primer for XPages Application Development, Debugging, and Performance

By Martin Donnelly, Maire Kehoe, Tony McGuckin, Dan O'Connor

ISBN-10: 0-13-294305-0
ISBN-13: 978-0-13-294305-5

A perfect portable XPages quick reference for every working developer. Straight from the experts at IBM®, *XPages Portable Command Guide* offers fast access to working code, tested solutions, expert tips, and example-driven best practices. Drawing on their unsurpassed experience as IBM XPages lead developers and customer consultants, the authors explore many lesser known facets of the XPages runtime, illuminating these capabilities with dozens of examples that solve specific XPages development problems. Using their easy-to-adapt code examples, you can develop XPages solutions with outstanding performance, scalability, flexibility, efficiency, reliability, and value.

Related Books of Interest

XPages Extension Library
A Step-by-Step Guide to the Next Generation of XPages Components

By Paul Hannan, Declan Sciolla-Lynch, Jeremy Hodge, Paul Withers, Tim Tripcony
ISBN-10: 0-13-290181-1
ISBN-13: 978-0-13-290181-9

XPages Extension Library is the first and only complete guide to Domino development with this library; it's the best manifestation yet of the underlying XPages Extensibility Framework. Complementing the popular *Mastering XPages*, it gives XPages developers complete information for taking full advantage of the new components from IBM.

Combining reference material and practical use cases, the authors offer step-by-step guidance for installing and configuring the XPages Extension Library and using its state-of-the-art applications infrastructure to quickly create rich web applications with outstanding user experiences.

SOA Governance
Achieving and Sustaining Business and IT Agility

Brown, Laird, Gee, Mitra
ISBN: 978-0-13-714746-5

Being Agile
Eleven Breakthrough Techniques to Keep You from "Waterfalling Backward"

Ekas, Will
ISBN: 978-0-13-337562-6

Common Information Models for an Open, Analytical, and Agile World

Chessell, Sivakumar, Wolfson, Hogg, Harishankar
ISBN: 978-0-13-336615-0

Disciplined Agile Delivery
A Practitioner's Guide to Agile Software Delivery in the Enterprise

Ambler, Lines
ISBN: 978-0-13-281013-5

Getting Started with Data Science
Making Sense of Data with Analytics

Haider
ISBN: 978-0-13-399102-4

Patterns of Information Management

Chessell, Smith
ISBN: 978-0-13-315550-1

Social Media Analytics

IBM PRESS

Social Media Analytics

Techniques and Insights for Extracting Business Value Out of Social Media

Matthew Ganis
Avinash Kohirkar

IBM Press
Pearson plc

New York • Boston • Indianapolis • San Francisco
Toronto • Montreal • London • Munich • Paris • Madrid
Cape Town • Sydney • Tokyo • Singapore • Mexico City

ibmpressbooks.com

IBM Press Program Managers: Steven M. Stansel, Ellice Uffer

Cover design: IBM Corporation

Associate Publisher: Dave Dusthimer

Marketing Manager: Dan Powell

Executive Editor: Mary Beth Ray

Editorial Assistant: Vanessa Evans

Development Editor: Box Twelve Communications

Technical Editors: Deborah DeLosa, Ajay Raina

Managing Editor: Kristy Hart

Designer: Alan Clements

Project Editor: Andy Beaster

Copy Editor: Chuck Hutchinson

Indexer: Ken Johnson

Senior Compositor: Gloria Schurick

Proofreader: Sarah Kearns

Manufacturing Buyer: Dan Uhrig

Published by Pearson plc

Publishing as IBM Press

For information about buying this title in bulk quantities, or for special sales opportunities (which may include electronic versions; custom cover designs; and content particular to your business, training goals, marketing focus, or branding interests), please contact our corporate sales department at corpsales@pearsoned.com or (800) 382-3419.

For government sales inquiries, please contact governmentsales@pearsoned.com.

For questions about sales outside the U.S., please contact international@pearsoned.com.

Library of Congress Control Number: 2015949068

ISBN-13: 978-0-13-389256-7
ISBN-10: 0-13-389256-5

Text printed in the United States on recycled paper at R.R. Donnelley in Crawfordsville, Indiana.
First printing: December 2015

To the Ganis Gang—Always and Forever

—Matt Ganis

I dedicate this book to my mother, a person who has given me so much and who at age 80 is still one of the most inquisitive persons I know!

—Avinash Kohirkar

Contents

Appendices

Foreword

In the decade since social networking was born, we have seen the power of platforms that unite humanity. Across our professional and personal lives, social platforms have truly changed the world. Social media has been the tool to ignite revolutions and elections, deliver real-time news, connect people and interests, and of course, drive commerce. In 2005, industry analysts were skeptical about how blogging and its successors could ever be used in business; today every single social channel has both B2C and B2B offerings sprinkled generously throughout the content.

As businesses figured out that they could use social networks to interact directly with their customers and prospects, questions were immediately generated about efficacy and ROI. Was it just hype and noise, or were new audiences being reached and new opportunities created? For the first several years, the only way to answer these questions was anecdotally. Many brands and businesses viewed social media warily, feeling that nothing good could come from engaging in online discussions directly.

Things changed as the technology matured to offer tools for social listening. Whether for business, politics, or news, organizations learned they could identify trends and patterns in all the flotsam and jetsam of online content. Another leap forward occurred as analytics engines were applied to the vast stream of unstructured data, when suddenly big-picture profiles and behaviors could be identified.

Today, organizations of all sizes and missions are looking for ways to make sense of the information available on the social web. Analyzing social media, the right way at least, is now just as important as a brand presence or advertising strategy. When done correctly, the insights available can shape decisions, make organizations more responsive, and quell negative press before it takes off.

In *Social Media Analytics*, Matt Ganis and Avinash Kohirkar have set out a thorough approach to gaining business insights from social media. Matt and Avinash understand this challenge. Each has built his career on data analysis and insights, and they have specifically looked at social content for the last several years. They have examined key vectors of social participation, including reach, eminence, engagement, and activation. They understand how to filter out noise and focus on relevant insight, building the right tools and conducting the right studies to demonstrate trends, correlations, and results.

Social Media Analytics provides much-needed understanding of both what can be accomplished by examining social streams and why such insights matter. In the first part, the book looks at data identification, sources, determining relevancy, and time horizons. In Part II, several chapters explain ways to find data—what tools, how to understand output, and getting deep into the insights themselves. Part III goes further into interpreting data, looking at potential shortcomings of social analysis and useful ways of sharing insight through visualization.

Social media has evolved quickly from the initial hype, through the naysayers, and to a point where it is no longer viewed as optional. Today, however, there are so many social channels, devising a strategy for sharing and leveraging the online conversation can make the difference between success and failure.

I invite you to think back nostalgically to the days of focus groups, printed surveys, and controlled messages. As those tools of the past have faded out, they've been replaced with a veritable deluge of information. *Social Media Analytics* will help you devise the right strategy to make data-driven decisions rather than reacting to that one nasty tweet, looking at the overall story your customers and prospects are sharing online.

Ed Brill
Vice President, Social Business
IBM Corporation
Chicago, September 2015

Preface: Mining for Gold (or Digging in the Mud)

In *The Adventure of the Six Napoleons* by Arthur Conan Doyle, the famous sleuth Sherlock Holmes remarks to his sidekick, Watson:

> "The Press, Watson, is a most valuable institution, if you only know how to use it."

That statement, when applied to the wealth of data in social media channels today (loosely, "the press"), has never been more true. Companies are always looking for an "edge" in an attempt to find ways to remain relevant to their ever more vocal set of constituents. They are struggling to position themselves as trusted advisors or suppliers in a cut-throat environment of competitors, where consumers use public opinion (both good and bad) to share information and experiences at the speed of light (literally). When looking to explore this deluge of social media data, we must think and act like detectives. Careful investigations can, at times, lead to many revealing insights. This can be both time consuming and complex; it is work that requires a careful, methodical effort and not only requires patience and perseverance, but at times also requires a creative streak or spark of insight.

This book, aimed at executives (or analysts) responsible for understanding public opinion, brand management, and public perceptions, attempts to look at the processes and insights needed when attempting to answer questions within this massive amount of unstructured data we call *social media*.

Just What Do We Mean When We Say Social Media?

A social media website doesn't just give you information, but rather it is built around a way to interact with you while allowing access to the information. This interaction could be collecting comments or suggestions on a blog or voting on a specific topic—allowing users to have a voice in a conversation as opposed to simply reading others' opinions—this is why we call it a *social media conversation*.

Think of print media or a static web page or website as a one-way street, much like reading a newspaper or listening to a report on television; you have very limited ability to give your thoughts on the matter. (Radio talk shows at least allow users to call in to express their opinions—although ultimately they have the ability to limit the conversation by cutting off the call at any point.) Social media can be considered a two-way street that enables communication between end users. Social media gives users on the Internet the ability to express their opinions and interact with each other at speeds unheard of in the past with traditional media. This popularity of social media continues to grow at an exponential rate.

Why Look at This Data?

Consider one of the most famous cases of using Twitter to watch for customer satisfaction issues: @ComcastCares. As *BusinessWeek*'s Rebecca Reisner [1] said, Frank Eliason is probably the best known and most successful customer care representative in the world (or at least the United States). In April 2008, Eliason's team started monitoring Twitter traffic for mentions of his company, Comcast, made by disgruntled customers. (Comcast is one the largest providers of entertainment, information, and communications services and products in the United States, providing cable television, broadband Internet, and telephone services.) His tactic was to watch Twitter and immediately reach out to these customers who expressed dissatisfaction with Comcast's customer service. The idea was to quiet the spread of any negative sentiment amongst Comcast customers, while providing a sense of personal touch to these frustrated clients.

According to a 2011 report (Eliason has since left Comcast for greener pastures), the new Comcast customer care division processed about 6,000 blog posts and 2,000 Twitter messages per day, which resulted in faster customer response times that directly translate into improved customer satisfaction indexes. While Comcast is not analyzing social media per se, it is watching issues related to perceived poor quality so that it can quickly address issues and interact with these customers.

How Does This Translate into Business Value?

According to Eliason, Comcast was able to understand issues on Twitter far in advance of their call centers (that is, when customers would call in to tell of a problem) [2]. For example, during the NHL playoffs, a sports network carried by Comcast went off the air. People used Twitter to complain about Comcast, claiming the problem was poor service. However, in reality, all of the other networks were offline as well due to a lightning strike. The Comcast call center was able to find out the reason within a few minutes of it happening and was able to put up an automated message telling people what happened. In this case, Comcast estimated that it was able to save $1.2 million by putting up a message about the outage. Customers were able to listen to the message and hang up rather than call in to complain, thus using valuable call center resources.

As another example, consider a new product launch. The marketing team spent hundreds of hours determining the best way to disseminate the message of your new offering, and the company has spent millions on advertising, yet there appears to be lackluster acceptance.

Why?

One way to listen to the man on the street is to scan various social media outlets such as discussion forums, blogs, or chatter on sites like Twitter or LinkedIn. Perhaps you can pick up on messages or customer perceptions of your product or brand. Perhaps when you look at the discussion around your product, you'll see something similar to the situation shown in Figure I.1.

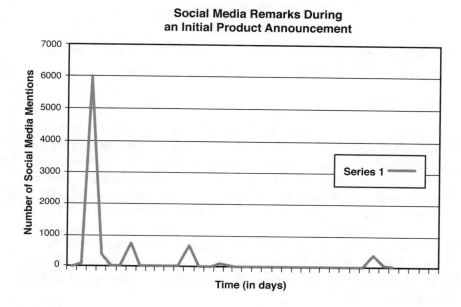

Figure I.1 Social media remarks during an initial product announcement.

This graph was produced for one of the projects we worked with during its launch. Note the steep rise in conversation at the initial launch. Social media conversations went from 0 to more than 6,000 mentions over the course of a few days. This is great! But look at what happens next. The level of conversations fell off rapidly, with just a few isolated spikes in conversation (which were later revealed to be additional announcements). So in this case, it wasn't so much that potential customers didn't like what they saw in the marketplace (of course, that may be the reason for the lack of conversation), but it appears more likely that the marketing campaign wasn't resonating with the public to pick up and carry on the conversation. We look at this particular case in a bit more detail later, but the message here is that a simple analysis within social media can quickly reveal where your business plan might have gone awry.

The Book's Approach

"I keep six honest serving men; they taught me all I know; their names are What and Why and When and How and Where and Who."

—Rudyard Kipling [3]

The process of social media analysis involves essentially three steps: *data identification, data analysis,* and finally *information interpretation.* In explaining each of these steps, we provide important insights and techniques that can be used to maximize the value derived at every point during the process. The approach we take is to first define a question to be answered (such as "What is the public's perception of our company in the light of a natural disaster?"). In attempting to analyze these questions, we suggest that analysts think like detectives, always asking the important questions "Who? What? Where? When? Why? and How?" These questions help in determining the proper data sources to evaluate, which can greatly affect the type of analysis that can be performed.

Data Identification

Any social media investigation is only as good as the data in which you are searching. The first part of this book explores proper *data identification*—or where to look in this vast social media space. In searching for answers, keep in mind that we will be searching through massive amounts of unstructured data, all in an attempt to make sense out of what we find in the process. Once we uncover some interesting artifacts, we will be transforming them into (hopefully useful) information. In the long run, the ultimate business objective is to derive real business insight from this *data,* turning the *information* we've gleaned from these sources into actionable *knowledge.*

In the first part of this book, we explore the source of the data that will be under analysis. To ensure that what we are collecting is the proper data or it explores the correct conversations, we look into questions such as these:

- Whose opinions or thoughts are we interested in?
- Where are the conversations about the topic in question happening?
- Do we need to look at the question back in time or just current discussions?

Data Analysis

In Part II of the book, we explore the data analysis techniques that can be utilized in answering questions within the data collection. Again, putting on our detective hats, we return to our "honest serving men" as described previously by Rudyard Kipling and explore a variety of topics.

How we want to look at this newly uncovered information is important. A data model is used to represent the unstructured data we collect and is an important (and complex) part of answering our questions. These data models are living and breathing entities that need to change over time or when newly discovered insights need to be incorporated into the model. These relatively long-running models tend to be complex and difficult to finalize, and as a result, many people may want to take a less-detailed view of the information. Many choose a real-time view of the data, where watching metrics or trends in real time (or near real time) provides a valuable, yet low-cost, set of insights. As an alternative between long-running analysis and a real-time view lies a structured search model that allows for the searching of common words or phrases within a dataset in an attempt to reveal some insightful information. Each type of analysis has its pros and cons, many of which are explored within this section.

In an attempt to understand *what* people are saying, we begin to explore some of the interpretations of the data, looking at simple metrics such as:

- In a collection that contains Twitter data related to a new product or service, what is the top hashtag?
- Are those hashtags positive or negative in their sentiment?
- What is the volume of conversation about the product or service? (Are people talking about it?)

Other techniques used to discern what people are talking about include the use of word clouds or the collection of top word groups or phrases. These visualizations can help analysts understand the types of conversations that are being held about the company or service in question. More advanced analysis may include the use of a relationship matrix that attempts to understand the interrelationship between concepts or terms (for example, how is the public's view of customer service correlated with perceived cleanliness of a store?).

Marketing teams will be sponsoring advertising campaigns or coming out with press releases at strategic points during a new product release or during a particular point in time—all in an effort to attract new customers while exploiting the loyalty of their existing customer base. But is their message reaching the intended audience? The question of *where* people are talking becomes important in evaluating the outlets that people use when discussing a topic. If the company is advertising mainly in trade journals but there is a large amount of conversation happening in Twitter, would the message be better spread via microblogging? (Or perhaps the use of microblogging can augment the marketing message?) Along those same lines, if we stand on a box in the center of a square and preach our message, do we want to do it in the middle of the night when the square is empty, or at lunchtime when the square is bustling with traffic. The same is true in the social media space: *when* we choose to disseminate information may be just as important as *where*.

Information Interpretation

Once we have all of this data reduced into information nuggets, making sense of the information becomes paramount. In Part III, we demonstrate that the insights derived can be as varied as the original question that was posed at the beginning of the analysis. In some cases, the goal is not only to identify *who* is doing the talking in our analysis but, more importantly, who is *influencing* the conversation or who is influential in their thoughts and opinions. It's important to remember what SunTzu once said: "Keep your friends close, and your enemies closer." The identification of the "movers and shakers" can be important in social media; these are the individuals we want to follow or attempt to get closer to in order to have them use their influence for us as opposed to against us. In other cases, *what* people are saying about a particular issue or topic is the object of the research. For example:

- Are people excited about the newly designed web experience that our company just released, or are they talking about the difficulty in finding information within our website?
- How critical are the outsourcing decisions that we just made to the brand perception of our company or product?

- What were the key issues or topics that people cited when they were expressing negative sentiment?

In our experience, we have also encountered cases in which the *where* is the most important finding. For a newly launched marketing campaign, is the conversation happening more in company-sponsored venues, or is it also happening in neutral venues? Analysis and insights around *when* are also important. For example, is the sentiment for your company becoming negative around the same time as the sentiment for a key competitor (perhaps indicating a downturn in your market)? More importantly, has sentiment for your company or brand gone negative while the competition has gone positive?

Why You Should Read This Book

According to *Merriam-Webster, Definition of SOCIAL MEDIA: forms of electronic communication (as Web sites for social networking and microblogging) through which users create online communities to share information, ideas, personal messages, and other content (as videos)* [4]. Use of social media has grown exponentially over the past eight years (see Figure I.2) [2]. Thus, social media is a major contributor to the explosive growth of big data in our world.

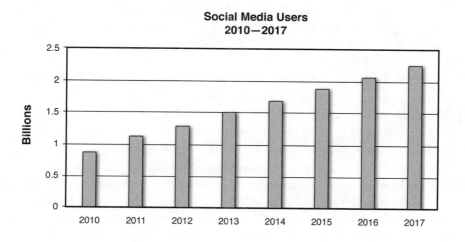

Figure I.2   Growth of social media users 2010–2017

Research has shown that the growth of social media use is far from over. According to Internet Statistics and Market Research Company eMarketer, in a report published in June 2013 [5], the current prediction is that one in four people across the globe will participate in social media by 2014. That's an incredible number. Consider also:

- Asia-Pacific will have largest social network population worldwide through 2017.
- The Middle-East and Africa will have the second largest audience starting next year, because their population penetration rates are among the lowest.
- Asia-Pacific has the largest user base with 777 million people, where 44.8% of social network users are expected at the end of the year.
- The higher penetration of Internet users in India, Japan, Australia, South Korea, Brazil, Mexico, Russia, Middle-East, and Africa has helped to revise the estimated number of social media users in 2013 by 100 million.
- In 2014, the Middle East and Africa (MEA) region emerged as the second largest social media hub, with more than 248 million users surpassing Latin America in regions in the next year.
- By the beginning of 2015, India was expected to surpass the United States as the second largest social media country after China.

IBM CEO Ginni Rometty has called big data the next great natural resource [6]. Getting in on the "ground floor" of anything can be challenging, but if you want to turn this natural resource into business value "gold," you should read this book.

This book will serve the needs of a number of business users. Those users who are new to the subject will get a good overall understanding of the domain by reading the entire book. Those users who have some familiarity with either one or more of the sections of this book will be able to get additional techniques and methodologies to add to their repertoire.

To enable you to apply the content from this book to your unique situation, we have included a number of case studies. The techniques and findings we present here are primarily based on over three years' worth of hands-on experience in executing a variety of social media analytics projects for IBM and IBM's clients. To protect proprietary information, we've edited the cases for illustrative purposes.

For example, we analyzed Twitter content for about a month before the 2014 Grammy Awards were announced and identified a list of potential winners. When the actual results came in, every single one of them was in the top three choices that we had predicted.

These are just some of the examples of value that people are finding by mining this new natural resource. We cover a variety of these use cases throughout the book. People have even used this new capability to fine-tune multimillion dollar marketing campaigns. And, in some cases, people have used analysis of Twitter data during the first two days of a conference and created talking points for an executive presentation on the third day.

By reading this book, you will get a broad understanding of the following topics:

- What are the various types of social media analysis that can be done?
- How do we collect the right kind of data for a project?
- How do we analyze the data using a variety of tools and techniques to get the value from it?
- How do we interpret the results and apply them for real business value?

What This Book Does and Does Not Focus On

A lot of good books out there are targeted at social business marketing managers and focused on how to effectively utilize social media channels to market their brand, their goods, and their services. We do not focus on that approach in this book.

This book is also not directed at technologists, architects, and programmers looking to implement the most effective technology solutions for social media analytics. We provide some information that might be helpful for this type of an audience, but this book is not primarily directed toward them.

This book also does not focus on a single technology platform or a single tool and therefore does not serve as a user manual for one of these products. The intention is to provide enough information to business users so that you can either build your technology solutions or buy solutions to serve your needs for extracting business value out of social media and textual content.

Even though this book is primarily targeted to business users, we cover several technical aspects at length to equip business users with enough knowledge to extract value from this book. Subsequent chapters cover enough detail, but what follows is a list of some of these key technology concepts with a high-level description.

- **Big Data**—Big data is usually characterized by a large volume of data, a large variety of data, and data that is moving at a large velocity (speed). For example, this includes the content flowing through the cables of your local cable TV provider during prime time or content being streamed by Netflix during the screening of an episode of *House of Cards*!

- **Natural Language Processing (NLP)**—NLP involves analysis of words used in our language. A simple application of NLP is a word cloud. A more complex example of NLP includes analyzing streams of conversations and identifying dominant themes.

- **Sentiment Analysis**—This is a special case of natural language processing. In this case, the content is analyzed by software and interpreted to identify if positive, negative, or a neutral sentiment is being expressed. For example, the sentence "I am very happy with the latest release of Product XYZ" is treated as expressing a positive sentiment, whereas the sentence "The installation process for Product XYZ is very difficult" is treated as negative. An example of neutral sentiment is "Product XYZ is supports platform A and system B."

Endnotes

[1] Reisner, Rebecca. Comcast's Twitter Man, *Business Week*, January 2009.

[2] Bernoff, Josh, and Ted Schadler. *Empowered: Unleash Your Employees, Energize Your Customers, Transform Your Business*. Harvard Business Press, 2010.

[3] Kipling, Rudyard. *The Elephant's Child: From the Just So Stories*. ABDO, 2005.

[4] "Social Media." Merriam-Webster.com. Merriam-Webster, n.d. Web. Sept. 21 2015. http://www.merriam-webster.com/dictionary/social media.

[5] Social Networking Reaches Nearly One in Four Around the World. See more at: http://www.emarketer.com/Article/Social-Networking-Reaches-Nearly-One-Four-Around-World/1009976#sthash.B7RoQKQs.dpuf.

[6] Lenzner, Robert. IBM CEO Ginni Rometty Crowns Data As The Globe's Next Natural Resource, *Forbes*, March 2013.

Acknowledgments

Matt Ganis

To be able to work my whole career with the latest technology, in fields that blossom into multimillion dollar industries, is truly a dream come true for the geek inside me. However, to be able to work in that field with my good friend is truly a blessing. Thank you, Avinash. The last few years have been a very wild ride!

However, I could never have achieved the success I have (in both my professional and personal life) if it weren't for the love of my life, my wife, Karen. She's stood by me through thick and thin, and if there is one person in this whole world that I can always count on, it's her. No matter what the circumstances, whether good or bad, I know I can turn to her for advice, a smile, or a shoulder to lean on. I love you, Karen. You make each day special for not only me, but our family. If there was ever a glue that bound a family together, it's you.

I also want to thank my children, Matthew and Taylor. I know it embarrasses you when I cheer the loudest or ask the dumbest questions, but I hope you can forgive the proudest father in the world. Matthew, I may not have your brains, and Taylor, I may not have your athletic ability, but I can promise you I will always have an endless amount of love for you both.

It's said that every journey begins with a single step. My journey started many years ago—more than I'd like to remember. But for all the sacrifices they made, from putting me through college to slugging through the snow to look through my telescope at "little white dots," thank you, Mom and Dad. You've always been there for me. You never wavered in your encouragement and always showed a pride in everything I did. Thanks for starting me down this path.

Avinash Kohirkar

I remember the day in 2011 when I was discussing a new career opportunity with Steve Wright. He wanted me to co-lead an offering of Social Analytics within IBM with Matt Ganis. As I look back, that was a very key day in my IBM life. What ensued was a wonderful ride in the world of social media analytics. I have had the great privilege of working with Matt, a technologist at heart, with a unique drive and passion to extract business benefit out of technology. The idea of this book would not have been possible without Matt. Thank you, Matt, for asking me to collaborate on this project!

In 1988, I was working with System Software for Unisys in Camarillo, California. I remember telling my wife, "I enjoy what I am doing so much that I can't believe they pay me to do this stuff!" I have been extremely fortunate that in my entire career I have felt like that pretty much all the time. I thank my wife, Smita Kohirkar, for enabling me to have a career like this by providing me unwavering support in every facet of my life. There have been numerous times in my career when my work consumed me and my attention, and she took care of me and my family during these times with a smile on her face. I was always a techie and a geek, but I learned a lot about the rest of life from her. The last few months have been especially busy for me while working on this book, and I could not have done it without her understanding and her support. Thank you very much!

I also want to thank my children, Neeraj and Sneha. Despite being the best kids a dad can have, they have been an inspiration for me. Neeraj, who has an amazing ability to learn anything in a very short amount of time, inspires me with his unlimited enthusiasm and passion for life. Sneha, who was always wise beyond her years, never ceases to amaze me with her unique ideas and unique perspectives. I love you all so much!

Joint Acknowledgments

IBM, like many large companies, is full of all kinds of personalities and interesting individuals. To call it a unique place to work is doing it a huge injustice. We've had the distinct pleasure of working with (and for) a number of really special people.

Our career change into analytics and, in particular, social media analytics is due to one person: Stephen Wright. Steve was the visionary leader who saw the potential in analytics and was our chief supporter, cheerleader, and, when we needed it, critic. IBM needs more Stephen Wrights. IBM is lucky to have him, and we were fortunate enough to be able to work for him during this exciting venture into this world of big data, analytics, and cloud computing. Steve, if ever someone were owed a huge debit of thanks, it's you. It was a truly a career highlight being part of the Enterprise Web Strategy and Experience team under your leadership.

Of course, Steve wasn't alone in his desire to see analytics used within the enterprise. We owe a huge debt of thanks to our management chain, specifically John Rosato and Ajay Raina. These are two great leaders who were always willing to support and trust us as we developed our analytics offerings into a world-class operation. As our services grew in sophistication, we joined forces with Liam Cleaver and James Newswanger as they formed IBM's Social Insights Group. To both of you, thank you for your support and willingness to allow us to grow our customer base.

As authors, we are indebted to both Ajay Raina and Debbie Delosa for reviewing the entire manuscript and providing us with invaluable feedback and critiques.

Thanks as well to Santosh Borse, Mila Gessner, and Chris Gruber for their technical and analytics leadership in executing a variety of social analytics projects over the years. We have used examples in this book that were based on individual contributions of these highly skilled analysts and technical wizards. (Santosh, how you pull off some of your magic still amazes us to this day!)

About the Authors

 **Dr. Matthew Ganis**, a member of IBM's Academy of Technology, is currently an IBM Senior Technical Staff Member located in Somers, New York. His current areas of interest include social media analytics, the Internet of Things, and Agile software methodologies. He is an adjunct professor of computer science and astronomy at Pace University in Pleasantville, New York, where he teaches at both the undergraduate and graduate level.

Dr. Ganis holds a BS degree in computer science and an MBA in information systems from Pace University, an MS degree in astronomy from the University of Western Sydney, Australia, and a doctorate of professional studies in computing from Pace University. He has authored or co-authored over 40 papers in both of his fields of interest, ranging from programming techniques, computer system administration, computer networking, and topics on stellar evolution and radio astronomy. He is also the proud co-author of *A Practical Guide to Distributed Scrum* published by IBM Press.

In his 30-year career at IBM, he has been responsible for a number of technological advances such as the creation of the first enterprise firewalls for IBM; the creation of highly available World Wide Web platforms to support the Atlanta, Sydney, and Nagano Olympics (which secured Dr. Ganis and his team a spot in the *Guinness Book of World Records* for the highest sustained rate of Internet web traffic); and the proliferation of advanced software development techniques across IBM's worldwide development laboratories.

He can be found on LinkedIn (https://www.linkedin.com/in/mattganis), on Twitter as @mattganis, or on his blog at http://mganis.blogspot.com.

 **Avinash Kohirkar** is currently Manager of Social Business Adoption in IBM. His current areas of interest include deployment and adoption of social technologies within an enterprise, social engagement dashboards, and social media analytics. Avinash Kohirkar holds a BS degree in electronics and communications engineering from Osmania University (India), an MS degree in industrial engineering from NITIE (India), and an MBA in finance from California State University. He has contributed to IBM white papers and has given numerous presentations on social analytics in IBM and outside IBM. He has authored a number of articles on this subject that have been published in the *Cutter IT Journal* and *Infosys Lab Briefings*.

In his 19-year career at IBM, he has leveraged technologies such as e-business, Web 2.0, social collaboration, social graph technologies, big data, and social media and text analytics for the business benefit of IBM and IBM's customers. He is recognized as a thought leader in the project management profession within IBM and is certified as Executive Project Manager at the highest level within IBM. He has held several technical, business, and management positions during his career: Architect, Development Manager, Project Manager, Project Executive, Associate Partner, Project Executive, and Business Manager.

He can be found on LinkedIn (https://www.linkedin.com/in/AvinashKohirkar) and on Twitter as @kohirkar.

1

Looking for Data in all the Right Places

On two occasions I have been asked, "Pray, Mr. Babbage, if you put into the machine wrong figures, will the right answers come out?" ...I am not able rightly to apprehend the kind of confusion of ideas that could provoke such a question."

—Charles Babbage [1]

Somewhere around 1964, George Fuechsel is thought to have coined the phrase "garbage in, garbage out." This popular computer science slang expression comes from early programmer education. Fuechsel taught his classes that they must check and recheck their data and coding to ensure that the results they achieved were valid. In this new era of computing, programmers were trained to test each step in their programs and cautioned not to expect that a resulting program would do the right thing even when given imperfect input. This basic premise also is true today in data analytics. Simply stated, if you use the wrong data, the results will be wrong (or worse, inaccurate).

So while originally intended for programming, this expression is equally applicable to data analysis. In this chapter, we explore what is meant by data identification and describe how this concept fits into the overall landscape of social media analytics.

Data identification is the process of identifying the subset of available data to focus on for an analysis. A key element of choosing the appropriate data source is to take the time to understand the outcomes/results.

What Data Do We Mean?

Think of data as the raw material that is transformed into information and ultimately knowledge.

Data by itself as a concrete concept can be viewed as the lowest level of abstraction from which information (and then knowledge) can be derived. *Unprocessed data* refers to a collection of numbers, characters, and phrases (snippets of a blog, tweet, and so on)—think of this as "observations"—that are somewhat random and by themselves convey no meaningful information or knowledge. Many pieces of data, when combined together, analyzed, and processed, produce that next level of abstraction: information (see Figure 1.1).

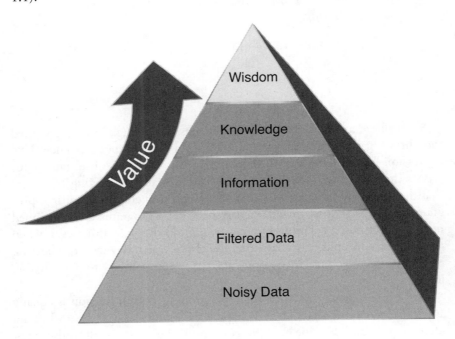

Figure 1.1   The value pyramid.

Data by itself is fairly useless; however, as we process it (or begin to interpret it), it begins to become useful as it conveys some kind of message. At this point, we deem it "information." Information is simply data that has been processed in such a way as to be meaningful to someone or something: it contains meaning, whereas data does not.

To make this concept easier to understand, let's consider a highly simplified version of a real project that we executed. The different levels of the value pyramid could be identified as follows:

- **Noisy Data**—There is a lot of conversation happening in the marketplace about our new product, related products, and competitors' products.

- **Filtered Data**—There is a lot of conversation happening in the marketplace about our new product.

- **Information**—The conversation about our product peaked during announcements or events but tapered off precipitously shortly after the events.

- **Knowledge**—The majority of the conversation that is taking place in the marketplace is being generated by our own marketing messages. The marketplace isn't picking up the message and engaging with it.

- **Wisdom**—Our marketing campaign for this particular brand of machines is really not working.

The end goal is to take all of the observations we can collect (our data), filter them so we look at only the relevant set of "puzzle pieces," and by applying some kinds of processing to it, convert, or organize, that data into meaningful information. By "meaningful," we mean it expresses the data in a way that conveys a new message or insight. Figure 1.2 shows a simple diagram that illustrates this concept.

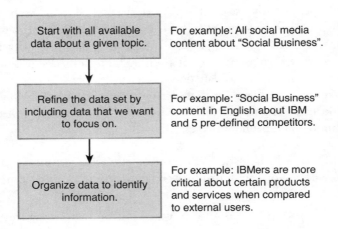

Figure 1.2   Goal of data identification activities.

According to the online *Merriam-Webster* dictionary, knowledge is

(1): the fact or condition of knowing something with familiarity gained through experience or association (2): acquaintance with or understanding of a science, art, or technique. [2]

That familiarity allows us to make better decisions based on the facts presented to us.

And it then follows that wisdom is the ability to think and act using this derived knowledge as well as our set of experiences, common sense, and insight.

It all starts at the bottom of that pyramid: the data. But we need to ensure we have the *right* data. As Chief Engineer Montgomery Scott (of the Starship Enterprise) says:

"How many times do I have to tell you? The right tool [or the right data source] for the right job!

What Subset of Content Are We Interested In?

In the context of social media analytics, data identification simply means "what" content are we interested in. In addition to the "text" of the content, we want to know:

- Who wrote the text?
- Where was it found (or in which social media venue did it appear)?
- Are we interested in information from a specific locale?
- When did someone say something in social media?

As an example, consider the following:

In 2012, Malala Yousafzai, a young girl from Pakistan, made national headlines as a result of the brutal attack against her by Taliban. She had taken a public stand on the rights for education for women in Pakistan. She has become widely known for her activism in Pakistan, where the Taliban had at times banned girls from attending school.

In 2009, Malala was working with the BBC and she created her blog. In this blog, she wrote of life under the Taliban rule in Swat valley, Pakistan, and her strong support for a woman's right to an education. The views of a 12-year-old girl on women's education and the Taliban regime caused quite a sensation. Many newspapers worldwide gave prominent coverage to her blog and her views. *New York Times* even created a documentary film about her life and views of the social situations in her region of the world. This obviously made her quite famous and her enemies quite upset. In October 2012, when Malala boarded her school bus, a gunman boarded the bus and fired three shots directly at her. She suffered major injuries to her face. She was in critical condition for several days. She was later transferred to a hospital in England for rehabilitation. Even though a lot of Islamic religious leaders came to her support after this incident, the Taliban was still intent on harming her and her family. This assassination attempt sparked an international outpouring of support for Malala, ultimately leading to her nomination for the 2013 Nobel Peace Prize [3].

So in this case, say we were trying to pose the question, "What is the reaction of the general population to Malala, the young girl from Pakistan who defied Al Qaeda, in the Western media?" Where should we look for relevant data to analyze?

The word *relevant* here is important. Remember the basic principle of garbage in, garbage out. We could pull data from "everywhere" in the social media space, but we want to be sure that the data we use in our analysis is relevant to the question we are trying to answer.

The data identification process would go as follows:

- We want to analyze content in the media, so we might choose to focus on popular news media and ignore blogs, bulletin boards, Twitter, and so on.
- We want to analyze content in the Western media, so we would focus on the content emanating from a region considered "West" and eliminate content from other regions.

The process of identifying relevant data can be accomplished in a single step, or it might take multiple steps, depending on the type of project we are working on. The process described in this section can be considered as follows:

- **Step 1:** What content are we interested in?

In subsequent sections, we discuss additional possible steps as follows:

- **Step 2:** Whose comments are we interested in?
- **Step 3:** What window of time are we interested in?

Whose Comments Are We Interested In?

A second possible step in the data identification process gets into more details. Considering the previous example, we need to think about issues such as the following:

- Should we eliminate content from sources that are known to be pro Al Qaeda because of negative bias?
- Should we eliminate all content from young girls because of positive bias?

Bias is a prejudice in favor of or against one thing, person, or group compared with another, usually in a way that is considered to be unfair. Being biased implies that we may have only one side of a story; thus, any conclusions we make from the data provided are bound to be biased toward one side. Being biased means that the entire data collected already had a preconceived opinion, and any analysis done on it would be useless.

For example, is there a segment of the population in our target audience, say young girls, who are so impressed by the inherent heroism in the stance taken by another girl against an organization that their comments may not be objective enough for our study?

What Window of Time Are We Interested In?

A third step in the data identification process considers the window of time for relevancy of the data. Would there be any sense in collecting data from three years ago? Should we include in the window of time Malala's address to the United Nations? There may be a case for doing that: if we want to look at the sentiment (or feelings) toward her over time. For example, has the public perception changed over time? But if we group all of the data about her and don't take time into consideration, we may find that the dataset is biased toward her as a "hero" (if the amount of conversation were considerably larger when she was nominated for the Nobel Prize) or perceived as a "villain" (if there were a huge outcry at the start of the incident and very little coverage of her as a Nobel Prize candidate).

Attributes of Data That Need to Be Considered

As the example that we have discussed so far illustrates, the "data identification phase" involves a variety of distinct steps. We discussed three of these steps so far. In the projects that we have executed, we have come across a number of attributes of data that come into play in the data identification phase. In this section, we address these attributes and describe how they help during the data identification phase.

Let's look at the following seven attributes of data:

- **Structure**
- **Language**
- **Region**
- **Type of content (blog, microblog, wiki, and so on)**
- **Venue**
- **Time**
- **Ownership of data (Private, Public, and Proprietary)**

Structure

The simplest way to define structured data is to think of it as data that resides in a fixed field within a record or file. The content of the dataset is very well known—so well known that we can define "columns" of elements in the data such that we will know ahead of time what the data looks like. It's so predictable that we can have any number of "rows" of this same format and know that it will be consistent across the dataset. This type of data is commonly contained in a relational database or a typical spreadsheet.

Various data manipulation and data analysis tools and techniques can be used for this type of data. One example of this type of data is survey results. If a company surveys its customers and collects their (well-defined) answers to specific survey questions, this data can be organized in a relational database since we know the question and we know all possible values of the answers. Some other examples are inventory records, sales forecasts, maintenance records, and so on.

Unstructured data, on the other hand, cannot be easily stored in a relational database to facilitate data manipulation or data analysis. For example, in the survey example shown in Figure 1.3, if the survey form includes a field for free-form comments, the responses to this field can be considered "unstructured data" because we have no way of knowing ahead of time what will be entered (other than it will consist of a string of characters).

Responses to a survey containing structured and unstructured content					
	Question 1	Question 2	Question 3	Question 4	Open-Ended Question
Response 1	1	2	1	A	don't know
Response 2	1	3	2	B	My favorite feature is the GUI
Response 3	2	1	1	C	none
Response 4	4	4	1	D	
Response 5	5	5	2	E	save before exit
....	....	....	....	....	....
Response N	2	1	2	A	?

☐ Structured Content
▓ Unstructured Content

Figure 1.3   Survey data: structured and unstructured.

A collection of tweets about a Super Bowl advertisement is another example. Some people will rave about it, but others will hate it. In either case, we have no idea of the structure of the comments or the format in which they will say it. Other forms of unstructured data include images, audio, and video files. In this book, we restrict the analysis of unstructured content to text.

Language

Consider these simple statements:

"I love the taste of the new Coke."
   and

"Pepsi is my favorite soft drink."

   In French, they become:

"J'aime le goût du nouveau Coke."
   and

"Pepsi est mon préféré softdrink."

If the objective of the project is to identify the number of mentions of Coke versus Pepsi in popular media, perhaps the exact language of the post (whether English or French) isn't all that important. However, if the objective of the project is to identify how many positive mentions of Coke there are as compared to Pepsi, the language becomes very significant. For example, if the tool for sentiment identification "detects" sentiment using a dictionary lookup of positive/negative terms, one needs to ensure the language used is supported for those dictionaries.

Region

While it may seem obvious, if the goal is to understand the issues associated with clean drinking water in South Africa, it is important to ensure that the data included in the analysis is only from that region of the world. On the other hand, one may be interested in a world view of clean water in an attempt to understand how South Africa is discussed within that context. In the former case, one needs to be able to filter the initial data source by the country or origin. Some sources of social media (such as Twitter, which uses location-aware technology on mobile devices) do that very well, although the amount of data is sometimes smaller than that from non-mobile devices. Of course, a native South African blogging from a site in the United Kingdom may be of interest in the analysis; in this case, the question (or problem) becomes: can one easily identify that blog author as South African?

Type of Content

A number of different data sources can be used in the analysis of consumer sentiment or in the understanding of any discussion around a particular topic. Each of these different data sources has its own unique challenges in terms of manipulation and analysis, and quite honestly, usefulness. For example, a tweet can be only 144 characters long, while a paper in a technical journal can span multiple pages. This is an attribute that really identifies a variety of different types of content. Consider some of the following sources of potential social media content:

- **Text**—Written text that is easy to read and understand if you know the language
- **Photos/pictures**—Scientific drawings, simple sketches, or photographs
- **Audio**—Audio recordings of books, articles, talks, or discussions
- **Videos**—Orientation, education, and training; "How to"

With the rise of social media outlets such as YouTube, Pinterest, and Snapchat, virtually every Internet user can become a publisher, broadcaster, and critic. With Facebook claiming about 1.5 billion active users—each with the average user posting 90 pieces of content a month—that averages out to about 7.5 billion pieces of social content to potentially be analyzed per month. But also consider nonprint content, specifically videos. YouTube's over 1 billion users upload more video content in a 60-day period than the three major US television networks have created in 60 years.

Consider the recording of a conference session on the use of specific tools or services. The off-the-cuff comments or live user feedback could reveal very interesting observations about a topic that, when overthought, may not make it into a white paper or published blog. A simple preprocessing of the data—what we like to call "data augmentation"—would take the audio/video content and transcribe it into text, where it can be treated like regular unstructured data from Twitter, Facebook, or LinkedIn.

While this book is about text analytics, the analysis of visual images can be equally important.

As Kyle Wong pointed out in *Forbes*, as more social media platforms (like Twitter) begin to emphasize photos and link them to purchasing opportunities (such as Pinterest), brands will need to measure visual content as a form of "word of mouth" marketing [6].

News, Press Releases, and Instructions

At first, the thought of using news stories for deriving customer sentiment or opinions doesn't seem very productive. Most news stories present the opinion of an organization (some will argue that the opinions of these organizations are biased) or simply report the news of a new product announcement using a company's marketing material. There is typically no room for understanding the sentiment of readers. However, evaluating the value of using news stories can be interesting for two reasons.

First, most news sites today post an article or story and allow readers to leave comments. Those comments and feedback are the content we may want to "mine" and analyze. If the story goes viral, the amount of feedback could be significant. The ability to derive meaningful inference and insight from comments is enhanced when the number of comments is large.

Another reason to look at the news is to understand the effect it has on the general population. One way to gauge the effect is via sentiment analysis. An analysis of the article could reveal a negative sentiment toward a product or issue. As we gather data within social media spaces that reference that news story, we may find that the general population doesn't have a negative sentiment toward the topic but perceives it just the opposite. Of course, if the topic at hand had a positive sentiment before the news story was released and then a negative sentiment afterward, we can assume (but perhaps not know for certain) that the news article had something to do with the change of heart. This is a valuable piece of knowledge for an organization. The understanding of who (or in this case, what news service) can change the public's perception of you or your product is an incredibly important factor when looking for an outlet to advertise products/services.

As an example of the influence that social media can have on issues of public opinion, consider the ethical issues around the use of animals in medical testing. Animal testing is a huge "hot button" issue with a large number of opinions on either side of the debate. On its own, it's an industry in which there are not only companies dedicated to the breeding of animals used for experimental purposes but also concerns around those companies that employ those techniques.

According to a study reported in *Science* [7] in early 2014, support for medical testing on animals had declined overall by 12% since 2001 (in the

United States), and according to the analysis, the researchers believed the Internet (specifically social media) may be responsible for the decline. The study, which was conducted by researchers at the advocacy group People for the Ethical Treatment of Animals (PETA) and Western Governors University, analyzed survey data from the previous 12 years looking at public opinion around this topic. A result of their work showed that 41% of American adults considered animal testing "morally wrong" in 2013, up from 29% in 2001. Opposition (luckily) to such testing has risen among all demographic groups, but the biggest jump has been among people aged 18 to 29, which jumped to 54% in 2013 versus just 31% in 2001. If we look at the social media impact, we see that animal rights organizations have a much stronger presence on social media than do pro-animal testing groups. PETA, for example, had more than 2 million followers on Facebook and nearly a half million on Twitter, as opposed to the Foundation for Biomedical Research, which has around 130,000 followers on Facebook and about 1,700 on Twitter at the time of the study. As a result, the researchers speculate, these organizations may be getting their message out more effectively, especially among young people.

Discussion Forums, Blogs, Wikis, and Microblogs

From a social media perspective (or the "true" voice of a customer), there is nothing better than social media sites where people express their feelings, anxieties, and joys 24 hours a day, 7 days a week (and usually many times per day).

Social media refers to the interactions among people or groups, where they create, share, and exchange information and ideas in an open and mostly public venue. The term *social media* also can be viewed in a much broader context of Internet-based tools and platforms that increase and enhance the sharing of information. This new communication vehicle makes the transfer of text (opinions), photos, and audio/video (marketing) increasingly easy among users and (with the growth of mobile devices) instantaneous.

Platforms such as Twitter, Facebook, and LinkedIn have created online communities where users can share as much or as little personal information as they desire with other members. Some are more "open" than others. For example, with Facebook and similarly LinkedIn, anything posted to your wall can be viewed by everyone in your community (your friends), which is a finite number. In the case of Twitter, anything said is instantly available to the over 289 million Twitter users on the planet [8]. The result is an enormous amount of information that can be easily shared, searched, and created on a daily basis.

Venue

Content is getting generated and shared in a variety of venues. There are popular news sites such as Time, CNN, and Huffington Post. There also are professional networking sites such as LinkedIn, social networking sites such as Facebook, and microblogging sites such as Twitter. Depending on the type of project you are working on, the venue becomes very significant. For example, if your project involves understanding sentiment about tennis players during a tennis match, a microblogging site like Twitter is probably a very good source of information. If, on the other hand, you are trying to understand which government contracts are insisting on accessibility features, you might have to target some specific venues to get to this type of information.

Following is a representative list of common venues that we typically encounter:

- News
    - Newspapers and magazines
    - News sites (CNN, Time, Huffington Post)
- Social networking/social sharing sites
    - LinkedIn
    - Google+
    - Facebook
    - SlideShare
- Blogs
    - WordPress
    - Tumblr
    - Microblogging platforms like Twitter
- Custom venues
    - Government procurement websites
    - Websites dedicated to legal or medical professionals

Time

Author Jarod Kintz once said, "Just because I liked something at one point in time doesn't mean I'll always like it, or that I have to go on liking it at all points in time as an unthinking act of loyalty [9]." This brings us to the temporal state of data.

When we think of the time attribute of data, we're referring to the currency of it. For your analysis, do you need content for the past week, month, or for the past 10 years? Sometimes for a project there is a need to access data in real time or near real time. For our purposes, we like to think of data in these two states:

- **Data at Rest** has been created and isn't changing (or actively being added to). For example, if you are trying to analyze Twitter content to determine which movie was the most popular among users in social media before the Academy Awards of 2011, most of the data would be "at rest," meaning the content is already created and the analysis can be done at your own pace.
- **Data in Motion** is real-time data created continuously and constantly. For example, if one is trying to identify the shifting sentiment between Barack Obama and Mitt Romney during the 2012 presidental debates, the data would be considered "in motion" during the course of the debate.

One variation of Data in Motion is something we call "near real time"; this data is collected in real time but is slightly late in its arrival. For example, we collect Twitter data in our lab in real time, but we copy the collected data to our analysis systems once every 5–10 minutes (due to some processing overhead). So this data is close (or near) to real time, but not instantaneous. Being able to get access to instantaneous data for analysis purposes requires a significant investment in storage and computing capacity. Often, near real-time data can serve the purpose at a significantly lower cost.

Ownership of Data

One way to look at the ownership of data is to think of data as "internal" (belonging to a company) or "external" (data in the public domain). Another way to think about it is to divide this area into these types:

- **Public Data**—A majority of the content shared by people on Facebook, Twitter, and other public venues is predominantly public data. People performing analysis of this kind of data still have to be careful. The venues where the content is created and disseminated have specific terms that define what constitutes the proper use of that data. For example, using a public Twitter feed, users can gain access to a variety of actual tweets being used by different people about a particular topic, but specific terms from Twitter govern how these tweets can be included or displayed on our own website. In addition, users of this data also need to adhere to the specific guidelines provided by each country about the use and handling of public content.

- **Private or Proprietary Data**—All of the social media content generated in a company's intranet should be considered either private or proprietary. There are specific terms of use for this data.

Summary

In this chapter, we discussed various issues surrounding the selection and inclusion of various data sources and data types in an analysis. Our view is that the selection of the "right" data will have a positive effect on your overall conclusions and insights. Others may argue that with the cost of computing on the decline, analysts shouldn't be concerned over what data they draw from; the analytics in the various software solutions can (and should) sort out the relevant from the irrelevant. And while this is true, from what we have seen, starting from a "cleaner" or perhaps more focused data source tends to produce more accurate results in a shorter time frame. There's nothing wrong with starting with a well-formed data source, deriving some results and then going back to add additional data sources (to perhaps expand the horizon of the analysis). Just be careful that you don't spend more time sorting through the garbage in the hopes of finding that diamond. We agree such diamonds may be there, but is the value spent on the search worth the value derived?

Referring back to the opening value pyramid in Figure 1.1, we believe the best conclusions or insights we can draw from the data we collect are only as good (accurate or meaningful) as the data we start with. This is the basic premise of the garbage-in, garbage-out model. We recognize that social media data, by definition, has a lot of noise. In this chapter, we have offered ideas on how to minimize the noise because the more relevant the data that goes in, the better insights will come out of the analysis process.

Endnotes

[1] Babbage, Charles, *Passages from the Life of a Philosopher* (New York: Augustus M. Kelley Pubs, 1864).

[2] See http://www.merriam-webster.com/dictionary/knowledge.

[3] See https://en.wikipedia.org/wiki/Malala_Yousafzai.

[4] See http://www.statista.com/statistics/264810/number-of-monthly-active-facebook-users-worldwide/.

[5] See http://www.youtube.com/yt/press/statistics.html.

[6] Wong, Kyle, "The Explosive Growth of Influencer Marketing and What It Means for You," *Forbes*, September. 10, 2014. See http://www.forbes.com/sites/kylewong/2014/09/10/the-explosive-growth-of-influencer-marketing-and-what-it-means-for-you/.

[7] Grimm, David, "ScienceShot: Is Social Media Souring Americans on Animal Research," *Science*, February 16, 2014. Retrieved from http://news.sciencemag.org/plants-animals/2014/02/scienceshot-social-media-souring-americans-animal-research.

[8] See http://www.statisticbrain.com/twitter-statistics/.

[9] Kintz, Jarod and Arod, Dora, *At even one penny, this book would be overpriced. In fact, free is too expensive, because you'd still waste time by reading it* (Kindle Edition, Kindle eBook, January 9, 2012).

2

Separating the Wheat from the Chaff

Knowledge is power, only if man knows what facts not to bother with.

—Robert Staughton Lynd [1]

To pick up on the thread from the preceding chapter (about looking for data in all the right places), just how do we separate the good from the bad or the useful from the not-so-useful data sources?

Ask any grain farmer if it's important to separate the wheat from the chaff in his harvest. As any good farmer knows, it's not only a useful saying, but it's critical to his success. In cereal crops such as rice, barley, oats, and wheat, the seed (which is what we eat) is surrounded by a husk. That husk is known as the *chaff*, which, when separated from the seed, is generally thrown away as useless. Thus, as farmers know, to generate a useful harvest, we must separate the wheat from the chaff. This metaphor of the chaff has long since represented a useless object or something to be discarded. It's the same with an initial data "harvest." Through the use of a search engine (or some other automated means), we retrieve useful data, but often, included with that useful material is irrelevant content that we need to remove.

In data analysis, we want to gather as much data as we can in the hopes of uncovering additional information, which will in the end help us make more informed observations. However, in that gathering process, we may inadvertently collect data that is totally useless to us during the analysis we are going to perform. As we said previously, we want to gather as much as we can and then try to separate the useless from the useful. You may have heard that in statistics, the larger the sampling of data, the more accurate the measurements will become. While that's true, what we're referring to here is not a diversity of opinion on a topic, but a separation of opinions on too many topics.

When conducting an analysis, we are looking to maximize the amount of data to analyze, but not sacrifice the quality (or relevance) of that data. Obtaining a sample size that is appropriate in both of those areas is critical for a number of reasons. Most importantly, a large sample size is more representative of the population we want to examine, which in turn will limit the influence of outliers or irrelevant observations. A sufficiently large sample size is also necessary to produce results among variables that are significantly different. For qualitative studies (such as text analytics), where the goal is to reduce the chances of discovery failure, a large sample size broadens the range of possible data and forms a better picture for analysis. Again, all this needs to be weighed against the introduction of too much unrelated data that can skew our results.

It All Starts with Data

We've all heard the saying "Knowledge is power, but wisdom is King." We need to remember that the source that power is built upon is the data that we use to derive our wisdom (or knowledge). We often describe this hierarchy to our clients as shown in Figure 2.1.

As an analogy, consider the building of a house. When we start construction, we start, obviously, from the ground up by laying a solid foundation. Every aspect of the future house depends on this foundation. If it's weak (perhaps not enough cement), the house could crumble under the weight of the additional floors that are added. This is true of a social media analysis also. If the data we collect is wrong, or erroneous, any conclusions we draw or assumptions we make could fall apart due to lack of supporting data. While the data is important in support of the conclusions we've drawn, in the final analysis what we see are the insights that were derived and the wisdom gained. No longer do we see the strong foundation of data or the information it represents. But it's important to remember and acknowledge that new wisdom we've uncovered is supported by a strong foundation.

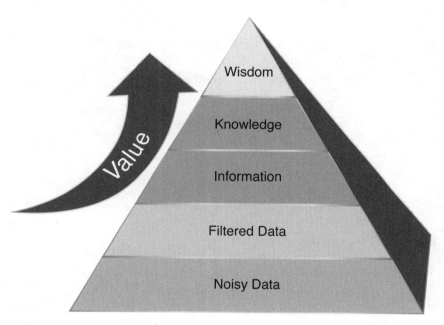

Figure 2.1   Value Pyramid: An Information hierarchy.

Casting a Net

When we are about to begin our project of analyzing a set of data in search of some nuggets of value, we obviously must start with a collection of data. We call this process "casting a net." Think of it like a fisherman would. The larger the net that is cast, the more fish we will haul in with each casting (see Figure 2.2). Harvesting social media data (or any data from the Internet for that matter) is the same. The wider, broader the search criteria we use, the more data we are likely to haul in for an analysis. What we need to understand when we cast this net is that some of the data we retrieve will be very relevant to the area we are looking to explore. Some of the data may be marginally useful, and some may be just plan worthless (the "chaff," if you will).

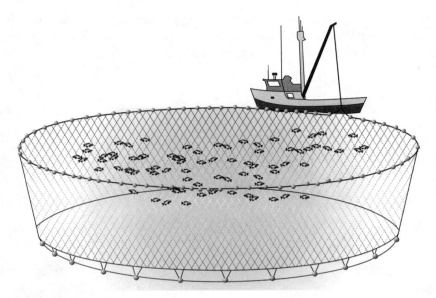

Figure 2.2   Casting a wide net.

There are two schools of thought on the data collection process:

- Gather with a very narrow focus and assume everything you have collected is relevant.
- Gather as much as you can, with a much "looser" set of collection criteria, and then "cleanse" the data, thus eliminating the extraneous results.

We believe there is a middle ground, where we should start with a wide net, evaluate the collection results and then modify the search criteria, and finally recast a net to hopefully retrieve a more intelligent sampling.

In thinking about data validity and only considering "correct" data, let's look at a simple example using numbers. Let's assume we have a list of numbers (see Table 2.1) that represent the number of visitors to a particular website every hour. To make the example a bit more realistic, let's assume we count web page accesses in a weblog and that we've done some kind of preprocessing on the weblog data to determine valid website accesses. That means we ignore robot searches and invalid web page accesses, and so on.

So using this method, we might come up with data that looks like Table 2.1 (remember, this is just a sample).

Table 2.1   Number of Web Page Accesses over a Five-Hour Period

Hour	Number of Web Accesses
1	5
2	8
3	3
4	25
5	6

So by adding together all of the web page visits (47 in total) and dividing by the time period (5 hours), we compute the average number of web visitors per hour to our site and come up with an average number of 9 visitors to our website every hour, as shown in Figure 2.3.

$$\frac{5 + 8 + 3 + 25 + 6}{5} = \frac{47}{5} = 9 \text{ Web visits/hour}$$

Figure 2.3   Computing the average number of web page visitors in a five-hour period.

But does that really make sense? If we empirically look at our data, we can see right away that most of the numbers in Figure 2.3 rarely went above 8 visitors per hour at our site, and often the number was around 5 or 6. If we look closely at the data we analyzed, it becomes obvious that one of the data points is quite different from the rest and appears to be an outlier in our data (that is, the sample that was reported at 25 hits per hour). This value may very well be correct, but based on the other samples around it, there is a distinct possibility that our process for computing the hits per hour was either flawed or was subjected to some other anomaly. Since the theme of this chapter is separating the wheat from the chaff, perhaps we should remove that value (as useless) and recompute our results. This gives us a value of 5.5 web page visits per hour (see Figure 2.4). This seems to be a more reasonable number for our average web site visitors per hour.

$$\frac{5 + 8 + 3 + 6}{4} = \frac{22}{4} = 5.5 \text{ Web visits/hour}$$

Figure 2.4   Computing what appears to be a more correct average number of website visits (after eliminating questionable data).

CAUTION

Please don't misunderstand this example. This is not about removing data in a set of observations that we just don't like or removing data to make our conclusions look better. This is about intelligently eliminating data that we truly believe was captured in error or, in the case of text analytics, is not related to the topic at hand but was perhaps collected because we cast too wide of a net in our collection process. But as Charles Babbage was once quoted as saying: "Errors using inadequate data are much less than those that use no data at all. [2]"

Our point is that we would rather eliminate what we believe is erroneous than allow what we know is erroneous to influence our results.

Let's look at another example (perhaps a bit more relevant to text analytics). Getting onto Twitter, we did a simple search (from the twitter.com search box) for "Apple." As this book was written, there were rumors flying around Twitter and the Internet that Apple was preparing to launch a 12.9-inch screen for its next iPad, so we thought we would quickly check to see if we could come up with a compelling wheat/chaff example around "Apple." Table 2.2 shows what we found (there are *many* more tweets; this is just a collection of the first seven tweets that showed up on our search).

Table 2.2   Sample Tweets Surrounding the Search Term "Apple"

Number	Tweet Contents
1	Apple said to prepare new 12.9-inch IPad for early 2015: .. *(url removed)*
2	Earbuds for Apple iPhone 5 5C 5S w/ Mic & Volume Remote Headphones - Full read by eBay: Price 1.34 USD (2 Bids) *(url removed)*
3	RT @BloombergNews Apple said to prepare new 12.9-inch IPad for early 2015: *(url removed)* $AAPL
4	I wanna be someone's cinnamon apple *(url removed)*
5	Apple is working on a bigger iPad with a 12.9-inch screen that will launch early next year *(url removed)*
6	Apple for the teacher, 2) Notebook and Pens – 3) Alibi ??? *(url removed)*
7	"Do these candles come in different scents" Well that one there's trout This one? Apple cinnamon Dont ask me why we carry apple cinnamon

Clearly, tweets number 1, 3, and 5 refer to the rumor about the size of Apple's iPad. And while tweet number 2 is about Apple products being sold on eBay, these products aren't particularly relevant to the analysis at hand (which is the reaction to the announcement about the screen size). Tweets number 4, 6, and 7 clearly have *nothing* to do with Apple (the company) and are completely irrelevant to the analysis we need to do here. So how do we solve this? We used a regular expression.

Regular Expressions

When we are looking to cleanse a dataset or limit the amount of data we collect as part of our gathering process, we need a simple way to indicate the data that we'd like to keep and which part of the data we want to discard. One way to specify this is with a regular expression.

A *regular expression* is a special text string for describing a search pattern. For those familiar with Microsoft Windows and the concept of wildcards, think of regular expressions as an advanced way to specify wildcards. If you're not familiar with wildcards, perhaps you've seen computer-savvy users list a set of files in a given Windows folder or directory by using the following command:

```
dir *.jpg
```

This is a shorthand notion for saying we want all of the files that end in .jpg or that are JPEG files (or pictures). The asterisk (*) indicates that any character will match (in this case) the filename, but that the file type must be .jpg. We could just as easily look for files that contain a specific prefix in their filename; for example:

```
PG32*.jpg
```

This command would give us all of the files that begin with PG32 and have a file type of .jpg. In this case, names such as the following all match this regular expression and, again, limit the number of files we see in a directory listing:

```
PG324356.jpg
PG3234.jpg
PG32-savedfile.jpg
```

Processing unfiltered (noisy) data uses similar techniques and relies on knowledge of regular expressions as a means to specify what part of the dataset we want to keep and which to remove. Before we dive into this topic, it's important to understand that the cleaning process may take several iterations before it is complete (see Figure 2.5). Even with several iterations, we may never get it 100% perfect. Remember, the goal is to take a dataset that is presumed to be noisy (that is, it contains data that is irrelevant to what we are looking to understand) and clean it in such a way that the majority of what we are going to analyze contains data directly relevant to the task at hand.

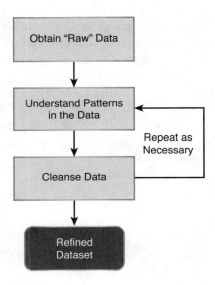

Figure 2.5   Iterative cleansing process.

For example, in Table 2.1, tweets about apple (the fruit) or candles (numbers 4, 6, and 7) are irrelevant and should be removed from the analysis.

So assuming we have a file with a list of tweets (as shown in Table 2.1), our first step at cleaning the data is to look for tweets that contain information about Apple (the corporation) as opposed to anything else. Remember, when this dataset was created, we did a Twitter search on just the word *apple*. Because we are interested in discussions around the latest iPad rumors, it stands to reason we should look only at tweets that contain *apple* (the whole dataset) and *ipad*.

NOTE

While this book is *not* about tools and specific software packages, we show some examples using a number of these utilities. Please note that, as a social media analyst, you are unlikely to use commands such as these directly. You are more likely to use open source or commercial tools for this purpose. However, the purpose of this section is to provide you with an understanding of how some of these tools work and how to express your requests in those other tools.

One of the tools frequently used by data scientists (and Linux system administrators) is called *egrep*. This program, which stands for Extended Global Regular Expressions Print, is part of most, if not all, Linux platforms (and is also widely available for Microsoft distributions). It scans any specified file, line by line, and returns all of the lines that contain a pattern matching a given regular expression.

Figure 2.6 shows an example of this Linux utility for text manipulation.

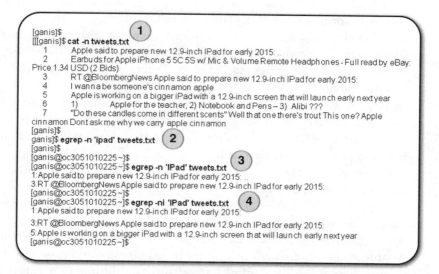

Figure 2.6 Example of a Linux utility for text manipulation.

Let's look closer at how regular expressions work. Figure 2.6 shows four steps in an attempt to look at some data we collected on some of Apple's iPad/iPod products.

1. In step 1 of Figure 2.6, we have our collected raw tweets in a file called tweets.txt. For the purposes of this demonstration, we use the Linux cat command to print them to the screen (with line numbers) so we can better understand our data.
2. At step 2, we use the egrep program to look for the word *ipad* in any of the lines of the file. If the program finds this word, it will print out the line (with the line number using the -n option). Practically, we wouldn't use the -n option because we would probably issue the command as follows:

```
egrep 'ipad' tweets.txt > refined.tweets.txt
```

This would run the egrep program and print each line in the file tweets.txt that contained the word *ipad* (ignoring the other lines). Rather than print them to the screen as we do here, we would redirect the output to a new file called refined.tweets.txt, thus creating a refined dataset that we will process later.

In any case, you'll notice from step 2 in Figure 2.6 that the egrep command produced nothing (there were no matches). Why is that? Looking closely at the data (step number 1), we see that the tweet in line 1 uses the word *iPad,* but the tweeter used *ipad* (all lowercase) instead of *Ipad,* so matching letter for letter, including case, there was no match.

3. In step 3, we see that pattern matching is more than just looking for similar letters; we have to be a bit more exacting. In step 3 we reissue the command (remember, we said that data cleansing is an iterative process), this time using *IPad* as our filter. The output of that command yields a cleansed dataset of two tweets that contain the word *IPad.* It's progress!

The problem is that there are many ways to express words. Sometimes people use all capitals or all lowercase. The word *iPad* appears in what a programmer would call "CamelCase." This is the practice of writing compound words or phrases in which every word or abbreviation begins with a capital letter (thus, the hump in a camel's back). Examples are commonly used words such as *iPhone, FedEx,* and *McDonald's.*

So how do we solve this? One brute-force approach is to specify all of the combinations we'd like to catch in our filtered stream, but that could be not only confusing but also complicated and error prone.

4. The simplest solution is to just assume that case doesn't matter. Using the -i option of egrep (which indicates that case should be ignored), our command now produces all of the tweets in the sample that we would expect (with someone referring to an *IPad* while others refer to an *iPad*).

Notice that by simply using the word *ipad* with the egrep command, we eliminate all of the other spurious tweets as well.

A Few Words of Caution

Be careful with the filters you use for your data. You may initially look at your original dataset and assume that because people are using the words *IPad* and *iPad*, you can simply filter on the *ip* part of the word, using, for example:

```
egrep 'ip' tweets.txt
```

This command would inadvertently give you the following output:

```
1: Apple said to prepare new 12.9-inch IPad for early 2015: ..
2: Earbuds for Apple iPhone 5 5C 5S w/ Mic & Volume Remote
Headphones - Full read by eBay: Price 1.34 USD (2 Bids)
3: RT @BloombergNews Apple said to prepare new 12.9-inch IPad for
early 2015:
5: Apple is working on a bigger iPad with a 12.9-inch screen that
will launch early next year
```

Notice the introduction of tweet number 2 (about the earbuds for an Apple iPhone) into your mix. That may be a correct dataset if you are looking to build a dataset about Apple products, but in this case, the iPhone discussion is irrelevant to the discussion about the iPad. It may be a simple example, but hopefully it points out a possible pitfall you could fall prey to.

It's Not What You Say but WHERE You Say It

Sometimes we need to filter our datasets based on the context in which a word or phrase is used. For example, during one of our engagements, we were trying to understand the discussions being held around a conference called "Sapphire Now." According to its Twitter account, it is "The world's premier business technology conference around business technology trends and innovations." When we first started collecting data, we simply searched on the word *sapphire* expecting to find all of our collected tweets referring to the show.

We forgot about:

- Sapphire, the gem
- Sapphire, the liquor
- Sapphire, the color
- and so on

So in the cleansing of this data, we had to look at all of our tweets that referenced *sapphire* and select just the ones that dealt with the conference or technology in general. In other words, the use of the word *sapphire* in the context of technology.

Using the sample dataset we had previously, we had the same problem. We had a set of data about "apple," and it came in a few "flavors":

- Apple, the corporation (and its products)
- Apple, the fruit
- Apple, as a sign of affection
- No doubt there would be others

One way we could sort out the data was to look for the word *apple* in the dataset and select just those tweets that discussed the iPad (or any of Apple's products).

Our egrep command could look something like this:

```
egrep -inh '(apple).*(ipad)' tweets.txt
```

In this case, we specify that we want all tweets that contain the word *apple* (remember, we use the `-i` option of egrep to ignore case) and then anywhere following that word (that's the use of the asterisk) the word *ipad*. The output of this command yields:

```
1: Apple said to prepare new 12.9-inch IPad for early 2015:
3: RT @BloombergNews Apple said to prepare new 12.9-inch IPad for
early 2015:
5: Apple is working on a bigger iPad with a 12.9-inch screen that
will launch early next year
```

Obviously, as before, specifying `(apple).*(ip)` would have included the tweet about the iPhone. The point is that looking for specific words when other keywords are present allows us to understand (or at least assume) our search words are being used in the proper context.

Many search engines allow for the filtering of keywords when other words are within a certain boundary (for example, if we see the word *apple,* the word *ipad* must be seen within three words; otherwise, it will not be considered a match).

Summary

What we discussed in this chapter could loosely be called the process of data cleansing. This is essentially the process of detecting and removing inaccurate data from a dataset (or database). It's an essential step in feeding our more complex "downstream" steps of analysis and interpretation. While we took you through some relatively simple examples, we hope we made our point: The accuracy of any analysis is only as good as its weakest link (if your datasets are corrupt, or inaccurate, the error or inaccuracies will only be magnified later). If you look to minimize the corruption or inaccuracies, hopefully the magnification of the minimized error won't be noticeable or too large as to skew your results in the wrong direction.

The question "How do we know if we have the right data?" is a difficult one to answer. The process of data cleansing, like the whole process of analysis, is iterative in nature (we discuss this issue further in Chapter 12, where we discuss things that can go wrong). At some point we have to decide that "enough is enough." If we've passed over the data three or four times in an attempt to clean it, and each pass produces less and less cleaning, repeating the process becomes a question of "Is it worth continuing to clean with less and less of a result?" There is no simple answer to that question other than your having a gut feeling that your data is ready for the next step.

Endnotes

[1] Lynd, Robert. *The Orange Tree: A Volume of Essays*. Metheun, 1926.

[2] Quote attributed to Charles Babbage (https://en.wikiquote.org/wiki/Charles_Babbage).

3

Whose Comments Are We Interested In?

All opinions are not equal. Some are a very great deal more robust, sophisticated, and well supported in logic and argument than others.

—**Douglas Adams,** *The Salmon of Doubt* [1]

Up to this point, we have concerned ourselves with what data to analyze while ensuring that what we selected is germane to our topic. In this chapter, we explore how important it is to determine *whose* comments we are interested in. A few examples are as follows:

- If we are interested in getting *objective* feedback on a product from a specific company, we might want to make sure that we can identify or exclude this company's employees from the pool of content under analysis.

- Similarly, we need to ask: Are we interested in comments from the general public, or are we interested in the comments of C-level employees (that is, chief marketing officers or chief information officers)?

- Also, are we interested only in people who have a positive bias toward a company or those with a strong negative bias?

Looking for the Right Subset of People

At the beginning of a social analytics project, analysts spend a fair amount of time thinking about the ultimate goals of the project and the results that we expect to get at the conclusion of the project. This upfront analysis will go a long way in determining the appropriate target segment of the analysis.

During the definition of a typical social media analysis project, requesters will (or should) explicitly point out the "who" (whose opinion are they interested in?) or will give the researcher or the model builder sufficient hints or guidance. Various attributes can be used to segment or target the audience that we're interested in. Some of them are described in the following sections.

Employment

Do we want the opinions of employees or nonemployees?

For example, if a company launches a new product or service and wants to see how the marketplace is reacting to that product or service in social media, it might prefer to exclude the comments of its own employees. In other situations, we might exclusively focus on the employee population if the intent is to learn how they are responding to a new product, service, or strategy. In a project that we worked on, IBM was interested in learning about the marketplace reaction of a brand-new product type. The marketing team specifically asked us to exclude the comments and sentiments of IBMers to understand sentiment from "neutral" people so as not to bias the results.

Sentiment

Are we looking for comments from people with a positive bias or negative bias?

For example, if the object of social media analysis is to detect customer support issues, it makes sense to focus only on posts with a clear negative bias. You might argue that highlighting positive customer experiences is just as important and probably needs to be considered as well. Another common use case involves trying to compare the sentiment about a variety of products that a company is providing to the marketplace. In this situation, we may consider opinions from all ranges of demographics and keep score about the number of positive, negative, or neutral comments. Sometimes, the purpose of a project is merely to find how many people or comments mention the company's product versus a competitor's product. In this case, we may (initially) ignore sentiment and consider all comments without exclusions.

A few years ago, there was a civil movement called Occupy Wall Street in the United States. Numerous people congregated around specific commercial buildings to express their silent protests against what they believed to be unfair practices. During this time, as a validation of some of our analytics capabilities, we built an experimental social listening model to detect whether there was any impact to an IBM location where some key customer meetings were being conducted. In this case, we built a model that focused on snippets of information that may have negative sentiment about IBM and then specifically looked for any mentions of protests or civil actions.

In many cases, sentiment is a result of an analysis phase. However, in some instances, the scope and nature of the project determine whether we should include comments only from people who have either a favorable view or an unfavorable view of our topic. In cases like these, we are able to take this information into account in the very initial phase of the project and focus only on a specific subset of people.

Location or Geography

Do we want to focus on comments from people who live in a specific location?

One of the projects that we were involved in dealt with issues around water in South Africa. In this particular project, we were clearly interested in comments from people in South Africa about the variety of issues and questions around the current and future needs and use of clean and healthy water. Sometimes we may be interested in comments from all over the world, but valuable insights can emerge when we classify the analytics by region.

Language

Is the language of the content important to us?

Some projects require us to understand what is specifically being said about a company's product or service in a particular local language. For example, if a company wants to do some market research around the market's appetite for a machine translation tool in Spanish-speaking countries, it will be interested in content contributed by individuals in the Spanish language.

Age

Is the age of content author important to the project at hand?

There is a lot of discussion in popular media about the work habits of Generation Xers. Those in Generation X (or Gen X) were born after the Western Post–World War II baby boom. As a point of reference, most consider those with birth dates ranging from the early 1960s to the early 1980s as being part of this demographic. If a company's Human Resources department wanted to study the experience of its newly hired Gen Xers, we would have to determine a way to segment the population based on age.

Gender

Are we specifically interested in comments of men or women?

Gender also becomes an important attribute upon which we may segment audience for a particular project. If an organization is creating training and educational materials to encourage more women to pursue higher studies in science- and mathematics-related disciplines, it may choose to focus exclusively on comments and feedback from women. Similarly, if a health-care company is undertaking research about male-pattern baldness, it would be served well by segmenting its audience to include only men.

In one case, we were asked to evaluate the comments that were made in social media during the introduction of a new movie trailer. Our client was interested not only in the reaction to the trailer, and by association the movie itself, but also if certain themes resonated with either males, females, or both. Again, the goal was to determine not only likeability of the movie, but also keys in how to market it.

Profession/Expertise

Do we need opinions from anybody in general, or do we need opinions from people who are working in a specific profession (such as the IT profession) in a specific industry (such as automotive)?

For example, if IBM is interested in learning about the reaction to the cognitive computing capabilities of IBM Watson in the area of health care, it is probably interested in the opinions of corporate users as opposed to home users.

Eminence or Popularity

Are we interested in opinions only from people of certain standing in the domain of the topic area?

A major aspect of a social media campaign for companies involves identifying who might be an "influencer" in a particular topic area or industry. For performing this type of analysis, we tend to spend a lot of time in developing rules to ensure we are able to narrow the solution space to identify a small subset of individuals that a company should target its marketing messages to.

Role

When dealing with social media analysis within a company's intranet, are we interested in segmenting based on a specific job role?

For example, we are working on a project that computes a social scorecard for employees based on their participation in social media. There are some roles in which the job demands a lot of collaboration in social media, and then there are some people who might be working on highly specialized or highly sensitive projects in which they may not be allowed to share information in social media. Here, the type of role is very important in interpreting scores.

Specific People or Groups

Are we really interested in narrowing down our analysis to comments about or comments from a specific individual or a specific set of individuals?

A couple of years ago, we were asked to build an application to capture and display sentiment in near real time about tennis players participating in the US Open. In this case, we used names of players, their nicknames, and a variety of other aliases to ensure we were targeting the right segment. In another example, we were asked to identify how people in social media were reacting to a Lance Armstrong interview with Oprah Winfrey.

Do We Really Want ALL the Comments?

In Chapter 1, we discussed the concept of bias—or the skewing of a dataset based on a potentially inappropriate set of authors. Perhaps *inappropriate* is too strong of a word, but in some cases you might want to exclude the comments of your company's employees. At IBM, we tend to look at ourselves as one of the best customers of our products and services, but sometimes IBMers are also among our most vocal critics. If we are looking to understand the true concerns or thoughts of our external customers and clients, we may want to exclude the subset of IBMers from the conversation. This is an example of the employment attribute that we discussed previously. Again, the purpose isn't to exclude because these comments aren't valuable, but in the spirit of openness and true sentiment or feelings, it may be useful to separate the comments.

In one example, we were asked to look at the social media activity around a new product launch. The client's concern was that while there was a tremendous amount of money and time being invested in the various marketing campaigns, the sales hadn't picked up as much as had been anticipated. A quick analysis of the discussion around the topic showed the level of activity over a four-week period (see Figure 3.1).

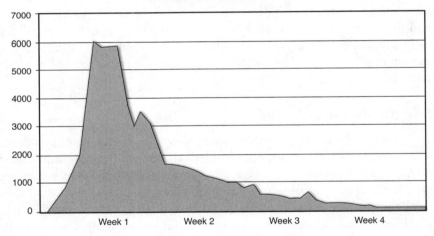

Figure 3.1 Social media remarks during an initial product announcement.

This graph shows the number of mentions of the particular product over time. It's rather clear from this simple graphic that in the beginning, there was quite a bit of hype or discussion around this product launch, but over a short period of time, the discussion continued to decline almost to zero mentions.

What was even more disturbing about this analysis was who was having the conversations. We quickly looked at the top contributors to this thread of conversation and turned up the list shown in Figure 3.2.

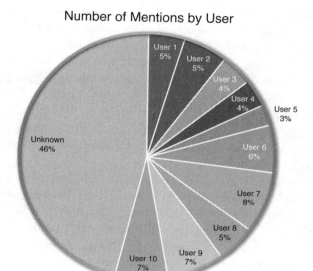

Figure 3.2 Top contributors to social media remarks during an initial product announcement.

A manual lookup of the top 10 users in this conversation revealed that at least 9 of them were employees of the company and represented nearly half the conversation (47%).

The conclusion we drew was that in the various social media and news venues, the employees were chatting about the new release, but given the slope of the curve in Figure 3.1, that conversation didn't sustain itself. After the employees stopped talking, there was virtually no conversation. Clearly, a new marketing plan was needed since what was being said wasn't being repeated, commented on, or perhaps even resonating with the public.

Are They Happy or Unhappy?

I'll never forget the time I [Matt] was traveling to Las Vegas to speak at a trade show. It was a long flight, but when we landed and the plane was taxiing to the gate, I simply tweeted "Viva Las Vegas" and was almost instantly greeted with a return tweet for a hotel/casino special. Someone was actually watching for conversation about the city, not just me, to send a special offer.

Watching or monitoring social media for customer issues is still a growing trend. It provides the ability to respond to issues in a timely fashion as well as gives opportunities for additional business opportunities.

Consumers are using Twitter to either ask questions about product- and service-related issues or to air complaints with increasing regularity. A study by Sprout Social found that social media messages eliciting a direct response from companies had risen by 178% from 2012 to 2013 [2]. To stay competitive, companies are choosing to watch for negative terms or concepts being used around a brand and head off a potential customer satisfaction problem later.

By listening to customer feedback in Twitter, companies like JetBlue have been able to build their reputation as responsive customer service organizations. Think about this from the consumers' perspective. Airline delays can be one of the most common causes of customer frustration. Not only do these delays happen often, but those being delayed or inconvenienced can be pretty vocal about their feelings, especially when there is nothing to do but sit in an airline terminal with their smart phones.

Acknowledging this fact, @JetBlue ensures the company is responsive to its customers because it understands the importance of continued customer loyalty. JetBlue not only engages with happy customers but also responds to and helps frustrated customers as quickly as possible.

According to an article in *AdWeek* [3], due to a downpouring of rain in the Northeast that grounded most of JetBlue's planes, the company was facing a public relations storm that seemed unlikely to go away anytime soon. On this particular occasion, passengers were trapped in their planes (on the tarmac) in New York City for hours—going nowhere and growing more annoyed by the minute. In many cases, passenger delays stretched into days while over 1,000 flights were ultimately canceled.

Needless to say, customer concerns and outcries ran rampant. However, through social media channels, then-CEO David Neeleman reached out to travelers of JetBlue to *personally* apologize for the issues and presented the company's plans to improve service. The use of social media outlets to enable an open atmosphere of communication coupled with the company's willing to admit (publically) its mistakes went a long way to turn a bad situation good.

The lesson?

Listening to the right content (in some cases, customer dissatisfaction) can provide an added vehicle to achieving customer loyalty and goodwill.

JetBlue leveraged YouTube (a popular video-sharing site) to explain the service failure and describe how it planned to improve its operations as a part of its effort to control the situation. Again, it did this by posting an apology by founder and then-CEO David Neeleman shortly after the trouble began. As a result, the company built a relationship with its customers.

This use of a social media source coupled with JetBlue's complete openness and willingness to take responsibility helped to push it over the media reports and resume its standing as a consumer favorite. What's important is that despite the negative news coverage and complaints by consumer advocacy groups, the airline was able to keep its place atop the J.D. Power North America Airline Satisfaction Study for low-cost carriers going on 11 years in a row [4]!

So when we think about who we want to listen to, the answer, of course, is everybody. But by segmenting the comments into those with positive sentiments and those with negative sentiments, we can quickly respond to those urgent customer issues.

Location and Language

There are times when understanding the mood or the thoughts of a particular region of the world is of main importance. For example, if we are interested in understanding the social opinions or concerns of youths in India, monitoring data from the United States isn't all that practical. Just to be complete in this thought, however, while we understand that there may be some spillover discussion in US-based traffic about conditions in India, the likelihood of finding any significant content is probably not worth the effort of having to discover it in a vast sea of other (unrelated) data. Obviously, this is a decision that needs to be made by each data scientist or organization; our intent is simply to point out where there may be value in looking only at a particular region in the world.

As an example, consider the diagram shown in Figure 3.3; it shows social media mentions for a particular bank we were working on an analysis for. The bank had recently made some announcements and was interested to see if there was an increase or decrease in social media traffic as (perhaps) a result of the media attention. Figure 3.3 shows a summary of the top 10 languages for all of the media mentions we were able to collect over the previous two days.

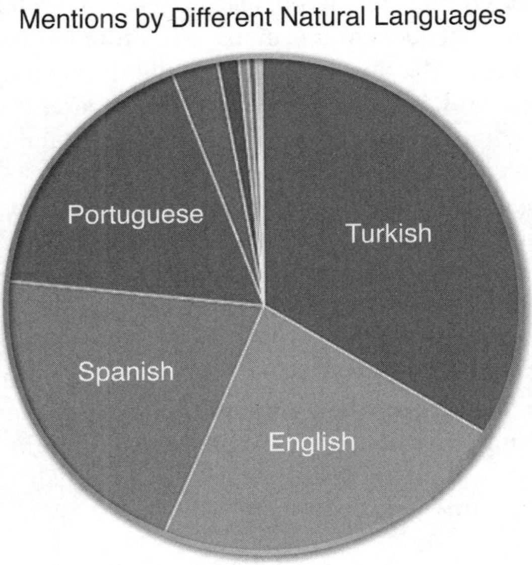

Mentions by Different Natural Languages

Figure 3.3 Top 10 languages used in mentions.

What we were able to see was a large amount of traffic coming not from English (US) speaking individuals, but from Turkish social media participants. Not only that, but it appeared that Portuguese and Spanish numbers were almost equally as high. What was more interesting was that the announcements were made in the United States.

One of the interesting facts to gather would obviously be the location of the individuals making the comments. In some cases, this information is easy to retrieve—for example, through the use of GPS technology on mobile devices. In the case of Twitter, the use of geolocation can allow someone to find tweets that have been sent from a specific location. This could be a country, a city, or multiple regions around the world. When a Twitter user opts in to allow location-based services on his or her Twitter account, Twitter uses geotagging to categorize each tweet by location and makes that information available to subscribers of the data. In theory, this would give users of that data the ability to track tweets sent from a specific city or country. Unfortunately, the statistics on the use of this feature aren't promising (yet), with only about 10% of the total population enabling the feature [5].

Lacking the exact geolocation, we could make the assumption that those posting in Turkish, for example, were originating their tweets from Turkey.

It may not be a perfect one-to-one match, but lacking any other information, it's the best we could do.

In this case, the bank in question had made an announcement (in the US press) about some branch closings in Europe. From the backlash we were able to mine from social media sources, it appears that those most widely affected customers were located in Spanish-speaking countries as well as Turkey. While we don't know exactly how the bank handled this situation (our job was simply to discover any potential issues), we do know it immediately focused customer relations on branches and banking in those regions in an effort to minimize any fallout from its announcements.

Age and Gender

Understanding the demographics of just who is using social media to communicate is an important step in being able to understand what is being said about a company or brand.

Some of the current data provided by the Pew Research Center [6] around social media can give us a better idea of who is generating all of the traffic (and who is listening). Let's not make a mistake here: according to this work, approximately 74% of Internet users are engaged in some form of social media (that's over 2.2 billion individuals). While we've tried to summarize some of the more simple statistics in Table 3.1[7], some numbers should stand out:

- In the 18–29-year-old bracket, there is 89% usage.
- The 30–49-year-old bracket sits at 82%.
- In the 50–64-year-old bracket, 65% are active on social media.
- In the 65-plus bracket, 49% are using social media.

Time spent online using social media shows [8]:

- The United States at 16 minutes of every hour
- The Australians at 14 minutes for every hour
- The United Kingdom users at 13 minutes

And while we're at it, remember that 71% of users' social media access comes from a mobile device [9], and women tend to dominate most of the social media platforms [10].

Table 3.1   Social Media Demographics of Prominent US Sites as of December 2014

Social Media Site	Percent of *Males* polled that participated	Percent of *Females* polled that participated	Ages 18–29	Ages 30–49	Ages 50–64	Ages 65 and older
Facebook	66%	76%	84%	79%	60%	45%
Twitter	17%	18%	31%	19%	9%	5%
Instagram	15%	20%	37%	18%	6%	1%
Pinterest	8%	33%	27%	24%	14%	9%
LinkedIn	24%	19%	15%	27%	24%	13%

Ultimately, we would like to include some of this demographics information in an analysis, but the knowledge of this information is just as useful. If, for example, we were wondering what the issues were surrounding health care (or other issues) post retirement in social media, we would be hard-pressed to find much discussion by that demographic in places such as Instagram or Twitter (since the number of participants in the 65 and older demographic seems to be quite low). That's not to say the chatter wouldn't be out there; there could be significant discussion by the children of those users in the 30–39-year-old demographic, but again, it may come with a different perspective. Similarly, based on this table, if we were interested in the content from females, Pinterest might be a good venue to consider.

Eminence, Prestige, or Popularity

What does it mean to be eminent? There are a number of online presentations and seminars on increasing your social media eminence, or "digital footprint." What are some attributes of eminent people? They tend to be in a position of superiority or distinction. Often they are high ranking or famous (either worldwide or within their social community or sphere of influence) and have a tremendous amount of influence over those who hear what they have to say.

For example, if the president of the United States (or any world leader) makes a comment on some social or economic issue, that comment is usually picked up by the press and is on everyone's lips by the time the evening news comes on (more so if it's a controversial topic). These leaders are highly influential and can literally change the minds or perspectives of millions of people in a relatively short time span. On the other hand, if coauthor Avinash Kohirkar makes a public statement about the same topic, the results are vastly different. He may influence family and friends, but the net effect of his comments pale in comparison to those that are viewed with a higher degree of eminence.

So what do these users do to lay claim to being popular, prestigious, or eminent?

People who are perceived to have a high degree of social media eminence publish high-quality articles or blog entries. Other users rush to see what they have to say (and often repeat it or are influenced by it). Highly eminent people are seen as those individuals who add value to online business discussions. Their eminence is further bolstered by others who have rated their contributions as valuable and have tagged them for reuse by others. In Chapter 11, we talk about how social analytics can be used to determine eminence!

It stands to reason that we would want to know what these people are saying. We also want to know if something was said in the social media concerning our brands or products. It does make a difference if a comment was made by a simple techie (such as Avinash) or a world leader.

One of the challenges in using eminence (or influence) as a metric is determining how to quantify it. There is a lot of discussion and debate in the industry about this topic, and there are lots of tools and approaches that people are using to measure influence [11]. To illustrate this point here, we are going to make some assumptions and come up with a simple formula.

In some of our work, we make the following assumptions:

- Influential people are those who often have their comments repeated.
- Influential people tend to have many people following them (that is, the interest in what they have to say is high).

Based on these assumptions, we defined a simple metric called "reach" that is a quantifiable way to determine how widespread someone's message could be. Reach, to us, is simply the number of things that a person has said multiplied by the number of people listening. Is this metric perfect? No. But it is something to watch for: a person with a large reach is saying a lot and is also reaching a wide audience. Granted, someone could be blabbering about some topic on social media and posting thousands of messages, all being received by a small handful of listeners. If that's a concern, simply look to modify the definition of influence to something like that shown in Figure 3.4.

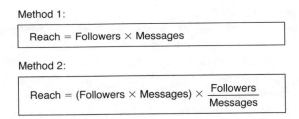

Method 1:

$$\text{Reach} = \text{Followers} \times \text{Messages}$$

Method 2:

$$\text{Reach} = (\text{Followers} \times \text{Messages}) \times \frac{\text{Followers}}{\text{Messages}}$$

Figure 3.4   Simple formulas for calculating influence.

It is possible for a company to use the concept of influencers to effectively communicate a key marketing message broadly. Consider the effect a well-known industry analyst who is constantly talking about security in financial institutions such as banks could have on the perception of various institutions. In addition, if we follow this analyst, we will come to understand the social media venues that this analyst and others like him or her participate in. As an example, let's assume that IBM acquired a company that specializes in fraud detection for banks. Our marketing teams in IBM will be served well by posting about this event on the venues that this analyst is already quite active in. If the analyst is impressed by the acquisition and chooses to "like" it or "share" it, that message will be received by a large number of his or her followers.

How do we measure how influential someone is? Or how do we measure how effective a person's messages are? We can look to see if that person has talked about a specific product or service and then measure the sales of that product or service to see if there is an increase (or decrease). However, that would be a difficult measurement and, quite honestly, wouldn't represent the image or perception of the product or service, which could, at a later date, affect the sales.

Instead, we chose to look at someone's reach, or how far and wide this person's message *could be* spread. Figure 3.4 shows an example of how reach could be computed in a message system such as Twitter (although it's equally applicable to any systems where a post is made and others follow that posting).

In Figure 3.4, we show that an individual's reach can simply be calculated in one of two ways:

- **Method 1**—Multiply the number of messages sent by the number of people that could read that message. If someone sends 1,000 messages and 10 people are following that person, the combined message has a calculated score of 10,000 (see Table 3.2).

- **Method 2**—Multiply the number of messages sent by the number of people that could read the message and then multiply that result by the ratio of followers to messages.

Table 3.2   Example of Determining Someone's Reach in Social Media

Followers	Messages	Reach (Method 1) (Followers * messages)	Ratio	Reach (Method 2)
10	1,000	10,000	0.01	100
200	50	10,000	4	40,000

In method 2, we've add another factor to our equation: the ratio of the number of followers to the number of messages produced. Doing so effectively gives more weight to the person with a larger following. This produces perhaps a more meaningful score for our metric, where we might be more inclined to focus on the comments of the second user rather than those of the first.

Summary

As you can see, as we're moving forward in these chapters, we're trying to get more and more specific about the data that is under analysis. In this chapter, we discussed the concept of the individual in the conversation, or the who. It's a huge point that we need consider in any kind of analysis we're looking to perform. Remember, if you're looking to understand the societal issues in, say, India, does it make sense to include opinions or thoughts of those people in the United States? Perhaps. But at a minimum, we believe you should at least consider breaking out the views of Indians to better understand your question at hand.

If the public chatter about a new movie contains the words *childish, silly,* or *waste of time,* is it relevant? That depends. If the movie is geared for children, and those are the views of adults, perhaps not. Remember, sometimes it's not what is said, but who is saying it!

Endnotes

[1] Adams, Douglas, *The Salmon of Doubt,* 2002, Random House Publishing.

[2] McCauley, Andrew, "Nice to Tweet You: 3 Ways to Use Twitter for Customer Service," *Modern Marketing Blog,* April 22, 2014. Retrieved from http://www.responsys.com/blogs/nsm/social-media-marketing/nice-tweet-3-ways-use-twitter-customer-service/.

[3] Giantasio, David, "JetBlue Knows How to Communicate with Customers in Social, and When to Shut Up: Mastering the Transparency Game," *AdWeek,* September 9, 2013.

[4] Maxon, Terry, "J.D. Power Study Puts Alaska Airlines, JetBlue Airways at Top of Customer Satisfaction," *The Dallas Morning News,* May 13, 2015. Retrieved from http://aviationblog.dallasnews.com/2015/05/j-d-power-study-puts-alaska-airlines-jet-blue-airways-at-top-of-customer-satisfaction.html/.

[5] "An Exhaustive Study of Twitter Users Across the World," Beevolve, Inc., October 10, 2012. Retrieved from http://www.beevolve.com/twitter-statistics/.

[6] "Social Networking Fact Sheet," *Pew Research Center,* 2014. Retrieved from http://www.pewinternet.org/fact-sheets/social-networking-fact-sheet/.

[7] See http://www.pewinternet.org/2015/01/09/demographics-of-key-social-networking-platforms-2/.

[8] See http://www.computerworld.com/article/2496852/internet/americans-spend-16-minutes-of-every-hour-online-on-social-nets.html.

[9] See http://blogs.adobe.com/digitalmarketing/mobile/adobe-2013-mobile-consumer-survey-71-of-people-use-mobile-to-access-social-media/.

[10] Clifford, Catherine, "Women Dominate Every Social Media Network—Except One," *Entrepreneur,* March 4, 2014. Retrieved from http://www.entrepreneur.com/article/231970.

[11] Bullock, Lilach, "What Are the Best Tools to Measure Social Media Influence?," Yahoo Small Business. Retrieved from https://smallbusiness.yahoo.com/advisor/best-tools-measure-social-media-influence-153738338.html.

4

Timing Is Everything

Time flies over us, but leaves its shadow behind.

—Nathaniel Hawthorne [1]

Most people think of social media outlets (Twitter, Instagram, Vine, and so on) as an "in the moment" type of media. What does that mean? Well, think about this: You walk into your favorite store and encounter one of the most unprofessional sales assistants you've ever come across. What do you do if you're active in social media outlets like Twitter? You open your smart phone and tweet something like this:

Worst customer service I've ever encountered—shame on you #company

There are times when we feel compelled to express our thoughts and feelings in this fashion and more often than not, someone listening to our rants responds with a sense of sympathy or consolation. By "in the moment," we're referring to being mindfully aware of what is going on right here and now.

This ability to immediately share our thoughts is one of the great powers of social media. This power, in turn, can be leveraged to derive business value. For example, we can monitor the pulse of a community of individuals pertaining to a specific event that is occurring right now. Trending topics are those being discussed more than others. These topics are being talked about—in Twitter or any other social media venue, for example—more right now than they were previously. This is the reason that Twitter lists the trending topics directly on its site. This list allows users to see what a large group of individuals are talking about. In addition to identifying trends, we are able to perform additional analytics to derive insights from such conversations. We cover these types of analysis in more detail in Chapter 6 of this book.

So far, we have talked about communications happening right now, but what about communications that have already occurred at some point of time in the past?

- Have people talked about that particular topic in the past?
- Has the sentiment surrounding the topic changed over time?
- Are there different themes surrounding the topic now as opposed to, say, last year?

In Jay Asher's book *Thirteen Reasons Why*, character Hannah says:

"You can't go back to how things were. How you thought they were. All you really have is…now." [2]

Luckily for us, this isn't the case in social media analytics. As a matter of fact, looking back in time is often just as important as (if not more so than) looking at the present.

Predictive Versus Descriptive

Most of what we think of when we talk about business analytics are what we would call "descriptive analytics." *Descriptive analytics* looks at data and analyzes past events for insight as to how to approach the future. Here, we look at past performance and, by understanding that performance, attempt to look for the reasons behind past successes or failures. Descriptive statistics are used to describe the basic features of the data in a sample. They provide simple summaries about the data and what was measured during the time it was collected. Descriptive analytics usually serves as the foundation for further advanced analytics.

Descriptive statistics are useful in summarizing large amounts of data into a manageable subset. Each statistic reduces larger "chunks" of data into a simpler, summary form.

For example, consider the analysis of a large block of social media data surrounding an industry trade show. If we break down the topics seen in all of the social media conversations from the show, we could produce a set of descriptive statistics similar to those shown in Table 4.1.

Table 4.1 Social Media Conversations by Topic

Topic	Percentage of Overall Discussion
Mobile Security	35%
Cloud Computing	15%
Internet of Things	10%
Analytics	20%
Social Computing	5%
Miscellaneous	15%

In this case, the metric "Percentage of Overall Discussion" describes what the conversations are generally about. We could have just as easily reported on the number of males or females who made comments or the number of comments made by people claiming to be from North America, Europe, or Asia Pacific (for example). All these metrics help us understand (or describe) the sample of data; thus, they are descriptive statistics. The purpose of descriptive analytics is simply to summarize a dataset in an effort to describe what happened. In the case of social media, think about the number of posts by any given individual, the number of mentions by Twitter handle, a count of the number of fans or followers of a page, and so on. The best way to describe these metrics is to think of them as simple event counters. We should also remember that the ultimate business goal of any analysis project will drive the data sources we are interested in as well as the aspects of the data we need to focus on. This dimension of time helps us collect a suitably large set of data depending on the goal of the project.

Predictive Analytics

Predictive analytics can be thought of as an effort to extract information from existing datasets to determine patterns of behavior or to predict future outcomes and trends. It's important to understand that predictive analytics does not (and can NOT) tell us what will happen in the future. At best, predictive analytics can help analysts forecast what might happen in the future with an acceptable level of reliability or confidence.

Refer again to the value pyramid from Chapter 1. The supposition was that as we continued to refine a data source (over time), the more valuable the residual, or resulting, dataset would become. Perhaps that same diagram can be drawn with respect to time, as shown in Figure 4.1. The more temporal the data becomes, the wider view we obtain, and therefore the greater understanding can be derived. If we are focusing on a given data source, we can improve our level of understanding of that dataset by not only gaining a wider understanding, but perhaps by modifying our perception of the data as it evolves over time. For example, if we are monitoring conversations in a community about a new email system that has been rolled out to all employees, over a period of time, we get an idea of which features are being talked about more than others, which types of users are having difficulties with a certain set of features, and who are the most vocal about their experience. This is possible because over time, we are able to refine our filters to look at the most relevant data, and then we are able to revise and refine our analytics model to expose key combinations of parameters that we are interested in.

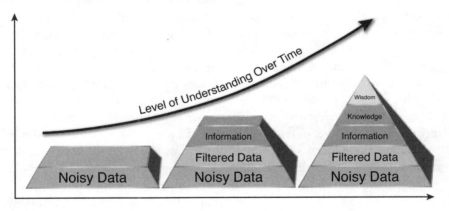

Figure 4.1   Understanding increases over time.

Often, when we are looking at trends or predictive behavior, we are looking at a series of descriptive statistics over time. Think of a trend line, which is typically a time series model (or any predictive model) that summarizes the past pattern of a particular metric. While these models of data can be used to summarize existing data, what makes them more powerful is the fact that they act a model that we can use to extrapolate to a future time when data doesn't yet exist. This extrapolation is what we might call "forecasting."

Trend forecasting is a method of quantitative forecasting in which we make predictions about future events based on tangible (real) data from the past. Here, we use time series data, which is data for which the value for a particular metric is known over different points in time.

As shown in Figure 4.2, some numerical data (or descriptive statistic) is plotted on a graph. Here, the horizontal x-axis represents time, and the y-axis represents some specific value or concept we are trying to predict, such as volume of mentions or, in this case, consumer sentiment over time. Several different types of patterns tend to appear on a time-series graph.

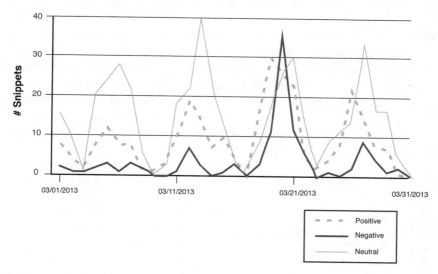

Figure 4.2 Consumer sentiment (positive, negative, or neutral) over time.

What's interesting in this graph isn't the size (or amount) of positive, negative, or neutral sentiment over the month of March, but the pattern that seems to emerge when looking at this data over time. This analysis of industrywide mentions of topics in and around cloud computing was done by Shara LY Wong of IBM Singapore (under the direction of Matt Ganis as part of a mentoring program inside of IBM). A close inspection of this temporal representation of the data shows that every 10 days or so, there is a peak of activity around the topic. All three dimensions of sentiment (positive, negative, or neutral) seem to peak and rise at the same time in a fairly regular manner. Given that the leader of the metrics in all cases is the line representing neutral sentiment, we were able to quickly determine that on a very systematic schedule, there are a number of vendor advertisements around the topic, most with a slant toward positive sentiment. One anomaly appears to be the March 21 discussions that generated not only the largest spike in discussion, but also the largest negative reaction by far.

The essence of predictive analytics, in general, is that we use existing data to build a model. Then we use that model to make predictions about information that may not yet exist. So predictive analytics is all about using data we have to predict data that we don't have. Consider the view of consumer sentiment about a particular food brand over time (in this case, a 20-month period). We've plotted the values obtained for the positive sentiment with respect to time and done a least-squares fit to obtain the trend line (see Figure 4.3). The solid line in this figure is drawn through each observation over a 20-month period. The broken line is derived using a well-known statistical technique called linear regression analysis that uses a method called least-squares fit. In this simplistic example, it is easy to see that the trend line can be utilized to predict the value of positive sentiment in future months (like months 21 and 22 and so on). We can have confidence in this prediction because the predictions seem to have been quite close to reality in the past 20 months.

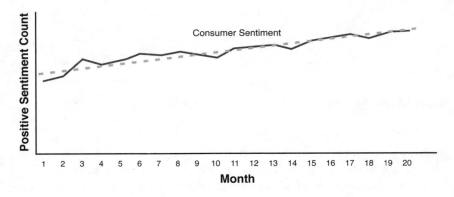

Figure 4.3   The trend line.

From high school math, this derived trend line is nothing more than the familiar equation for a straight line:

$Y = mx + b$

where the value of *m* is the slope of the line and *b* represents the y-intercept (or the point where *x*—in this case, time—is zero) are constants. From this, we can examine any time in the future, by substituting a value for *x* (in this case, we would use a value of *x* greater than 20 to look into the future, since anything less than 20 is already understood) and, with a fairly good level of confidence, predict the amount of positive consumer sentiment (the value of *y*). While simple in nature, this is a perfect example of a predictive model.

If we want to know what the sentiment will be around this brand over the next 24 to 36 months (assuming conditions don't change), this simple relationship can be a "predictor" for us. As we said previously, it's not a guarantee, but a prediction based on prior knowledge and trending of the data.

Descriptive Analytics

When we use the term *descriptive analytics*, what we should think about is this: What attributes would we use to describe what is contained in this specific sample of data—or rather, how can we summarize the dataset?

To further illustrate the concept of descriptive analytics, we use the results from a system called *Simple Social Metrics* that we developed at IBM. It's nothing more than a system that "follows" a filtered set of Twitter traffic and attempts to provide some kind of quantitative description of the data that was collected (we talk more about this in Chapter 8, where we address real-time data).

In this example, we use a dataset of tweets made by IBMers who are members of IBM's Academy of Technology. The IBM Academy of Technology is a society of IBM technical leaders organized to advance the understanding of key technical areas, to improve communications in and development of IBM's global technical community, and to engage its clients in technical pursuits of common value. These are some of IBM's top technical minds, so an analysis of their conversation could be quite useful.

One of the first questions we want to answer is this: "Who is contributing the most?" or rather, "Who is tweeting the most or being tweeted about?" One way to do this is to analyze the number of contributions. We simply call this the "top authors," and for the month of November, a breakdown of the top contributors looked something like that shown in Figure 4.4. Even though this diagram tells us which author had the most number of tweets, we need to go beyond the machine-based analysis and leverage human analysis to determine who really "contributed" the most.

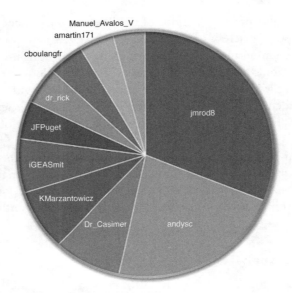

Figure 4.4   Top 10 authors from IBM's Academy of Technology during November 2014.

While this data is interesting, we need to remember that these types of descriptive metrics represent just a summary over a given point in time. The view could be quite different if we look at the data and take the time frame into consideration. For example, consider the same data, but a view of the whole month versus the last half of the month (see Figure 4.5).

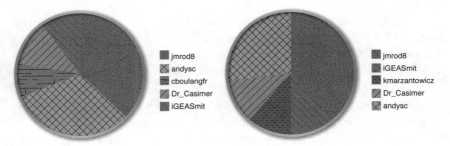

Figure 4.5   Top authors during the whole month and just at the end.

An important fact that comes across here is that one of the users, kmarzantowicz, came on strong during the last half of the month with a heavy amount of tweeting to move into the top five of all individuals. Perhaps this person was attending a conference and tweeting about various presentations or speeches; or perhaps this person said something intriguing and there was a flurry of activity around him or her. From an analyst's perspective, it would be interesting to pull the conversation that was generated by that user for the last 15 days of the month to understand why there was such a large upsurge in traffic.

Sentiment

One of the more popular descriptive metrics that people like to use is *sentiment*. Sentiment is usually associated with the emotion (positive or negative) that an individual is feeling about the topic being discussed. In this chapter, which is focused on time, we discuss sentiment as it changes over time.

Sentiment analytics involves the analysis of comments or words made by individuals to quantify the thoughts or feelings intended to be conveyed by words. Basically, it's an attempt to understand the positive or negative feelings individuals have toward a brand, company, individual, or any other entity. In our experience, most of the sentiment collected around topics tends to be "neutral" (or convey no positive or negative feelings or meanings). It's easiest to think about sentiment analytics when we look at Twitter data (or any other social site where people express a single thought or make a single statement). We can compute the sentiment of a document (such as a wiki post or blog entry) by looking at the overall scoring of sentiment words that it contains. For example, if a document contains 2,000 words that are considered negative versus 300 words that are considered positive in meaning, we may choose to classify that document as overall negative in sentiment. If the numbers are closer together (say 3,000 negative words versus 2,700 positive words—or an almost equal distribution), we may choose to say that document is neutral in sentiment.

Consider this simple message from LinkedIn:

Hot off the press! Check out this week's enlightening edition of the #companyname Newsletter http://bit.ly/xxxx

A sentiment analysis of this message would indicate that it's positive in tone. The sentiment analysis being done by software is usually based on a sentiment dictionary for that language. The basic package comes with a predefined list of words that are considered as positive. Similarly, there is also a long list of words that can be considered negative. For many projects, the standard dictionary can be utilized for determining sentiment. In some special cases, you may have to modify the dictionary to include domain-specific positive and negative words. For example, the word *Disaster* can be a negative sentiment word in a majority of contexts, except when it is used to refer to a category of system such as "Disaster Recovery Systems."

Understanding the general tone of a dataset can be an interesting metric, if indeed there is some overwhelming skew toward a particular tone in the message.

Consider the descriptive set of metrics of sentiment shown in Figure 4.6, taken from an analysis we did for a customer in the financial industry over a one-month period. This represents the tone of the messages posted in social media about this particular company.

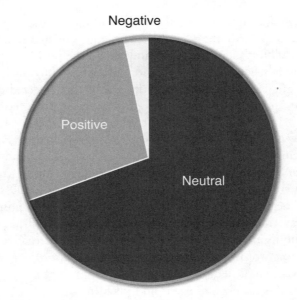

Figure 4.6 Customer sentiment over a one-month period.

On the surface, this looks like a good picture. The amount of positive conversation is clearly greater than the amount of negative, and the neutral sentiment (which is neither bad nor good) overwhelms both. So in summary, this appears to be quite acceptable.

However, if we take the negative sentiment and look at it over time, a different picture emerges, as illustrated in Figure 4.7.

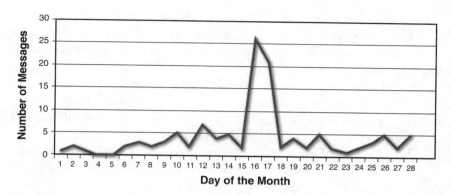

Figure 4.7 Plot of one month's count of negative sentiment.

While cumulatively the negative sentiment was much smaller than the positive, there was one particular date range (from approximately the 16th to the 18th of the month) when there was a large spike in negative messaging centered around our client. While just an isolated spike in traffic, the event could have lingering effects if not addressed.

Time as Your Friend

Access to historical information can be vastly informative (and useful) if utilized in the proper way. Up until this point in our discussion, we've described the collection of data as it appears but really haven't mentioned the use of a data store or the collection of historical information.

We talk more about this topic in the later chapters, but for now the question to ask is: How could we take advantage of a historical data collection? One answer is that we could look for a baseline so that, as we take measurements now, in the present, we can better understand if those measurements have any real meaning.

For example, in the previous example where we discussed positive versus negative sentiment, on average for the month shown, we had a ratio of 1:8 negative to positive comments (for every one negative comment, we were able to see eight positive comments).

The question is: Is that good or bad? The answer to this question depends on the specifics of the situation and also on the goal of the social analytics project that we are working on. Looking back in time, we were able to compute that in previous months, the ratio remained relatively constant. So there was no need for alarm in seeing the negative statements (note that this is not to say we need to ignore the negative things being said—far from it—but there doesn't appear to be an increase in any negative press or feelings).

But there is another interesting use case for data stores, and it's that of validating our models.

In one interesting use case we had, we were asked to monitor social media channels in an attempt to identify a hacker trying to break into a specific website. The idea sounds a bit absurd: What person or group would attempt to break into a website and publish their progress on social media sites?

While we didn't have high hopes for success, we followed our iterative approach and built an initial model that would describe how people might "talk" when (or if) they were attempting a server breach. It was a fairly complex model and required a security specialist to spend time looking over whatever information we were able to find. Over the months of running our model, watching as many real-time social media venues as we could, we ended up returning a large number of false positives.

This inevitability leads to the question: Is the model working, or is it just that nobody is trying to break in? It's a valid question. How do we validate that we can detect a specific event if we don't know that the event has occurred?

Well, we took the data model and changed it to reflect IBM. We wanted to run the model against a site that had been hacked in the past, and a widely reported incident around IBM's DeveloperWorks site defacement was a perfect candidate.

Using a data aggregator called Boardreader (which is closely integrated with IBM's Social Media Analytics [SMA] product), we pulled data from around January 1, 2011, until January 31, and processed that data within our model. Sure enough, we saw that our model identified the hacking instance almost as soon as it was reported (within minutes). This data was important to us because it served to validate our model and assure us to a certain degree that if a group was going to do this again (to our client), we could at least catch it as soon as possible.

Summary

In this chapter, we discussed how the concept of time can be factored into an analysis in several ways:

- Accumulation of larger datasets
- Descriptive analytics

- Predictive analytics (establishing trends and using the trends to predict the future)
- Validation of hypotheses using historical data

In general, the level and depth of analysis are directly proportional to the amount of properly selected and filtered data that went into that analysis. However, in some use cases, it is important to get a quick "point in time" analysis, as we discussed with a trade show or presentation and audience reactions. Of course, if we want to deliver a more relevant message, our datasets for analytics may need to look back over time to establish a trend. For example, if IT professionals had been discussing security around cloud computing for the last several months, chances are, that's a topic they would be interested in hearing about during a presentation.

One perhaps not-so-obvious use of historical data could be to validate models for an upcoming analysis. Many times we assume we have configured models and data engines to capture the "right" data, but do we know for sure they work? Using historical data provides an easy testbed to ensure, or at least test, that our assumptions and models are correct so that our current analysis can be as accurate as possible.

Endnotes

[1] Hawthorne, Nathaniel. *Transformation: The Marble Faun, And, The Blithedale Romance*. George Bell and Sons, 1886.

[2] Asher, Jay. *Thirteen Reasons Why*. Ernst Klett Sprachen, 2010.

5

Social Data: *Where and Why*

Variety's the very spice of life, That gives it all its flavor.

—William Cowper

When you think of the word *data*, what comes to mind?

At a very simplistic level, data is nothing more than a collection of facts, measurements, or observations that, when combined, form or create what we might call information. At its core, data is a raw, unorganized set of facts that need to be processed into something more meaningful. A set of numbers (or data points) such as those shown in Table 5.1 is relatively meaningless until we put them into context. The numbers 45.3, 39.1, 35.9, and so on mean nothing to us until we realize (from Table 5.2) that they are measurements of temperature. So, by combining data (values in a table) with the additional contextual data that the values represent temperature, we are able to extract "information."

Table 5.1   Raw Data

Data
45.3
39.4
35.9
32.1
30.6
29.3
27.4

Table 5.2   Temperature Data

Temperature
45.3
39.4
35.9
32.1
30.6
29.3
27.4

By labeling the column of data with the word *Temperature*, we at least have a bit of content. The numbers by themselves could represent literally anything—from distances between a specific city and nearby towns or cities, average test scores, water levels in a reservoir, or any other measurable entity.

But they're still not useful.

- Are those temperatures at a specific location?
- When were the measurements taken? (At night, during the sunlit day, under water?)
- How is the temperature measured? Is it degrees Fahrenheit or Celsius, or is it measured in kelvins?

Table 5.3 provides even more context and tells us that these are observations about temperature (in degrees Fahrenheit) at various points in time on a particular day in 2014. This table now helps us realize that on the particular date in question, around 5:30 p.m. there was a sharp decrease in temperature—the derivation of a new piece of information. Each column represents a piece of data, meaningless when it stands alone but relevant when understood *within a context*.

Table 5.3 Temperature Readings as an Example of Data

Temperature	Scale	Timestamp
45.3	Degrees Fahrenheit	2014-12-10 17:30pm ET
39.4	Degrees Fahrenheit	2014-12-10 18:00pm ET
35.9	Degrees Fahrenheit	2014-12-10 18:30pm ET
32.1	Degrees Fahrenheit	2014-12-10 19:00pm ET
30.6	Degrees Fahrenheit	2014-12-10 19:30pm ET
29.3	Degrees Fahrenheit	2014-12-10 20:00pm ET
27.4	Degrees Fahrenheit	2014-12-10 20:30pm ET

Structured Data Versus Unstructured Data

Even though data comes in a variety of shapes, sizes, and forms, for the purpose of our analysis, we can think of data as coming in essentially two categories: *organized* and *unorganized*. That may be a bit of an oversimplification. A data scientist would call them *structured* and *unstructured*.

Think of structured data as data that contains a high degree of organization: We can define a data model for it and allow it to easily be placed into a database system. Once in a database, the data is readily searchable by simple, straightforward search engine mechanisms. Consider the example shown in Figure 5.1.

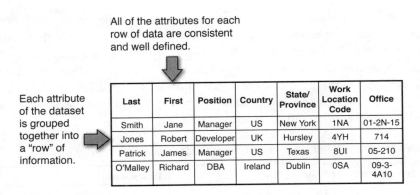

Figure 5.1   Example of a structured database table.

This example illustrates a table from a structured database. Each row in the column represents an *observation* (a specific employee), and each column is an *attribute* that describes the row of data (the person's last name, position in the company, work location, and so on). We call it structured because each record or row has the same attribute. Each one can be interrogated because we know the type of data held in each attribute. For example, we know the country column has a well-known set of values, as does the work location code and position. This table can be stored in a database, so querying or evaluating the data is relatively straightforward using standard database querying tools that are available in the marketplace.

Unstructured data is essentially the opposite of structured. The lack of structure makes collecting this data a time- and energy-consuming task due to the nonuniformity of the data.

In the case of social media, the data takes the form of unstructured data, or data without a specific format. Unstructured data often includes text but more often than not can contain additional multimedia content. In the case of social media, this could include likes, URLs in messages, and pictures or references to other individuals. One contradiction to consider is that different data sources may have a specific "application structure"; that is, data from one source can all look similar (as if it was structured). But because the data that these sources contain doesn't fit neatly into a database or across multiple applications, we still refer to it as "unstructured." Consider the Twitter example in Figure 5.2.

While some social media (in this case, Twitter) has a number of structured or well-defined attributes, for an analyst, what's more interesting is the free-form text of the tweet or payload.

User Handle	Date	Time	Tweet
ITGuy	Jan 1, 2015	15:40:22	Wondering how #productname is suppose to work
AliceR	Jan 1, 2015	15:43:13	Loving my new installation of #productname
BigGuy	Jan 1, 2015	15:45:03	Does anybody have a preference #productname or #otherproduct
LuvData	Jan 1, 2015	15:45:54	@alicer – I agree – I think its fantastic #productname

The commentary is essentially free-form text, meaning that there is nothing to query or examine that allows us to identify attributes of the message. It's essentially "unstructured" in that we have to deduce what is being said.

Figure 5.2   Example of Twitter data as unstructured data.

While this data looks similar to that of the previous example of structured content, the real value of the Twitter data (or any other social media content) comes from an analysis of the unstructured portion of the "record," in this case, the tweet.

Big Data

According to an article by Gil Press of *Forbes* [2], the first documented use of the term *big data* appeared in a 1997 paper by scientists from NASA, in which they were describing the problem they had with the visualization of their datasets:

[A large data set] provides an interesting challenge for computer systems: data sets are generally quite large, taxing the capacities of main memory, local disk, and even remote disk. We call this the problem of big data. When data sets do not fit in main memory (in core), or when they do not fit even on local disk, the most common solution is to acquire more resources. [3]

The term *big data* also appeared in a 2008 paper by Randal Bryant, Randy Katz, and Edward Lazowska that made the following bold statement:

> Big-data computing is perhaps the biggest innovation in computing in the last decade. We have only begun to see its potential to collect, organize, and process data in all walks of life. [4]

There a number of definitions for big data:

> "Big data is the derivation of value from traditional relational database-driven business decision making, augmented with new sources of unstructured data." —Oracle Corporation [5]

> "Big data is the term increasingly used to describe the process of applying serious computing power—the latest in machine learning and artificial intelligence—to seriously massive and often highly complex sets of information." —Microsoft [6]

The National Institute of Standards and Technology (NIST) argues that "Big data refers to digital data volume, velocity, and/or variety that exceed the storage capacity or analysis capability of current or conventional methods and systems" (in other words, the notion of "big" is relative to the current standard of computation) [7]. No matter how we slice it or describe it, big data is the latest craze in the Information Technology industry. It's a term (or concept) that attempts to describe the voluminous amount of data available (most likely on the Internet) that can be used to mine for information. Most pundits in the industry define big data through the use of the *Three Vs*: the extremely large *volume* of data, the wide-sweeping *variety* of types of data, and the various data sources and the *velocity* at which the data is appearing (or being created) and therefore must be processed. Others include a fourth dimension, *veracity* (or the quality of the data), and still others attach *value* as an attribute (see Figure 5.3). No matter what definition we use to describe this phenomena, it is clear that we are being inundated with data, and choosing the right data source can be crucial to a social media analytics strategy.

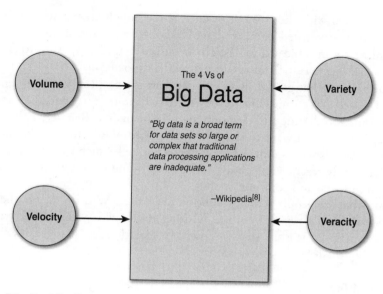

Figure 5.3   The 4 Vs of big data.

Social Media as Big Data

The term *social media* can be viewed as an umbrella term that can be used for several different venues where people connect with others directly on the Internet to communicate and exchange views and opinions or participate in any type of social commentary.

It is important to understand why people use these websites, as there is a variety of demographics represented on these sites. Some people use them for business purposes, to network, and to find new deals. Others use social networking sites for purely personal reasons and are totally oblivious to the fact that there is a business presence in the social networking environment.

NOTE

The content created by employees within a company while collaborating with each other in their enterprise social network is also considered social media. We cover this aspect of social media in Chapter 11.

We started with the concept of data, and through an explanation of big data and unstructured data, we have described what social media data is. Before we get into the analysis aspects in future chapters, we want to explore why social media is such an important media to focus on.

Social media has gained in acceptance over the past few years for a number of reasons. We can point to the growth of the Internet and the concept of information sharing and dissemination. Humans, by their very nature, are naturally social and want to share what they know. Add to that the incredible growth of smart phones and mobile technologies such that we, as a society, have truly reached an "always on" culture—and it's no wonder we see a growth in social and community sites.

But what are people actually *doing* on these sites? Why do they bother?

In looking at a report by Anita Whiting and David Williams [9], we can see a number of reasons that Internet users participate in social media, as covered in the following sections.

Social for Social's Sake

While not in any particular order, the concept of participating on these sites can purely be for the social aspect of meeting new acquaintances and staying in touch with older ones. In our opinion, this is the primary reason for the rapid growth of sites like Facebook. The ability to allow others to share in our daily lives and stay abreast of our every move has a certain appeal and perhaps gives us a sense of community. In the same vein, we tend to be curious by nature, and through the windows of social media, we are able to see into the lives of others, perhaps living vicariously through them or just building a bond as we stay "in" each other's lives.

Social Media as Entertainment

Many people report that the use of social media is a way to unwind, to pass time, or just relax with others via the electronic highways of the Internet. Given that many of these social sites not only provide for the sharing of information in the form of pictures, short updates, and even longer blog-like postings, they also foster gaming, either with others in an immediate network or individuals. Through the use of games, many social media providers hope to keep participants coming back for more—and they obviously do. Many people simply look for relaxation or ways to alleviate stress and escape from reality, even if just for a little while.

Social Media as Sharing

Apart from socializing with others, we also like to share what we know with others or seek the advice of others when or if we have questions of our own. Not only that, but we do like to share our opinions and experiences with others in the hope of influencing them or perhaps steering them away from bad experiences. Social media can be a valuable tool, put in the hands of individuals, in a quest to spread praise or criticism of products or services.

In the case of blogging, millions of people are making their voices heard. The Internet has drastically changed how we, as individuals, can reach out to others. Never before has it been so easy to be able to reach a *global* audience with so little effort. Today, bloggers have the opportunity of reaching hundreds or even thousands of people every day and spreading their stories, opinions, and values. For individuals, there is a benefit of building their personal brand.

Think of this as *Consumer Reports* for individuals. From it own website, *Consumer Reports* defines itself like this:

> Consumer Reports has empowered consumers with the knowledge they need to make better and more informed choices—and has battled in the public and private sectors for safer products and fair market practices. [10]

How do writers at *Consumer Reports* form their opinions? Through their own independent tests and evaluations, which then get reported to individuals. It's not unlike posting a request for a local restaurant review on Facebook or Twitter and then making an informed decision based on what others have to say.

Now, to be fair, this is where the *V* for *veracity* comes in (and perhaps some pessimistic individuals). Obviously, there are those who will believe that since we can't ensure an unbiased review, how do we know we can "trust" the opinions or thoughts espoused on social media sites? Well, the short answer is: we don't. But if we see enough positive reviews versus negative reviews, we're likely to be swayed (obviously one way or the other).

Where to Look for Big Data

The next question, then, is Where do we look for big data?

There are large number of conversational sites on the Internet where even larger varieties of conversations are happening. Knowing where to look or what conversations to watch for can be a daunting task. Conversations can (and do) happen everywhere. They obviously occur in social media sites, but conversations and opinions are often found in comments made to news stories, online retail stores, obituary sites—virtually everywhere on the Internet. It's easy to get lost in the sea of sites when trying to collate all of this information. Often, organizations merge enterprise data with social data, linking together employees and their social commentary or product schedules and announcements with public discussions around the products. This can only compound the issue of trying to find the "right" conversations to analyze. While we acknowledge this is being done and it makes "big data" even bigger, within the context of this book, we don't address the additional issues of expanding the datasets' size by augmenting with additional data. This brings us to the next question: Which data source is right for my project?

Paradox of Choice: Sifting Through Big Data

In his book *The Paradox of Choice: Why More Is Less*, American psychologist Barry Schwartz purports that eliminating consumer choices can greatly reduce anxiety that many shoppers feel [11]. The idea that we have so many choices in life can actually cause us stress (stress over "Did I pick the right one?" or "Will this other option last longer?" and so on). According to *The Paradox of Choice*, when it comes to buying any kind of item, from a box of cereal to a new car, we have trouble making decisions. What's interesting is the fact that too much choice is actually harmful to our well-being. When there are too many options, we suffer, believing our choice is flawed or that we could have made a better one in the long run.

This suffering is the paradox of choice, and it describes how we become less satisfied the more choices there are. We bring up this topic not to discuss our buying habits, but to point out a similar situation in choosing where to look for the social media data that we would like to analyze.

Consider the graph in Figure 5.4. Here, we graph the number of users reporting to be registered in some of the more popular social media sites available on the Internet. We've taken just a snapshot of the more popular sites; it would be nearly impossible to show them all—partially because social media sites come and go and some might not be identified as traditional "social media" sites, so we don't know about them [12].

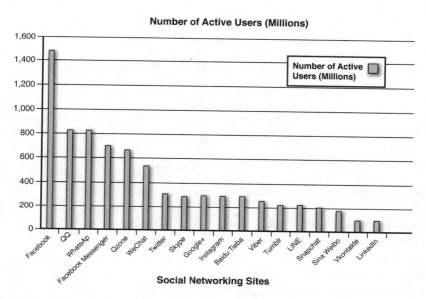

Figure 5.4   Number of users participating in various social media sites.

The question, however, remains: Which sites should we gather data from for our analysis?

The leader of social media content is clearly Facebook, which boasts of over 1.5 billion registered users at the time we wrote this chapter [13]. So the question analysts have to ask themselves is: Can I use data from just Facebook and ignore the rest? The short answer is no. To obtain a well-rounded opinion, we want to have as much relevant data as possible. So again, looking at the graph in Figure 5.4, we probably should focus on sites from Facebook to Baidu Tieba (or maybe Tumblr). But why not all of them? Where do we (or should we) stop?

On one hand, when we hear about big data, we immediately think of sifting through tremendous amounts of data, distilling it down to its bare essence, revealing some golden nuggets of truth. In some cases, this may be true, but in practice, we have found that as the amount of data rises, so does the noise in the data. An electrical engineer refers to this as the *signal-to-noise ratio*—or how much "relevant" information there is in a sample versus how much "noise," or nonrelevant information (see Figure 5.5).

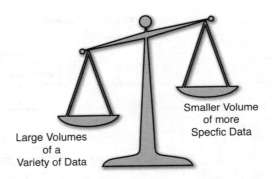

Figure 5.5 Trade-off between large (nonscoped) and smaller (scoped) datasets.

As a case in point, consider one analysis we were involved in during our early days here. We were approached by one of our internal divisions and asked for an analysis of IBM's BladeCenter product against its competitors. We were asked to look at this from a number of different angles including the sentiments toward/against IBM's product, the sentiment around its competitors, the trends over time, the topics of conversation, and even where, within the social media space, the conversations about the product were occurring most.

For this analysis, we ingested as much "relevant" data as we could find into our analytics tool and began the analysis. In one instance, we discovered one particular venue (social media site) where the discussions about BladeCenter were far outpacing the others (see Figure 5.6).

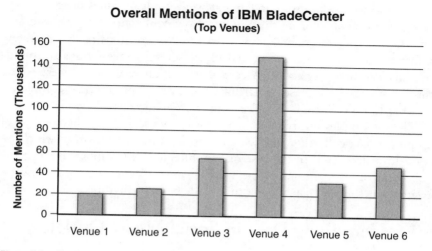

Figure 5.6 Number of mentions for BladeCenter in social media.

The interesting thing about that site is that it was a gaming site where users discuss various ins and outs of gaming: running sites, playing games, deploying strategies, and so on. This led to the (false) conclusion that the BladeCenter product was used heavily as a gaming platform, so we continue to "drill" into the specifics from that site.

Well, as any good data scientist will tell you: Your results are only as good as your data.

As we looked closer, it became apparent that the discussion on that social media site was indeed about Blades, but it wasn't a computer; it was a character in one particular game that was very popular. In other words, all of that conversation was completely irrelevant to our topic! In that particular case, we ensured that our data collection avoided gaming sites to make sure we had the correct data. Issues like these are usually picked up in the first few iterations of analysis, which is an essential part of the process. We highlight this point here for you as an issue to be aware of as you do a similar analysis on your own.

Of course, the obvious question is: What if there was substantial discussion on these gaming sites of the BladeCenter product? It would have meant a much more sophisticated data model that ensured any discussion of BladeCenter was in the context of computing (or perhaps cloud computing), but in this case, the easiest solution was to simply remove the data source.

In another case, we were looking at what kinds of issues or topics were being talked about during the SapphireNow conference (http://events.sap.com/sapphirenow/en/home) a few years ago. We got some really interesting information, but at first we started to see several conversations surrounding mixed drinks (cocktails). A careful inspection revealed we were seeing discussions (and advertisements) for Bombay's Sapphire Gin—completely unrelated to the IT conference we were interested in observing.

These examples illustrate what we mean by "scoping." The concept of scoping a data collection simply means to set a boundary within which we want to collect data. In the case of SapphireNow, we wanted to scope the collection of an mentions of the word *sapphire* to computer- or software-related issues rather than allow it to be wide open to anything.

Identifying Data in Social Media Outlets

When we talk about social media sites, we often have to be clear what type of data we would gather. It's important to understand how people interact on the site and how they exchange information with one another. In this section, we primarily discuss the sites that are most relevant in the United States. There are too many social media sites and venues to dive into the demographics of all of them. But it is useful to understand where we can go to find information from a specific region or demographic. The following tables provide a glimpse of the social media outlets for China (see Table 5.4), Europe (see Table 5.5), and India (see Table 5.6) [14].

Table 5.4   Social Media Outlets for China

Site Name	User Population	Type of Site
Qzone	712 million users	Blogs/content sharing
Tencent Weibo	507 million users	Microblogging
Sina Weibo	500 million users	Microblogging
Pengyou	259 million users	Social networking
51.com	200 million users	Gaming
RenRen	172 million users	Facebook-like site
Jiayuan	73 million users	Dating site

Table 5.5   Social Media Outlets for Europe

Site Name	User Population	Type of Site
Viadeo	55 million users	LinkedIn-like
Tuenti	14 million users	Facebook-like
Grou.PS	12 million users	Social networking
Bebo	11 million users (declining)	Facebook-like
Lokalisten	200 thousand users	Facebook-like
Hyves	100 thousand users	Gaming

Table 5.6   Social Media Outlets for India

Site Name	User Population	Type of Site
Bharastudent	44 million users	Social networking
Ibibo	29 million users	Facebook-like
Orkut	20 million users	Facebook-like
Zedge	3 million users (declining)	Site for mobile users
Shtyle	1.5 million users	Social networking
Hyves	100 thousand users	Gaming

Professional Networking Sites

Professional networking sites are just that: social networking sites where business professionals can go to meet or find others with similar interests or just stay connected with business contacts, all with a goal of building up a professional network. They are rich in profiling information such as education level, job history, and current position within companies. These sites often allow the users to be "introduced to" and collaborate with other professionals in an effort to enhance or improve their professional stature. LinkedIn is the dominant professional social network. It has become the de facto system of record for online résumés for many professionals. Want to hear what business professionals are saying about a topic? Look to LinkedIn (or other professional networking sites).

LinkedIn

User population: 332 million users

Demographics [15]:

- North America: 119 million
- Europe: 78 million
- Asia: 52 million
- South America: 46 million
- Africa: 15 million
- Middle East: 11 million
- Oceania: 8 million

LinkedIn is an online social network that was designed for business professionals. Because of this distinction, it tends to be different from other social networking sites such as Facebook or RenRen. LinkedIn users are looking to build or enhance their professional network. They are looking for or posting job opportunities, discovering sales leads, or connecting with potential business partners—rather than simply making friends or sharing content.

LinkedIn profiles are more like professional résumés with a focus on employment and education history. Like Facebook users, LinkedIn users are part of "invited networks" (in Facebook, users have "friends"; in LinkedIn, they are part of a network). Based on work history and education background (from a profile), LinkedIn can help identify others that (potentially) have similar interests or backgrounds to invite into your network. On LinkedIn, the people who are part of your network are called your "connections." A connection implies that you know the person well or that it is a trusted business.

Generally, user profiles are fully visible to all LinkedIn members who have signed into the site; all of this is configurable within LinkedIn. Typically, contact information such as email, phone number, and physical address is visible only to first-degree connections and members (those you have in your network). Users can control the visibility of their posts and other recent activity by adjusting their visibility settings, and most allow their comments/posts to be seen only within their networks.

Since LinkedIn does tend to be more professional networking, it's not clear that sentiment would be all that valuable. If users are on LinkedIn to potentially connect with future employers (or employers are looking for new employees), most of these users tend to be careful about what they say.

Social Sites

Classifying a social media site as social seems a bit redundant, but in this instance, we're referring to sites where people go to reconnect with old friends or meet new people with similar interests and hobbies. These sites enable users to create public profiles and form relationships with other users of the same website who access their profiles. These sites offer online discussion forums, chat rooms, status updates, as well as content sharing (such as pictures or videos). The king of social sites has to be Facebook with over 1.5 *billion* registered users [15]!

Facebook
User population: 1.5 billion registered users
Demographics [16]:

- 171 million users from the United States
- 66 million users from India
- 60 million users from Brazil
- 54 million users from Indonesia
- 41 million users from Mexico
- 35 million users from Turkey
- 34 million users from Phillipines

Facebook is the king of social media sites, claiming the largest number of registered and active users of all such sites. At first blush, this would seem like a goldmine for gathering data for a social media analysis, but in actuality it's not as useful, from a business perspective, as you would think.

Facebook is organized around a timeline, the things users say or post, and their friends. When users post something, typically the only ones who can see the content are those in that user's list of friends. That capability is wonderful for sharing information within a community of friends, but from the perspective of trying to look at public opinion or thoughts, these posts or timelines aren't available to the general public. While it is possible to set user controls to make all content publicly accessible, this setting is not generally used because most users want to keep their comments and conversations private, or within their own circles.

One alternative to the more private profile is a fan page. Businesses, organizations, celebrities, and political figures use fan pages to represent themselves to the public on Facebook. Unlike regular Facebook profiles and content, fan pages are visible to everybody on the Internet, which makes for a useful set of information to collect and analyze.

Facebook groups enable communication among a group of people to share common interests and express their opinions. Groups allow people to come together around a common topic to post and share content. When creating such a group, the owner can choose to make the group publicly available or private to members, but members must be Facebook users.

RenRen [17]

User population: 219 million users in 2014

Demographics: Predominantly Chinese

RenRen is the leading (real-name) social networking Internet platform in China. RenRen, which means "everyone" in Chinese, enables users to connect and communicate with each other, share information, create user-generated content, play online games, watch videos, and enjoy a wide range of other features and services. Most people refer to RenRen as the Chinese Facebook. Like Facebook, RenRen does not allow visitors or search engine spiders to view profile pages without being logged in (in other words, being a member). Of course, like Facebook, it does allow searching for public profile pages of brands and celebrities.

Information Sharing Sites

Most of the social media sites allowing sharing of status messages or content such as pictures or videos. Some, however, like Instagram, are almost solely focused on sharing (in this case, images). Other examples include sites like YouTube and Tumblr, and while they allow for commentary on the content posted, they are primarily content sharing.

YouTube

User population: 1 billion users

YouTube is a website that was designed to enable the general public to share video content. Millions of users around the world have created accounts and uploaded videos that anyone can watch—anytime and virtually anywhere.

Many businesses today have come to realize that the use of YouTube videos can help to increase their brand exposure while creating a personal connection with their audience. More importantly, these short videos can be an effective way to deliver information that users may find useful—perhaps leading to an increased brand loyalty.

What's most important is the number of views that videos achieve from the YouTube site. Looking at the top 10 countries viewing videos [18], we see:

- United States: 124 billion views
- UK: 34 billion
- India: 15 billion
- Germany: 15 billion
- Canada: 14 billion
- France: 13 billion
- South Korea: 12 billion
- Russia: 11 billion
- Japan: 11 billion
- Brazil: 10 billion

Video files can be very large and are often too big to send to someone else by email. By posting a video on YouTube, users can share a video simply by sending the other person a URL link.

Microblogging Sites

Microblogs are short postings or brief updates sent online. Think of them like text messaging. Unlike traditional blogs, microblogs are typically limited in the amount of text that can be posted (Twitter's limit is 140 characters). These updates often contain links to online resources, such as web pages, images, or videos, and more often than not, they refer to other users (called mentions). As is the case with most microblogging, when a message is posted, those updates are seen by all users who have chosen to "follow" the author who posted the message (submitter). In the case of Twitter, those posts are all public; you may not receive them if you don't follow the submitter, but you can search for a keyword or topic and find someone who is talking about a specific subject (and then perhaps follow that person if he or she seems interesting). Microblogging should not be confused with text messaging (or texting) on mobile phones, which is private and not recorded anywhere. Texting is typically one-to-one (or in the hybrid case, group chats among a small number of people).

Twitter

User population: 289 million users
Demographics:

- 180 million from the United States
- 23 million from the UK
- 16 million from Canada
- 8 million from Australia
- 6 million from Brazil
- 4 million from India

Twitter is the prototypical microblogging site. Users tweet using short bursts of messages out to the Twitterverse with the hope that their messages will be useful or interesting to others. Messages on Twitter, by definition, are limited to 140 characters, so they tend to be statements as opposed to conversations. There are threads of conversation where users reply to other tweets, but more often than not, we tend to see more retweeting of messages. This behavior can be viewed as an implicit agreement with the originator's view.

One of the draws of Twitter is the instantaneous delivery (and reception) of messages and information. Many people tweet about current events that are underway, during sporting events or talks at trade shows, for example. All of these message can be immensely important when trying to understand conditions surrounding an event in real time. From a historical perspective, looking back at tweets (or sentiment) when an event occurred (understanding the event in hindsight) can be particularly useful in trying to predict reactions to future events.

Blogs/Wikis

A blog is nothing more than an online personal journal or diary. It provides a platform for people to express themselves and their opinions. It is a place to share thoughts and passions. The Internet makes this information dissemination that much easier. In earlier days, someone with a strong opinion would stand on a raised platform (typically a box meant for holding soap) in a public square and make an impromptu speech, often about politics, but it could be about anything. Hyde Park in London is known for its Sunday soapbox orators, who have assembled at Speakers' Corner since 1872 to allow individuals to discuss any number of topics ranging from religion and politics to social themes. The modern form of this soapbox is a blog, which allows anyone, anywhere, to make a statement that can be heard by all (or ignored by many).

Blogs can range from personal experiences and observations to well-crafted marketing messages put out, seemingly, by individuals on the behalf of corporations. Of course, this is true for any form of social media. And as with any media, being sure to determine who is conveying the opinions and message is important.

Summary

As we have seen in this chapter, data can come in a number of different forms and from a wide variety of sources. Given the unstructured nature of social media content and the large number of possible sources, each requiring a unique analysis methodology, the complexity of this type of data can be overwhelming at times. The trick is to be able to understand what is being said in the unstructured content and to look for patterns (repetition of themes, sentiment, or perhaps customer satisfaction issues). We briefly touched on these concerns here but deal with them at length in Chapter 7. Once it is understood, we can process this data as if it's one large set of structured data, using standard relational queries and well-known techniques.

Endnotes

[1] Cowper, William, *The Task and Other Poems*, Published by David Huntington, 1814.

[2] Press, Gil, "12 Big Data Definitions: What's Yours?" *Forbes*. Retrieved from http://www.forbes.com/sites/gilpress/2014/09/03/12-big-data-definitions-whats-yours/.

[3] IEEE Computer Society Press, *Proceedings of the 8th Conference on Visualization '97* (Los Alamitos, CA: Author, 1998), 235-ff.

[4] Bryant, Randal, Randy H. Katz, and Edward D. Lazowska, "Big-Data Computing: Creating Revolutionary Breakthroughs in Commerce, Science and Society." *Computing Community Consortium*, December 22, 2008. Retrieved from http://cra.org/ccc/wp-content/uploads/sites/2/2015/05/Big_Data.pdf.

[5] See http://www.ecampusnews.com/top-news/big-data-definition-224/.

[6] See https://news.microsoft.com/2013/02/11/the-big-bang-how-the-big-data-explosion-is-changing-the-world/.

[7] NIST Big Data Definitions and Taxonomies, Version 1.0, Definitions & Taxonomies Subgroup, NIST Big Data Working Group (NBD-WG) August, 2013.

[8] See https://en.wikipedia.org/wiki/Big_data.

[9] Whiting, Anita, and David Williams, "Why People Use Social Media: A Uses and Gratifications Approach," *Qualitative Market Research: An International Journal* 16.4 (2013): 362–369.

[10] *Consumer Reports*. Retrieved from http://www.consumerreports.org/cro/about-us/index.htm.

[11] Schwartz, Barry, *The Paradox of Choice: Why More Is Less*, Harper Collins Publishers, 2004.

[12] Statista, "Leading Social Networks Worldwide as of August 2015, Ranked by Number of Active Users (In Millions)." Retrieved from http://www.statista.com/statistics/272014/global-social-networks-ranked-by-number-of-users/.

[13] Carrasco, Ed, "The Top 10 Countries in YouTube Viewership Outside the USA [INFOGRAPHIC]," *New Media Rockstars*, March 18, 2013. Retrieved from http://newmediarockstars.com/2013/03/the-top-10-countries-in-youtube-viewership-outside-the-usa-infographic/.

[14] Kemp, Simon, "Digital, Social & Mobile Worldwide in 2015." *We Are Social*, January 21, 2015. Retrieved from http://wearesocial.net/blog/2015/01/digital-social-mobile-worldwide-2015/.

[15] Techner, Isobel, Blog, LinkedIn Usage By Country 2014, http://linkhumans.com/blog/linkedin-usage-2014.

[16] See http://worldknowing.com/top-10-most-facebook-user-country-in-the-world/.

[17] See http://www.chinainternetwatch.com/10928/renren-q3-2014/.

[18] See http://sysomos.com/sites/default/files/Inside-Twitter-BySysomos.pdf.

6

The Right Tool for the Right Job

2014 will just be about the improved use of data to drive insight, action, and value in a huge number of ways. The last few years have been about putting the systems, technology, and people in place. There will still be an ongoing war for data talent but the use of data across organizations will finally become more 'business as usual' in 2014.

—Ashley Friedlein, *Econsultancy* [1]

Data analysis is the critical set of activities that assist in transforming raw data into insights, which in turns leads to a new base of knowledge and business value. A review of the current literature on social media analytics reveals a wide variety of use cases and types of analysis.

Many different types of analysis can be performed with social media data. In our own work, we have found it beneficial to categorize and classify these different types of analysis in a number of "buckets." In this chapter, we present our recommended taxonomy schema for social media analytics as well as the types of insights that could be derived from that analysis. This taxonomy is mainly based on four dimensions:

1. The depth of analysis (the complexity of the analysis)
2. The machine capacity (the computational needs of the analysis)
3. The domain of analysis (internal versus external social media)
4. The velocity of data (the rate at which data arrives for analysis)

This proposed taxonomy is then examined through the use of several sample metrics derived from a number of engagements we have worked on in the past [2].

The Four Dimensions of Analysis Taxonomy

A taxonomy is a valuable construct for the categorization and organization of attributes used to describe similar entities. There have been many attempts to classify the type of analysis possible in the social networking analytics space [3] and, recently, an attempt to classify the types of data used [4]. In the case of social media analysis, various tools and techniques are used to aid analysts in drawing conclusions from these data sources. Understanding the type of analysis that is required is important when comparing tools or services that would be needed for any future analysis projects.

The taxonomy is mainly based on four dimensions:

- **Depth of analysis**—Simple descriptive statistics based on streaming data, ad hoc analysis on accumulated data, or deep analysis performed on accumulated data.

- **Machine capacity**—The amount of CPU needed to process datasets in a reasonable time period. Capacity numbers need to address not only the CPU needs but also the network capacity needed to retrieve data.

- **Domain of analysis**—The vast amount of social media content available out there can be broadly classified into internal social media (all of the social media content shared by company employees with each other that typically stays inside a firewall) and external social media (content that is outside a company's firewall).

- **Velocity of data**—Streaming data or data at rest. Streaming data such as Twitter that is being posted in real time about a conference versus accumulated data from the past five minutes, past day, past week, past month, or past year.

For each distinct type of analytics specified in the taxonomy, we describe the type of analysis that can be performed and what types of techniques can be utilized for the analysis. In future chapters, we take some of these salient types of analytics and provide more complete treatment based on real-life examples.

Depth of Analysis

The depth of analysis dimension is really driven by the amount of time available to come up with the results of a project. This can be considered as a broad continuum, where the analysis time ranges from a few hours at one end to several months at the other end. For the sake of simplicity, we can consider this as three broad categories: small, medium, and large.

In cases in which the depth of analysis is small, we typically use a system called Simple Social Metrics (SSM). SSM allows us to look at a stream of data and come up with some simple and quick metrics that yield useful information. For example, if we are monitoring Twitter data on a given topic, say cloud computing, SSM will be able to answer the following questions at the end of the day:

> How many people mentioned *IBM* in their tweets?
> How many people mentioned the word *Softlayer* in their tweets?
> How many times were the words *IBM, Microsoft,* and *Amazon* mentioned during the day?
> Which author had the highest number of posts on *cloud computing* during the day?

In cases that could be classified as having a medium depth of analysis, we can take the example of projects in which we have to do ad hoc analysis. Consider, for instance, the case in which our marketing team has been collecting information from social media channels, including Twitter, over the past three months. Now the team wants the analysts to answer the following questions:

> Which IBM competitor is gathering the most mentions in the context of social business?
> What is the trend of positive sentiment of IBM over the past three months in the context of mentions of the term *social business*?

And, lastly, cases that could be considered as having a large depth of analysis are varied and are really project specific. For example, a group within IBM that is responsible for releasing new features for a specific product wants to do an in-depth analysis of social media chatter about its product continuously over a period of one year. This group may do a baseline analysis for three months, where it just collects social media data and counts the number of mentions and assesses sentiment. Then, in response to a specific new feature release, the group wants to see how the same metrics change over a period of three or six months. The group also wants to understand how the sentiment is influenced by some other attributes in the marketplace such as overall economy or competitors' product releases.

Machine Capacity

The machine capacity dimension considers the network and CPU capacity of the machines that are either available or required for a given type of use case.

In subsequent sections of this chapter, we discuss aspects of network use and CPU use in the context of the four main dimensions that we have considered in the taxonomy. Table 6.1 shows a summary view of Network and CPU requirements.

Table 6.1   Summary of Network and CPU Requirements

Category	Network Use	CPU Use
Real time	High bandwidth	High CPU
Near real time	Moderate bandwidth	Moderate CPU
Ad hoc exploration	Low bandwidth	Moderate CPU
Deep analysis	Low bandwidth	High CPU

Real-time analysis in social media is an important tool when trying to understand the public's perception of a certain topic as it is unfolding to allow for reaction or an immediate change in course. The amount of data to be processed can be very large in such cases. During one of the debates between President Barack Obama and Mitt Romney during the 2012 presidential election, there were about 20,000 related tweets per second [1]. The need to collect, store, and analyze information at such velocities causes us to rate the bandwidth and the CPU requirements as high within our taxonomy.

In the case of *near real-time analysis*, we assume that data is ingested into the tool at a rate that is less than real time. As a consequence, the bandwidth requirement is less than that of a real-time component, and the CPU requirement also becomes less.

An *ad hoc analysis* is a process designed to answer a single specific question. The product of ad hoc analysis is typically a report or data summary. An ad hoc analysis is typically used to analyze data at rest—that is, data that has previously been retrieved and ingested in a non-real-time manner. These types of systems are used to create a report or analysis that does not already exist, or drill deeper into a specific dataset to uncover details within the data. As a result, the CPU requirement can be moderate while the network bandwidth requirement would be relatively low.

A *deep analysis* implies an analysis that spans a long time and involves a large amount of data, which typically translates into a high CPU requirement.

Figure 6.1 presents a graphical view of the machine capacity requirements.

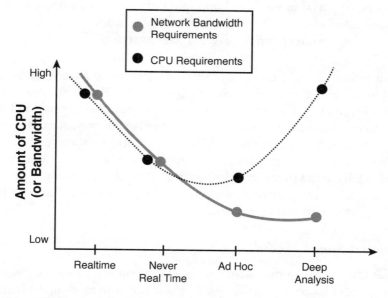

Figure 6.1   CPU and network requirements by system type.

Domain of Analysis

The domain of analysis is broadly classified into the following two categories:

- **External social media**—In this book, we have spent quite a bit of time describing and focusing on external social media.

  Most of the time when people use the term *social media*, they usually mean external social media. This includes content generated on popular social media sites such as Twitter, Facebook, LinkedIn, and so on (see the discussion on various social media venues in Chapter 5).

- **Internal social media**—For a number of years now, many companies have been investing in enterprise social networks as a way to open communication channels between employees.

An enterprise social network (ESN) is an internal, private social network used to assist communication within a business [5]. As the number of companies investing in ESNs grows, employees are discovering more and more ways to conduct business in a more social and "open" way. According to an IDC Study in June 2013, about 79% of the companies surveyed had enterprise social networks [6]. Internal social media, also known as enterprise social media, refers to the variety of contributions (blogs, forums, communities, and so on) made by company employees with each other utilizing ESNs as the platform for communication.

External Social Media

Let's first focus on the external social media domain. There are two broad analysis types based on whether the data is at rest or in motion. And, in each of these cases, we consider use cases for simple social metrics, ad hoc analysis, and deep analysis.

Data in Motion

Earlier we described the velocity of data, or the rate at which new data arrives. The term *velocity* implies something in motion (such as the arrival of new entries in a data stream). Consider the buildup to a major sporting event, say the finals of a World Cup Soccer match. Prior to the event, there may be a small amount of discussion leading up to the match, but as the day of the match approaches, the amount of conversation around the topic will grow, sometimes to a feverish pitch. This increased rate of arrival of motions is what we refer to as the velocity of the data, or its increased rate of motion.

Simple Social Metrics (SSM)

There are several use cases in which we may want to understand what is happening in real time. For example, consider the host of a large conference or trade show that is attended by customers, press, and industry insiders. The success or failure of such an event can be critical to the hosting organization. During the conference, a dedicated team of customer service professionals may be able to watch a live Twitter feed to stay on the lookout for any tweets related to a customer service or dissatisfaction issue. In another case at this same conference, a technology consulting firm that specializes in fraud prevention in the financial industry may be looking for leads by looking at any tweets that mention the terms *fraud, financial, bank*, and so on. In this use case, the focus is on timely processing of information that is streaming through. In both of these examples, the need for real-time alerts or analysis is required to complete these tasks.

In thinking about the machine capacity and the real-time nature of the data, the network bandwidth and the CPU capacity required for this type of analysis can be quite high. By network capacity, we are referring to how fast of a network connection is required to keep up with the data rates from a high-velocity feed. For example, a typical T1 network connection (about 187,500 characters per second) would be consumed (fully used) if the velocity of a Twitter feed exceeded approximately 1,340 tweets per second.

CPU bandwidth, on the other hand, is the amount of compute time needed to perform the text analytics on the tweets received from a feed. If the CPU can't "keep up" with the arrival rate of the data, the ability to analyze tweets in real time suffers as the data "queues" up waiting for CPU to free up for the next analysis.

If, instead of real time, we are allowed to have a delay of one to five minutes (near real time), the network and CPU requirements become more moderate. The reason is that we are allowed to process the tweets we've already received in whatever time we have available.

Ad Hoc Analysis and Deep Analysis

Because of the short amount of time available for processing, deep analysis or ad hoc analysis usually is not possible in such cases. In our taxonomy, we use the term *ad hoc analysis* to describe an analysis that is produced one time to answer a single specific business question. This type of analysis refers to dealing with situations as they occur rather than ones that are repeated on a regular basis. The assumption is that there is a data store or collection of raw data that these queries or analysis can "run over."

Data at Rest

Data at rest refers to use cases in which data has already been accumulated. This can include data from the past day, week, month, or year. This also includes custom windows of time—for example, social media data around a "water day" event in South Africa several months back for a duration of one month.

Simple Social Metrics (SSM)

SSM analysis is characterized by simple metrics, computations, and analytics. The focus is on generating some quick results. Following are some sample use cases with the SSM type of analysis:

- **Duration of analysis**—1 day

  During the IBM Insight 2014 conference in Las Vegas, at the end of the day, we wanted to identify the top hashtags, top mentions, and top authors in discussions around the topics *cloud, analytics, mobile, social,* and *security.*

- **Machine capacity**—The network bandwidth and the CPU capacity required for this type of analysis are low.

Ad Hoc Analysis

- **Duration of analysis**—1 month

  During the first month after the release of a new version of an IBM Software product, we wanted to understand the trend of "volume of conversations."

- **Duration of analysis**—3 months

  For a given IBM Software product, during any continuous time period, we may want to understand the "volume of conversations" around IBM. This analysis is often called the "share of voice" in a conversation, or how much of the conversation includes mentions of, say, *IBM*, and how much contains mentions of its competitors.

- **Machine capacity**—The network bandwidth required is quite low, but the CPU capacity is typically low to moderate, depending on the amount of total data that we will be processing.

Deep Analysis

A deep analysis is a full-fledged social media research project typically spanning a period of weeks to months. The amount of data processed in each iteration of the analysis could be relatively small or large, but the duration of the study is usually large. This type of analysis is characterized by an approach that starts with raw data and some limited goals. But as the analysis progresses through the various iterations, the team progressively becomes aware of the hidden insights, and the solution focus areas get narrower and narrower. We described one example from our experience here.

In this case, we collected data from a conference and analyzed it in an attempt to identify dominant themes. Once the themes and topics were identified, using tools that support sophisticated statistical capabilities, we established correlations between various topic pairs. The resultant table is shown in Figure 6.2. The data has been modified for illustrative purposes so that no "real" conclusions can be drawn about the named entities here.

Affinity Matrix					
Class Name	Class Size	Product 1	Product 2	Competitor 1	Competitor 2
Analytics	1114	0	489	21	0
Big Data	403	0	236	0	1
Cloud	2602	2	1160	1	17
Database	436	30	275	2	1
Mobility	726	0	2	1	4
Other	2597	3	10	1	23
Totals	7878	35	2172	26	46

Red = High Affinity	Orange = Med Affinity	Yellow = Low Affinity	Dark Red = No Affinity

Figure 6.2   Relationship matrix (results of deep analytic analysis).

In many cases, a deeper analysis of a set of data involves combining several specific terms under a single umbrella, or concept. For example, when mining unstructured data for words such as *computer, computing, computer networking*, or *cloud*, we could group them together to form a single concept called "Information Technology." The increased CPU intensity attribute for the deep analysis comes from this extra pattern matching and text analytics code. In the case of the relationship matrix (see Figure 6.2), all of the concepts are compared to compute an affinity matrix between concepts in an attempt to determine if there is a low affinity (relationship) between concepts or a high affinity. Since it is quite possible that new terms or words could be uncovered during the analysis that would be relevant to a particular concept, the data models would need to be modified and rerun. This, in turn, also drives the high CPU utilization (in hindsight, this could also point to another extension of the taxonomy: time to deliver results). Table 6.2 contains a summary of different types of use cases involving External Social Media.

Table 6.2 Summary of Use Case Involving External Social Media

Domain	Velocity of Data	Type of Analysis	Examples
External social media	Data in motion: real time	Simple social metrics	Watching tweets in real time for customer support issues
External social media	Data in motion: real time	Ad hoc analysis	Not applicable
External social media	Data in motion: real time	Deep analysis	Not applicable
External social media	Data in motion: near real time	Simple social metrics	Number of mentions of the word *fraud* in the tweets associated with a conference
External social media	Data in motion: near real time	Ad hoc analysis	Ranking of positive mentions of Barack Obama versus Mitt Romney at the end of the 2012 presidential debates
External social media	Data in motion: real time or near real time	Deep analysis	Not applicable
External social media	Data at rest	Simple social metrics	Tracking of top hashtags, top mentions, and top authors, and so on during a live event (like a conference)
External social media	Data at rest	Ad hoc analysis	Share of voice, competitive analysis
External social media	Data at rest	Deep analysis	Multiple iterations of analysis are conducted with more and more refinements of the model and goals as more insights are generated progressively

Internal Social Media

Let's now focus on the internal social media domain. IBM uses its own product, called IBM Connections, as its enterprise social network platform to facilitate collaboration among all the employees inside the firewall. Even in this domain, there are two broad analysis types based on whether the data is at rest or in motion. And, in each of these cases, we consider use cases for simple social metrics, ad hoc analysis, and deep analysis.

Data in Motion

With more than 500,000 profiles enabled on the IBM Connections platform, there tends to be quite a bit of activity occurring throughout the day. Activity ranges from the simple posting of a status message to notifications of new product announcements, recognition of employees, and just general awareness of things happening inside of IBM.

To watch for potential employee dissatisfactions, we have implemented a simple application that analyzes content in this platform and can capture and highlight any IT support issues that could arise with a new release of an internal computing application. For example, if a new version of Lotus Notes is rolled out to a broad section of the employees, the IT support team can configure this application to watch for positive or negative sentiment words being mentioned together with the name of the product.

- **Machine capacity**—Given the real-time nature of the data and the network bandwidth needed to keep up with incoming data, the CPU capacity required for this type of analysis is quite high. If, however, instead of real time, we introduce a delay, say one to five minutes, we can significantly reduce the network and CPU requirements because our computing infrastructure doesn't need to process in real time. This is what we would call "near real time."

Simple Social Metrics (SSM)

Similar to the Simple Social Metrics discussed previously, IBM's research team in Haifa has created a simple pie chart that shows a breakdown of the sentiment of all the content streaming through IBM Connections into positive, neutral, and negative sentiments. As of this writing, 38% percent of the posts are positive, 60% are neutral, and 2% are negative. These kinds of metrics allow us to understand the general feeling within IBM; this analysis doesn't need to be on a real-time basis, since the change in mood of a large workforce changes over time, not instantaneously.

This Social Network Analysis application also continuously updates trending topics and trending words in real time because they can be predictors of things to come.

- **Machine capacity**—The network and CPU requirements are moderate in this case.

Ad Hoc Analysis

The IBM Research team has built an application that continuously monitors and analyzes all of the content that is streaming through IBM's enterprise social network: IBM Connections. This social network analysis application has an interface that enables users to specify any topic, and the application will show these users an interactive view of all the conversations (including counts) relevant to that topic over the past 30 days (see Figure 6.3). This can be a very handy tool to gauge how well a certain topic has been resonating with the employees in the past month or so.

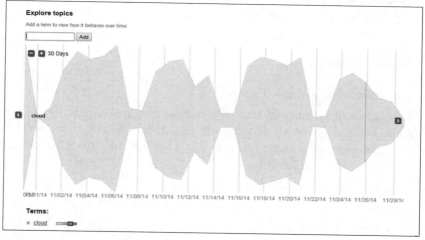

Figure 6.3   Volume of conversations over time.

Deep Analysis

Because of the short amount of time available for processing in these types of projects, deep analysis is usually not possible.

Data at Rest

Data at rest refers to use cases in which data has already been accumulated. This can include data from the past day, week, month, or year. This also includes custom windows of time—for example, social media data around a "water day" event in South Africa several months back, for a duration of one month.

Simple Social Metrics (SSM)

IBM conducts online courses on key topics for very large audiences every month. The industry refers to these as massive open online courses (MOOCs). These courses are accessible to all employees. A new course is launched on the first Friday of each month. During the course of this day, we collect comments from all IBMers about this topic and about this specific course in the IBM Connections platform. At the end of the day, we compute some simple social metrics and come up with the following: top 10 hashtags, top 10 mentions, top 10 authors, and overall sentiment.

- **Machine capacity**—The network bandwidth and the CPU capacity required for this type of analysis are low.

Ad Hoc Analysis

- **Duration of analysis**—1 month

  During the first month after the release of a new MOOC, we perform an analysis of all posts made by IBMers in IBM Connections and come up with some reports. For a course on cloud computing, we produced the following:

  - Volume of conversations over time
  - Volume of conversations by geography of the author
  - Percentage of posts about cloud computing, in comparison to other similar words
  - Percentage of positive, neutral, and negative comments
  - Percentage of discussion by business unit and role

- **Machine capacity**—The network bandwidth required is quite low, but the CPU capacity is typically low to moderate, depending on the amount of total data that we will be processing.

Deep Analysis

There are a variety of possibilities for use cases in the deep analysis category.

Since IBM has implemented an enterprise social network to facilitate communication and collaboration with and among employees, the next logical question becomes: What new insights can we derive through an analysis of the conversations? A few possible analytics projects have been proposed, but to date, we haven't implemented them due to time constraints. We thought it might be of interest to see what kinds of projects would be possible given this rich source of data:

- What is the correlation between the level of social activity and the likelihood of increased innovation?
- What is the correlation between the level of social activity and the likelihood of getting selected for a customer advocate role?

We cover the details of this use case in a subsequent chapter. Some of the high-level steps in implementing an internal social analytics practice include:

1. Establish an enterprise social network inside the corporate firewall. If the intent is to use an external platform, take care to ensure employees understand the risks of inadvertently releasing sensitive information to the public. But if an external platform is chosen, keeping a record of employee identifiers in that platform is critical to enable the retrieval of their information and ensure the analysis contains information from just the employees and not those outside the company.
2. Ensure a widespread adoption of the capabilities by employees.
3. Establish a metrics program that measures people's participation in social activities.
4. Map these activities to behaviors and identify key performance indicators (KPIs).
5. Establish algorithms to compute the scores for each key performance indicator.
6. Establish a baseline.
7. Establish a metric for measuring innovation—for example, the number of patents.
8. Establish a metric for the customer advocate role—for example, names of people who got selected for a customer advocate role.
9. Establish a window of time for the study and analysis.
10. Measure the change in KPI values during the window of time.
11. Apply regression analysis and draw conclusions.

- **Machine capacity**—The network bandwidth required is usually low, but the CPU capacity required for this type of analysis is usually high.

Table 6.3 shows use cases for internal social media.

Table 6.3   Summary of Use Cases for Internal Social Media

Domain of Analysis	Velocity of Data	Depth of Analysis	Examples
Internal social media	Data in motion: real time	Simple social metrics	Watching posts in real time for IT support issues
Internal social media	Data in motion: real time	Ad hoc analysis	Not applicable
Internal social media	Data in motion: real time	Deep analysis	Not applicable
Internal social media	Data in motion: near real time	Simple social metrics	Continuous tracking of sentiment (one-minute delay) at any time during the day
Internal social media	Data in motion: near real time	Ad hoc analysis	
Internal social media	Data in motion: real time or near real time	Deep analysis	Not applicable
Internal social media	Data at rest	Simple social metrics	Tracking of top hashtags, top mentions, top authors, and so on during a live event (like a conference)
Internal social media	Data at rest	Ad hoc analysis	Share of voice, competitive analysis
Internal social media	Data at rest	Deep analysis	Multiple iterations of analysis are conducted with more and more refinements of the model and goals as more insights are generated progressively

Velocity of Data

We briefly discussed time as an attribute of data in Chapter 1. We broadly divided this into two categories: data at rest and data in motion. In the following sections, we look at the dimension of time from the perspective of analysis. The dimension of velocity of data also can be divided into two parts: data in motion and data at rest.

Data in Motion

As an example of data in motion, during a US Open tennis match between two players, we might want to understand how the sentiment of the general population is changing about the two players during the course of match. Is the crowd conveying positive sentiment about the player who is actually losing the game? In such cases, the analysis is done as the data arrives. Our assumption, as shown in Figure 6.4, is that for a constant time interval, the amount of detail produced increases as the complexity of the analytical tool or system increases.

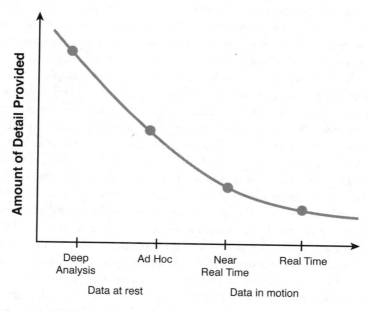

Figure 6.4 Amount of detail provided by system type.

Data at Rest

A second type of analysis in the context of velocity is what we call "analysis of data at rest." For example, we can collect social media conversations around IBM products and services before, during, and after a specific event to understand the public's opinion. Once the data is fully collected, we can then perform analysis on this data to provide different types of insights; some examples follow:

- Which of your company's products has the most mentions as compared to others?
- What is the relative sentiment around your products as compared to a competitor's product?
- Is there a strong correlation between the marketing of a product or service and the number of positive comments about the brand itself?

In these two cases (data at rest and data in motion), there are trade-offs that we need to consider time and the cost-to-deliver those results.

For example, if the results of such an analysis are needed in real time or near real time, the amount of time available for processing is, of course, limited and that will have an influence on how deep we can go with the analysis. We have observed that valuable insights can be derived quickly by providing some lightweight analytics in these real-time use cases. Simple metrics such as popular hash tags, most prolific authors, top mentions, and so on can provide some revealing insights without a large investment in computing (and analysts') time. This usually translates into lower infrastructure costs because we are processing relatively small amounts of data in a small chunk of time.

When we are performing analysis of data at rest, the amount of data available for analysis (the volume) has a strong bearing on the time needed for the analysis to complete and hence the costs of that analysis. The amount of data could range from the one day to several weeks, months, or years. In such cases, we are usually interested in topics in aggregate, such as "How has the sentiment about a company's brand changed over the given time period as compared to its competitors?" rather than a very specific topic or question.

The business benefits gained from a social analytics project aren't always directly proportional to the cost. We have observed that, even though a lightweight analytics solution may cost much less than a deep analytics solution, the business benefit is still highly dependent on the specifics of the project that we are working on. For example, if a company is monitoring social media for any negative press about itself, its products, or its executives, and it detects a sudden surge in negative sentiment, the public relations department can be prepared with an appropriate response in a very short time. As any good public relations staff will tell you: "Forewarned is forearmed."

Summary

Data analysis is the phase that takes filtered data as input and transforms that into information of value to the analyst. In this chapter, we presented a taxonomy of the various analytical situations we can run into and also discussed in general some of the analysis techniques that can be used in each situation. In subsequent chapters, we pick some specific situations and provide a fuller treatment of the analysis phase.

Endnotes

[1] Shiveley, Kevin, "10 Quotes from Analysts About the Future of Social Analytics and Measurement," *The Simply Measured Blog*, March 24, 2014. Retrieved from http://simplymeasured.com/blog/2014/03/24/10-quotes-from-analysts-about-the-future-of-social-analytics-and-measurement/.

[2] Ganis, Matthew, and Avinash Kohirkar, "Taxonomy for Social Media Analysis, Infosys Lab Briefings," Volume 12, Number 1, 2014. Retrieved from http://www.infosys.com/infosys-labs/publications/Documents/social-media-computing/taxonomy-social-media-analysis.pdf.

[3] Chelmis, C., and V. K. Prasanna, "Social Networking Analysis: A State of the Art and the Effect of Semantics," *Privacy, Security, Risk and Trust (PASSAT)*, October 2011, 531–536.

[4] Schneier, B., "A Taxonomy of Social Networking Data," *Security & Privacy, IEEE*, 8, no. 4 (July–August 2010), 88.

[5] Kitt, Denise, "What Is An Enterprise Social Network?, CRM Switch—CRM," May 24, 2012. Retrieved from http://www.crmswitch.com/social-crm/enterprise-social-network/.

[6] Thompson, Vanessa, "Worldwide Enterprise Social Software 2013–2017 Forecast and 2012 Vendor Shares: From ESS to ESN," *IDC*, June 2013.

7

Reading Tea Leaves: Discovering Themes, Topics, or Trends

In wisdom gathered over time I have found that every experience is a form of exploration.

—Ansel Adams [1]

Discovering themes and patterns from social media content can be a very exciting endeavor. This is the part of analysis where the detective in the analyst really comes out. This chapter focuses on the common goals of a majority of social data analysis projects. These goals fall into two broad categories: validation of hypothesis and discovery of themes. In the first category, the researcher already has a hypothesis (a prediction of what the likely outcome will be) in mind that he or she wants to validate. In the second major category, discovering themes or topics or trends, there is no preconceived notion of what the researcher is likely to find. The analyst begins the analysis with an open mind and attempts to discover what the data is implying either in terms of definitive insights or answers to specific questions, or in terms of the trends being implied by the underlying data. Here, we discuss the analysis steps that are typically taken to satisfy these goals in the context of some specific project examples.

Many social media analysis projects require an iterative approach. We have made reference to this approach throughout this book, and we refer to it in this chapter also. Toward the end of this chapter, we have included a discussion of iterative methods and how we recommend applying this method for social media analysis projects.

Validating the Hypothesis

Many social media analytics projects start with some preconceived idea of the results or insights they are expecting to find. With that as a starting point, the analyst identifies the appropriate datasets and performs analysis iteratively to arrive at the conclusion. At the end, the results might either confirm the hypothesis or reject it. It is possible that an analysis may end up with inconclusive evidence, so the analyst may have to refine the approach and try again. In the following sections, we look at a few examples and describe the process end-to-end to highlight the specific steps that need to be taken.

We discuss three specific examples:

- **Youth unemployment**—In this example, we describe a project that we executed for a marketing team in Europe. The subject was youth unemployment in Europe. The hypothesis was that we would be able to find evidence in social media to support the conclusions being reported by official government reports.
- **Cannes Lions 2013**—In this example, we describe a project that we executed for a marketing team in the United States. The hypothesis was that a very popular movie in general media would win an award in this competition.
- **56th Grammy Awards**—In this example, we describe a project that the social media analytics team executed as an experiment to test the hypothesis that social media chatter could give very effective clues about who would ultimately win an award.

Youth Unemployment

A marketing team in Europe contracted our IBM social media analytics team to see if social media analysis could be used to confirm or deny youth unemployment in Europe. At the time of this project, the topic of youth unemployment in Europe was dominating the news media. The IBM marketing team was interested in exploring the benefits of IBM's social media analysis tools and techniques in an effort to see what could be uncovered in this space. The theory was that if our team could identify some insights by just using data that is freely available (social media content), it could be used in a case study discussing product or service opportunities with some of our government clients in Europe. The hypothesis was that there would be a sufficient amount of chatter across the social media sites to corroborate the reports that were being generated by the official channels in the countries being severely affected by this problem. As we have discussed before, these projects required an iterative analysis. Based on this concept, our approach for this project included the following steps:

1. Identify the relevant data sources.
2. Develop or modify a set of keywords to bring in the most appropriate data from these sources.
3. Develop or modify a model to classify and categorize the information.
4. Evaluate the results.
5. If the results are satisfactory, the project concludes. If not, we go back to step 2 and iterate.

Data Identification and Data Analysis

Given that this project focused on the views of Europeans, we needed to look at all of the social media content originating in those countries. With location as the first filter, we needed to identify content that matched a known set of keywords that would indicate discussion around the term *youth unemployment*. We utilized the service of a data aggregator called Boardreader to search and discover social media content matching our keywords. We started with an initial set of keywords based on input from the marketing team and the judgment and experience of our lead analyst, Mila Gessner [2].

From a data identification perspective, we came up with a list of countries that we needed to focus on: Spain, Italy, Ireland, France, Portugal, and Slovakia. We configured the data identification tool to select content from these countries.

We then needed to come up with an initial set of keywords that we were going to use to pull in content from the social media universe: *youth, unemployment*. We configured the analysis tool to focus on search keywords like *youth, young*, and *teen*. We used regular expressions to ensure all variations of these terms were captured and included in our data model. In Chapter 2, we discussed the method of using regular expressions to "cleanse" the data, or to limit that data that we collected for further analysis. We demonstrate a few more examples of regular expressions here. See Table 7.1.

Table 7.1 Keyword Model

Search Term with Regular Expressions	Explanation of the Syntax
Youth	This would capture all content that has the word *youth* anywhere in the post, comment, or article.
worker.{0,1}	This would capture the word *worker* by itself or *worker* with up to one additional letter, which would include words such as *workers*.
(young|younger|youngest) .{0,80} worker.{0,1}	This would capture content that included references to the words *young* or *younger* or *youngest* in close proximity (80 characters) with another word; in this case, *worker*.

The tool also allows the analyst to specify related context keywords, ensuring that only content relevant to the project is included. For example, in our initial model, we used context keywords such as *unemployment* and *unemployed*. This ensured that we captured all conversations that referenced young people but within the context of talking about topics of "unemployed" or "unemployment."

We took the results of this phase forward and conducted our analysis. For the sake of discussion, let's call this iteration 1. We quickly learned that we were missing much of the relevant content because our search keywords were too limiting. For example, we learned that we needed to add the word *graduates* to our mix (implications of being young). We also learned that we needed to add a few additional context keywords like *jobless* and *out of work*.

During this phase, we also learned that quite a bit of irrelevant content was being captured in the model. The analysis tools allowed us to exclude that irrelevant content by using "exclude" keywords, or keywords that, when found, cause the content to be ignored. As a result, in the next iteration, we used exclude keywords such as *movie*, *cricket*, and *world war* to eliminate content that perhaps matched our keywords and context words but was not relevant for our analysis.

We hope this discussion gives you an indication of how a typical analysis phase, with multiple iterations, is executed on projects. Rarely does a first attempt work without any changes to the model or collection.

Here, we have reproduced the final model at the conclusion of this project.

Countries of interest:

EU, Spain, Italy, Ireland, France, Portugal, Slovakia

Keywords:

```
youth
grads
graduates
(young|younger|youngest) .{0,80} worker.{0,1}
worker.{0,1} .{0,80} (young|younger|youngest)
(young|younger|youngest) .{0,80} (adult|adults)
(adult|adults) .{0,80} (young|younger)
youngsters
(young|younger|youngest) (worker|generation|people|folks|individual
s|citizens|adult|adults).{0,1}
(young|younger|youngest) .{0,80} generation.{0,1}
generation.{0,1} .{0,80} (young|younger|youngest)
(young|younger|youngest) .{0,80} people.{0,1}
people.{0,1} .{0,80} (young|younger|youngest)
(young|younger|youngest) .{0,80} folks
folks .{0,80} (young|younger|youngest)
(young|younger|youngest) .{0,80} individuals
individuals .{0,80} (young|younger|youngest)
(young|younger|youngest) .{0,80} citizens
citizens .{0,80} (young|younger|youngest)
```

Context terms for keywords:

```
unemployment
unemployed
jobless
joblessness
not employed
(looking|searching) for work
(looking|searching) for job.{0,1}
no job.{0,1}
no employment
without employment
without job.{0,1}
unwaged
out-of-work
```

```
out of work
between jobs
(looking|searching) for .{10} work
(looking|searching) for .{10} job.{0,1}
without work
```

Exclude keywords:

```
Cypriot
prophet
World War.{0,3}
Stalin
Holy Roman Empire
mortgage.{0,1}
obesity
gay.{0,5}marriage.{0,1}
football
Pistorius.{0,2}
soccer
horse.{0,5}
.{0,1}baseball.{0,3}
fashion.{0,20}week
topless
Vatican
marathon.{0,2}
league.{0,1}
Pope
film
drone strike.{0,1}
drone.{0,1}
movie
cartoon
{0,1}World.{0,1}Cup.{0,1}
mandela
Cricket.{0,1}
```

Once the model is ready, then we need to look at the results to see if they are ready for interpretation. One common issue that we run into in projects like this is called "duplicates." A particular piece of content may be referenced in different social media venues by different sets of people. We typically have to weed out these duplicates to ensure clean analysis.

Based on the amount of content we were obtaining from our aggregator, we decided to limit the analysis to a duration of three months (January to March 2013). At the end of this phase, we identified a number of qualified mentions about youth unemployment from a number of European countries. These mentions were then ranked by the countries that showed evidence of high incidence of youth unemployment. We then compared this data with official unemployment data published in Europe by the Heritage Foundation.

The results are shown in Figure 7.1.

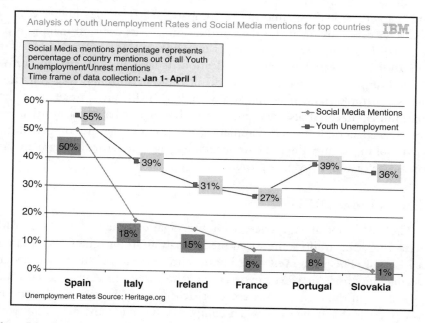

Figure 7.1 Analysis of youth unemployment rates.

Results

From this analysis, we were able to conclude that indeed there was a strong correlation between countries with high levels of youth unemployment and the chatter related to youth unemployment in social media venues.

This use case is an example of validating a predetermined hypothesis. In this particular case, we were able to confirm the hypothesis.

So what's the big deal?

That's a good question. Just because we've shown a relationship exists between the social media postings of unemployed youth and the real unemployment number doesn't really answer any questions for us (or quite honestly, provide any business value on its own).

The important thing is that we have shown we have a working model that would contain social comments made by individuals who are unemployed. So if we want to target them in marketing campaigns, blogs, or social media, we can use this model to understand the issues concerning them, such as education, health care, cost of living, and so on.

This is the point where there is a close tie between social media analytics and marketing. Let's assume that a company that provides higher education services is looking at this data during some of its decision-making processes. If that company is trying to get members of this segment to consider educational classes or additional education, it launches a marketing campaign. Using the concepts in this model, it could perform a before-and-after analysis to understand if its marketing message made any inroads into the community. It could also determine if its message is having a positive (or negative) effect on its intended audience. The point is that the company now has a tool to measure the pulse or general feeling of a particular segment. As we said before: knowledge is power.

Cannes Lions 2013

The IBM Social Analytics team was again contacted by the IBM Marketing team to do some social media analysis around the Cannes Lions 2013 event. This is an event that honors and celebrates creativity in media. During this time, an IBM movie called *A Boy and His Atom* was creating quite a stir in the media. We were approached to see if we could determine how popular this movie was when compared to other campaigns that were receiving a similar buzz at the festival.

Since this was a real-time event, we built a model analyzing Twitter data that was being generated during the event. We first noticed that *A Boy and His Atom* was receiving mentions (27 to be precise) in the context of *IBM* (342 total mentions). To us, this meant that the movie was clearly being noticed and being talked about in the context of technology companies (in this case, IBM). See Figure 7.2.

Next, we compared the mentions of this movie as compared to others in the same category, and we realized that it was nowhere in the top (see Figure 7.3).

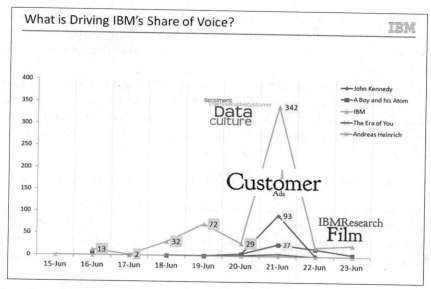

Figure 7.2   What is driving IBM's share of voice?

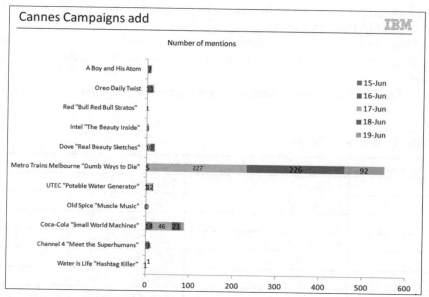

Figure 7.3   Cannes campaign advertisements.

So, the conclusion at this point was that our hypothesis was rejected. There was clearly a lot of external media buzz about this particular movie, but other movies in the category had many more mentions within social media channels.

We've seen this scenario time and time again: a topic is discovered in an analysis, and we assume that it is relevant based on the frequency of use. But what always has to be considered is the context in which that topic is discussed. So naturally, when users of social media were referencing the movie *A Boy and His Atom*, they probably posted something like this:

Check out IBM's "A boy and his atom"—a great piece of work.

So the movie was discussed in the context of *IBM* (in other words, when we looked for mentions of the word *IBM*, we also found discussion about this movie). This is logical and makes perfect sense. But what that means is that in the context of *movies*, it gained far less traction (and perhaps appeal).

56th Grammy Awards

In 2013, we challenged our social media analytics team to see if they could use the tools available to predict the winners in Grammy awards based on chatter in social media.

Hypothesis: There is a correlation between the number of mentions (and positive sentiment) in social media about an artist and the fact that he or she won.

Table 7.2 shows some sample categories and the nominations in those categories.

Table 7.2 Nominees by Category

Number	Category	Nominee
1	Record of the year	*Get Lucky*
2	Record of the year	*Radioactive*
3	Record of the year	*Royals*
4	Record of the year	*Locked Out of Heaven*
5	Record of the year	*Blurred Lines*
6	Album of the year	*Random Access Memories*
7	Album of the year	*The Blessed Unrest*
8	Album of the year	*Good Kid, M.A.A.D City*
9	Album of the year	*The Heist*

10	Album of the year	*Red*
11	Song of the year	*Royals*
12	Song of the year	*Just Give Me a Reason*
13	Song of the year	*Locked Out of Heaven*
14	Song of the year	*Roar*
15	Song of the year	*Same Love*

We analyzed content in social media and public media up to one month prior to the day of awards. About 81 categories were identified. There were an average of 5 nominations in each category.

We captured mentions about each category and each person nominated. We then tabulated the winners that were determined purely by number of mentions in social media. We compared this list with the eventual winners. We observed that in 62 out of the 81 categories (77%), the eventual winner was in the top three list based on social media mentions. We concluded that in a majority of cases, the winners identified by social media analysis prior to the actual announcement were in the top three of the actual winners.

So, what is the business value of this experiment?

The first important lesson our analysts learned from this experiment was that social media mentions are quite powerful. Even when they had no idea of the real process that was utilized to select the winners, they were able to obtain a prediction about who the winners might be (in a majority of the cases) by listening to public opinion. From a business perspective, social media analytics becomes a tool that can be leveraged for some quick analysis using publicly available data before spending large amounts of money in focus groups or other formal information-gathering mechanisms. Consider that a company with many established products in the marketplace could perform a quick market reaction analysis of its products without spending much money before deciding on further formal research that may be needed. Thus, perhaps it could make an educated guess before proceeding.

Discovering Themes and Topics

So far, we have discussed some actual use cases that satisfy the goal of validating hypotheses. Here, we look at a use case in which we do not start with a predetermined hypothesis, but we keep an open mind and try to discover and understand what the data is telling us. In these types of cases, the project team is usually not sure of what to expect. Team members are truly open to discovering new information from the analysis. The content utilized in this project cannot be considered as social media content; however, the content is unstructured text and the techniques used and conclusions drawn are equally applicable to text captured via social media.

One of the divisions in IBM had initiated an award for the best-managed project in that division. A number of project managers submitted their projects for consideration of this award. A panel of judges evaluated the applications and designated one project as the best project of the year.

As part of this process, the project management profession leaders of that division wanted to analyze the project submissions to discover attributes of top projects based on the information submitted. What made one project stand out against others? What were the common attributes of projects that were perceived to be better than others?

As input to our analysis, we started with the content that was submitted by each of the 100 projects. The format of the input file contained the following fields:

> Name of Project:
> Email Address of the Project Manager:
> Name of the Manager:
> Business Value: Free-form text

Business Value of Projects

To give you an idea of the content available for this project, we include here one random example of an entry for a project that we utilized in our analysis. This is basically the text that the person who submitted the application included in the Business Value field.

Sample Entry

This Project implemented best practices in Scope Management, Planning, Monitoring including Status Reporting. In addition to using Fasttracking wherever possible, the PM created an Excel-based visual dashboard for displaying project scope up to the task level on each of the multiple components (Work Breakdown Structure), status of the task, and the date when it was expected to complete. It facilitated stakeholders and the PM to get a quick understanding of which tasks and which components were behind schedule.

This sped up monitoring as well as control and communication to stakeholders, and thereby identified action items that could control the deviations in the schedule. This saved quite a bit of time during reviews with stakeholders and enabled the team to focus more on resolving issues, minimizing risks, increased planning, and better decision making and implementation. The quantitative business value was the setting up of a new I/T infrastructure of 22 servers from scratch (including capital and hardware procurement) and deploying IBM's business-critical CRM (Customer Relationship Management) application which produces reports that are utilized by executives and our CEO in just 10 weeks, which normally would have taken close to a year.

Analysis of the Information in the Business Value Field

We then analyzed this information using a text analytics tool called IBM Content Analytics (now, Watson Text Analytics). IBM Content Analytics (ICA) is an advanced search and analytics platform that enables users to derive insight and create better decision-making models from any type of content (enterprise content, social media, plain text, and so on). IBM's Content Analytics solutions allow users to understand the meaning and context of human language and rapidly process information to improve knowledge-driven search and surface new insights from that content. Content Analytics uses the same natural language processing (NLP) technologies as IBM Watson DeepQA, the world's most advanced question-answering machine.

Our Findings

Once the model was defined in this tool, the tool was able to analyze all of the content and, based on the frequency and co-occurrence of the words, come up with themes suggested by the content. For example, there was a lot of discussion associated with projects being executed "on budget," "under budget," or with "cost savings." Our analyst collected a list of such words and categorized them in our model under the attribute "Financial Planning" of a project. This process was continued, and nine attributes were identified across all the projects that were submitted for consideration. The following list shows the name of the attribute and the key words that we used to include a particular textual description under the given attribute of project performance:

- **Financial Planning**—On budget, under budget, cost savings, accurate revenue-cost forecasting, financial management cost savings, decreased costs, no cost overruns, cost reduction for the client, under estimated cost
- **On-Time Delivery**—On time, on schedule
- **Strong PM**—Implemented strong PM practice, strong PM, PM capabilities, PM discipline, PM resolution, PM approach, WWPMM, The IBM Worldwide Project Management Methods Project MGMT Disciplines
- **Agile Methodology**—Agile methodology, agile development framework
- **Control Management**—Agile Scope Control, monitoring, tracking, tight control framework
- **Risk Management**—Risk management plan, minimize the risk of failure, risk management, reduce risk
- **Defect Resolution**—Eliminate constraints, address clients' issues, fix incapability and dependency, minimize disruption, cutover, zero escalation, manage defect, reduce defect, fix framework
- **Milestone Adherence**—Meet key deadlines, key project milestones, meeting of planned deliverables, deliverable management mobilizing resources in a timely fashion
- **Target Adherence**—Project performance measured against the project plan on a weekly basis, systematic tracking of goal, target adherence, ongoing evaluation results, refine requirements at the beginning of each spiral

We then calculated the percentage of projects that referenced these key attributes, as shown in Figure 7.4.

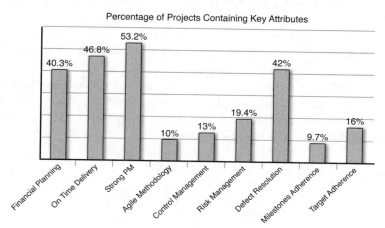

Figure 7.4 Key performance attributes

This analysis showed that the top three attributes of successful projects were strong project management discipline, on time delivery, and good processes for defect resolution. These results were fed back to the Project Management Education and Training program for that division to further reinforce the importance of these attributes in successful execution of projects.

Using Iterative Methods

Many times when we start out on a project, we have a clear vision, and with a little forethought, we establish a course of action that enables us to achieve our desired results. Of course, as Robert Burns once said: "Sometimes the best-laid plans of mice and men oft go awry." Mice, men, or even social media analysts—it's all the same! Sometimes the ideas we have, the questions we've posed, or the plan of attack that we've devised needs to be modified. We have to be flexible because sometimes we're just plain wrong, or we've picked up a screwdriver to drive a nail. Things just aren't right.

An iterative method of working, be it the creation of a model, the writing of software, or even of writing a book, is one in which we do not attempt to start with a full specification of requirements or plan. We don't define steps 1 through 100 and then proceed in order creating our solution. Instead, we begin by specifying and implementing just part of our solution, which can then be reviewed and evaluated in order to identify further requirements or changes. This process is then repeated, producing a new version that is hopefully an improved version of the previous release. We continue cycling through iterations of our product, software, or solution until we believe we've achieved success.

As we work iteratively on a project, we create a rough draft or rough set of results in a single iteration. We then review it, decide on changes to (hopefully) improve it in next iteration, and continue until we've finished. Figure 7.5 visually describes the iterative method.

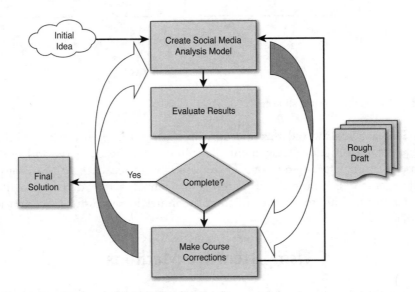

Figure 7.5   Visual depiction of the iterative method.

In the iterative model, we are building and improving the final analysis step-by-step. In this way, we can address deficiencies in our model or analysis early on in the process. This allows us to perhaps change our model, look for additional data, or perhaps change the question in a way that is more relevant. The most important aspect is the ability to obtain feedback as we progress.

A feedback loop is something we use to gather feedback about what we're doing, learn from the feedback, and then make changes based on that feedback. The sole purpose of a feedback loop is to improve a project based on the current plan of attack. These loops are important because they allow us a systemized approach to observing our results and learning from them.

Using this approach helps us to avoid those awkward moments that can happen when we present our analysis and the customers simply look on with a blank stare and comment, "That's not what I asked for." If they can see the progress (and perhaps help shape the final analysis), there are no surprises at the end.

Summary

For projects in which we are validating a previously formed hypothesis, the analysis is complete as soon as we find enough evidence that either proves or disproves the hypothesis. For projects in which we are discovering the themes, the end is not so clear. The team that is performing the analysis has to work with the stakeholders iteratively to determine if the level of detail analyzed and the types of conclusions derived are in line with stakeholder expectations. There are also projects in which, even after validating a hypothesis, there is considerable business value to be gained by discovering other themes that the team had not considered before.

Endnotes

[1] Spaulding, Jonathan. *Ansel Adams and the American Landscape: A Biography.* University of California Press, 1998.

[2] Mila Gessner is an analyst who works at IBM. Many of the examples used in this chapter are based on the specific work she did on these projects. These examples are reproduced here with her knowledge and permission.

[3] The Heritage Foundation, "2015 Index of Economic Freedom." Retrieved from http://www.heritage.org/index/country/france. To locate a specific country, use the following URL, supplying the name of country where indicated: http://www.heritage.org/index/country/*name of country.*

8

Fishing in a Fast-Flowing River

The value of a moment is immeasurable. The power of just ONE moment can propel you to success and happiness or chain you to failure and misery.

—Steve Maraboli [1]

This chapter delves into the concept of real-time and near real-time data analysis. We look at it from a few perspectives. For example, we look at real-time tweets during a televised presidential debate, and analysis of data in what we call near real time (think of feedback from attendees at a live conference), or any simple yet powerful analytics that can be computed and presented in a short timeframe for analysis despite the limited amount of time afforded for analysis.

There are two main reasons to consider analytics systems when dealing with evolving information in real time and near real time. One reason is to sense and respond. In these situations, we want to monitor data to get a sense of what is happening in order to respond to it in a timely fashion. A second reason is to implement an early warning system. This includes timely collection and analysis of data, resulting in prompt interventions. We look at examples of both of these scenarios in the following sections. We also describe the concept of stream computing and describe a specific analytics system that we built using the principles of stream computing to harness the analytics from real-time and near real-time systems.

Is There Value in Real Time?

During the 2008 US presidential debates, a TV channel used a real-time public opinion display (see Figure 8.1) to depict the averaged reactions of 32 supposedly undecided voters. They expressed favor or disfavor for the candidates by turning handheld dials as they watched the debates live. The results of those public opinions were immediately converted into a real-time computer-generated graph. This graphic, also referred to as the worm, was displayed at the bottom of millions of television screens to give an indication of the public's approval or disapproval of the comments the leaders were making. This could be considered an example of a sense-and-respond system. We are sensing in real time the opinions of a small group of individuals, and in response, we are translating that into a graphic that is being shared with millions of users.

Figure 8.1   The "worm" (graph) from the TV presentation of the 2008 US presidential debate (re-created) [2].

While on the surface, this system seems like an interesting ruse to keep the attention of viewers, it is really validating an individual's opinion with that of others.

But what if this kind of technology could actually sway voters or public opinion one way or another? That's exactly what British psychologists, Colin Davis, Amina Memon, and Jeffrey Bowers, of the Royal Holloway University of London believed.

In a simple experiment, Davis and his team had two groups of subjects watch an election debate that included the worm as an indication of others' (supposedly undecided voters') opinions. To test their hypothesis that the worm could influence public opinion, Davis and his team presented their subjects not true public opinion but fake data that would show the supposed opinion in favor of one candidate over the other.

Their results were intriguing, to say the least [3]. What they found was that the worm did have a huge influence on their subjects' perception of who won the debate. The two groups had completely different ideas about who had won the debate, and their opinions were consistent with what the worm had been telling them (which, again, was manipulated by Davis and his team). So the group that saw a worm which favored Gordon Brown thought that he had won the debate, whereas the group that saw the worm which favored Nick Clegg overwhelmingly thought that he was the winner. Interestingly, when the research team asked their subjects about their choice of preferred prime minister, it was clear that, if people had been voting immediately after that debate, the manipulation could have had a significant effect on how those people voted!

WARNING

We're not suggesting in any way that anyone use (falsified) real-time analytics in an effort to sway public opinion. Please don't misunderstand our intention here.

We highlight this example to showcase the power of real-time analytics. If public opinion can be swayed by the opinions of others, it only stands to reason that from a business perspective, we would be served to understand the pulse of our constituents and look to re-emphasize the positive and correct the negative as soon as possible.

Real Time Versus Near Real Time

We draw a distinction between *real time* and what we like to call *near real time*. Think of real time as being instantaneous access to data: The second someone says or does something, we are notified right away. In the case of near real time, we assume there is some delay in between the time an event occurred and our notification or observance of the event. What makes it "near" real as opposed to analyzing prior data is that the time between the event's occurrence and our observation is minimized. Basically, we acknowledge the fact that most of what we observe in real time isn't instant, simply due to the processing or analysis that must be done to make sense of the event.

In the example in Figure 8.1, the sample audience members had a specialized device that allowed them to change their "feelings" about a candidate using a simple dial or switch. This data was polled and the results sent back to a central station to be aggregated and quickly displayed on national television. This type of scenario is pretty close to real time since there is no additional processing to take place, and the "signal," or opinion, is fed right to the source (in this case, CNN).

In Chapter 6, where we discussed a taxonomy of data analysis types, we briefly discussed a type of analysis called Simple Social Metrics (SMM). Later in this chapter, we further discuss the SSM system as applied to a stream of tweets over a period of time. Because the data comes to us (or anybody) in essentially a random fashion, real time doesn't make sense, so we aggregate it over a five-minute interval so that changes in the data are more apparent.

For example, Figure 8.2 shows the top distribution of topics of conversation from Twitter made by a select group of IBMers. This data represents the topics as they were discussed at the time of the sampling, which was delayed by five minutes. Because the number of participants was low, the chance of the graph changing appreciably in real time was low, so we simply show it in near real time.

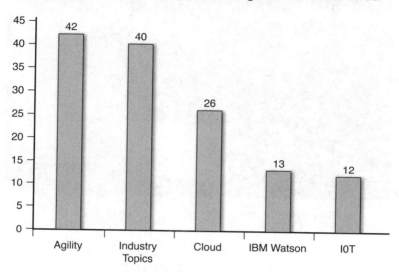

Figure 8.2 Topics of tweets made by a number of IBMers over a two-week period.

Forewarned Is Forearmed

So why look at data in real time? What value is there?

Consider the case of IBM's Always-On Engagement Center. Figure 8.3 shows an example of a display often used by IBM Engagement Center at various IBM events around the world. The idea behind the display is to highlight, in real time, various social media conversations happening at that moment around a given topic. While some insightful bits of information emerge, the Engagement Center allows a user, at a moment's notice, to gauge the pulse of a community or the thoughts or feelings around a topic. Using these techniques, command centers or call centers can, in theory, be ready for an onslaught of calls pertaining to a particular issue or incidence. So again, while not providing an insight into *why* something happened, we can be prepared for it by understanding *what* the discussion is around a particular topic. This can be considered an example of an early warning system.

Figure 8.3   The IBM Always-On Engagement Center.

Stream Computing

Stream computing is one of the latest trends allowing organizations to continuously integrate and analyze data in motion in an effort to deliver real-time and near real-time analytics. For the purposes of computing analytics, a stream is nothing more than a sequence of data elements delivered for processing over a continuous time frame.

Think of a stream like a conveyor belt that delivers packets of information, or data, in a continuous flow (see Figure 8.4). This doesn't mean the time between entries is consistent, but it does mean that data will continue to flow over time. As an item reaches the end of the belt (in our case, a system that can process data in motion), the item is processed, and then room is made to process the item on the belt in a sequential fashion.

Figure 8.4   Data arriving on a stream is like products arriving on a conveyor belt.

This analogy works well from a data-arrival perspective. But what makes stream computing sometimes difficult to grasp is that the concept of querying the data is turned around somewhat. If we wanted to capture and analyze data in a traditional environment, we would set up a feed to capture all of the data we are interested in first and then analyze it. This process involves capturing data, storing it into some kind of a database, creating queries to run against the data, and then executing those queries and deriving some information.

With a stream model, we define the queries or manipulation process of the data first using something like IBM's Streams Processing Language (SPL). We connect these nodes together in a directed graph (or a path for the data to flow through our system), and then rather than collect and query, we run the data over our graph and produce results as the data arrives.

Functions that operate on stream data are known as filters. Filters operate on stream data and then pass it along in the stream, continuing the flow, which results in another stream. A string of filters operating together is called a pipeline. Filters may operate on one item of a stream at a time or may base an item of output on multiple items of input from other parts of the stream. So, while we show a single stream in Figure 8.5, any number of streams of data may pass through an environment, combining items, separating items, and forming new streams along the way.

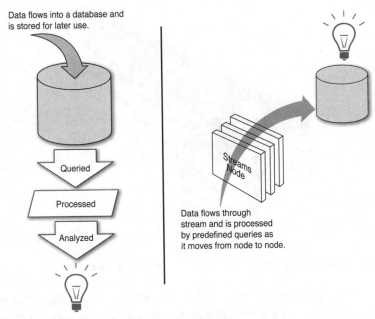

Figure 8.5   Traditional capture and query versus stream computing.

Stream computing can enable an organization to detect trends or signals in fast-moving data that can be detected or acted upon only at the time it occurs. With stream computing, we are able to process and potentially take action on rapidly arriving data because we are watching a data flow in its original sequence (in real time or near real time). As a result, we are able to analyze and act on issues before they are lost to history, or rather, before that needle gets lost in the haystack. As a result, there is now a paradigm shift as we move our processing data in batch (or operating on "data at rest") to processing data in real time, thus enabling faster insights.

IBM InfoSphere Streams

IBM InfoSphere Streams is a software platform that enables the development and execution of applications that process information in data streams. Streams enables continuous and fast analysis of massive volumes of moving data to help improve the speed of business insight and decision making.

Streams consists of a programming language and an Integrated Development Environment (IDE) for Streams applications and a runtime system that can execute the applications on a single or distributed set of hosts. The Streams Studio IDE includes tools for authoring and creating visual representations of the Streams applications.

Streams offers the IBM Streams Processing Language (SPL) interface for end users to operate on data streams. SPL provides a language and runtime framework to support streaming applications. Users can create applications without needing to understand the lower-level stream-specific operations. SPL provides numerous built-in operators, the ability to import data from outside streams and export results outside the system, and a facility to extend the underlying system with user-defined operators. Many of the SPL built-in operators provide powerful relational functions such as Join and Aggregate.

SPL Applications

The main components of SPL applications are as follows:

- **Processing elements (PEs)**—A processing element is an individual execution program that performs some function on the incoming stream. Processing elements are then tied together to create a work-flow of execution.

- **Tuples**—An individual piece of information in a stream is called a tuple. This is essentially the piece of data that is passed along the stream from one processing element to the next. This data can be structured or unstructured. Typically, the data in a tuple represents the state of an object at a specific point in time—for example, the running sentiment of a Twitter feed, the current topics of conversation, or the reading from external sensors.

- **Data streams**—These are the running sequence of data (in the form of tuples) that passes from one processing element to the next.

- **Operators**—An SPL operator manipulates tuple data from the incoming stream and produces results in the form of an output stream. One or more operators work together to form multiple streams and operators deployed in streams to form a data flow graph.

- **Jobs**—A job is an instance of a running streams processing application.

- **Ports**—A port is the place where a stream connects to an operator. Many operators have one input port and one output port, but operators can also have zero input ports (for example, if we read from an external source), zero output ports (if an operator is performing an operation and storing the results in a database as opposed to passing a tuple down the stream), or multiple input or output ports.

The tuple is the only data construct in streams. The data flow (streams) between the operators (processing elements) is made up entirely of tuples. We can say that the streams of a tuple are processed or manipulated to obtain the desired result. A tuple can have any number of elements (strings, numbers, and so on) within the construct and may even consist of another tuple. For the sake of simplicity, think of a stream as the data path and the contents of the stream being made up of tuples that get passed from one operator to the next (producing a new tuple to be passed on to the next operator).

Directed Graphs

A directed graph is a graph or set of objects (called vertices or nodes) that are connected together. When we think about streams, the nodes or vertices are essentially represented as processing elements (which are further composed of operators). These edges are directed from one vertex to another (passing tuples) along a data stream (see Figure 8.6).

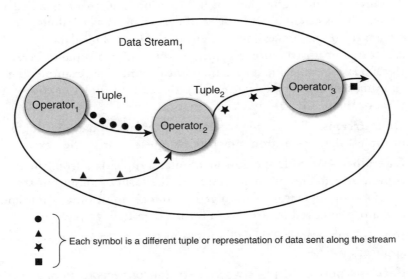

Figure 8.6   A stream is a directed graph of operators processing data objects called tuples.

The graph in Figure 8.6 is taken from our Simple Social Metrics application described later. Here, Operator$_1$ has received some information from the Internet. Because we don't require many of the fields that come in a standard feed from Twitter, our operator takes the raw data and creates a shorter subset of each tweet, Tuple1, and passes that data down the stream to Operator$_2$. It is important to understand that these processing elements, or operators, are purposely meant to be simple in function. This provides for an environment that is then easy to modify by simply rearranging the order that the operators are located in the stream.

Operator$_2$ in our application is a processing element that accepts two inputs: Tuple1 (the shortened form of the tweet from the Twitter stream) and another tuple, indicated by the solid triangle, that is the result of another operator. While we don't show it in this diagram, the operator's function is to take the tweet from the Twitter stream and perform a lookup in a table that we maintain. This list of special users is simply a list of known IBM tweeters, and if one of them has a tweet in the stream, we create a new tuple that contains not only that user's tweet and Twitter handle, but also an indication of the fact that he or she is indeed an IBM employee. This way, we can segment or separate IBM opinion or comments from our customers if the need arises. The function of Operator$_2$ is to merge that data, if necessary, and perform a sentiment analysis of the comment. The resulting data is represented as Tuple2 and then passed along the stream to the next operator.

In Operator$_3$, the incoming data is categorized based on a simple dictionary lookup of terms. This allows us to group similar discussion topics together. Again, the data stream is modified and passed on to the next node in the stream as a new tuple (represented by the dark square).

This is the beauty of streams. By turning as many functions into atomic or single-purpose functions as possible, we can quickly assemble a computational flow based on the type of analysis we are looking to perform.

Streams Example: SSM

As discussed before, we've created a simple but effective application based on InfoSphere Streams that we call Simple Social Metrics, or SSM. The idea behind this system is to capture a stream of tweets around a predetermined topic and provide summary analytics around the stream in real or near real time. Our system also supports an analysis of the stream in the past because we record our data to a standard SQL database, which in turn is front-ended by a number of REST Application Programming Interfaces

(APIs) for querying the data. REpresentational State Transfer, or REST, is an architectural style and an approach to communications that is often used in the development of Web services. The use of REST is often preferred over the more heavyweight Simple Object Access Protocol (SOAP) style because REST does not leverage as much bandwidth, which makes it a better fit for use over the Internet [4].

While we plan to show a simple example of how we use Streams to capture this data in near real time, our system is a bit more complex in practice. We show a few of the metrics we derive, but since this is a discussion about possibilities as opposed to a how-to guide, we chose to show a subset. In our live system, we are able to derive the following attributes (in real and near real time) within a stream of Twitter data:

- Top authors
- Top hashtags
- Top mentions
- Top negative sentiments
- Top positive sentiments
- Top known tweeters based on a predetermined list
- Top unknown tweeters based on a predetermined list
- Top retweeted users
- Top tweeted languages
- Top words
- Sentiment distribution (sentiment trend)
- Sentiment count
- Top reach (computed by author tweets multiplied by number of followers)
- Top categories
- Author information with top-used negative and positive sentiment, top categories
- Count trend over given period for tweets, hashtags, and mentions

For the purposes of this example, we discuss only top classifications, mentions, authors, and words. We have chosen only these four to illustrate the concept because they are some of the most commonly used metrics that we have encountered in our work. All of these metrics can be utilized to provide business value depending on the project at hand.

Figure 8.7 shows an example of our near real-time engine for analyzing Twitter streams. We labeled each of the distinct steps 1 through 8.

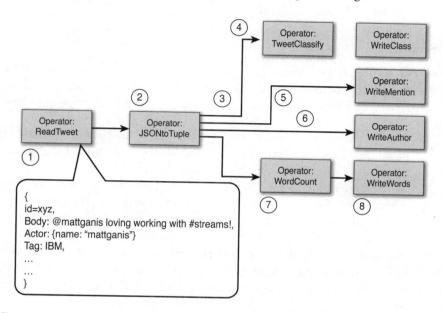

Figure 8.7 Directed graph representation of our near real-time Twitter service.

Let's look at the flow of data in a step-by-step fashion, using the following sample tweet:

```
@mattganis loving working with #streams!
```

Step 1

Streams has a number of built-in functions that allow a programmer to ingest data from a variety of sources. In this case, we connect to the Twitter source and read the tweets that we have collected that were a match to our search criteria. In many examples, we set up a Twitter feed and simply watch for a hashtag or small number of keywords that, when matched, will be collected by our search engine for later retrieval and ingestion (like we do here).

In this step, we start with an operator that receives a stream of tweets in the form of JSON data [5]. JavaScript Object Notation is a lightweight data-interchange format. It is easy for humans to read and write; plus, it is easy for machines to parse and generate. That data, in JSON format, is collected externally and read by our first operator (called ReadTweet). The data is separated by tweet (the input data source could be composed of a number of tweets) and formed into a tuple that is passed along the stream to the next operator (in this case, JSONtoTuple).

Step 2

The JSONtoTuple operator has an input port (for the incoming tuple, which contains the tweet to be analyzed) and several output ports (each of which has a different tuple placed on it). Here, we form four different tuples:

1. The first contains just the text of the tweet, also referred to as tweet payload. We use an external classifier in the next operator, but all we need for that is the text of the tweet itself.
2. In JSONtoTuple, we examine the tweet payload and look for any Twitter mentions in the stream. We want to keep track of who is being talked about in the Twitter stream, so we form a tuple that contains all of the *@userid phrases* that we encounter in the tweet.
3. We form a tuple that contains just the author of the tweet. This information is passed on to a separate operator that processes it alone (in this case, simply updating the author count in the database).
4. We create a tuple that contains all of the words used in the Tweet. That data is passed on to the next operator, and a word count is written to the database. This allows us to easily form *word clouds* based on the frequency of words used.

Step 3

It's important to remember that steps 3, 5, 6, and 7 all execute at the same time (in parallel). So even though they are labeled numerically (to help us understand this example), the power of stream computing is that tasks can happen simultaneously.

One of the outputs of the JSONtoTuple operator is the tuple we call *tweet*. It's a stream representation of the tweet payload we just received (in this example, `@mattganis loving working with #streams!`). At this point, it's placed in a stream that will take it to a classifier, so we can group similar tweets together. This same tuple is also sent (on another stream) at step 7, where it is broken down into the individual words for later use in a word cloud.

Step 4

We've found it useful to look at a large number of tweets and group them into "buckets," or classifications, based on their subject matter. Classification is a difficult problem, but we take advantage of the fact that Twitter (or any microblogging technology) uses short text for updates coupled with the fact that when we gather Twitter data, we are gathering it based on a predetermined set of filters. In the case of the tweet used as an example for this section, `#streams` will probably translate into a category called "Stream Computing". To explore this concept some more, let's consider a few other examples. For example, in the past we have captured all of the tweets that contain the word `#ibminterconnect`, so more than likely any mention of the word *cloud* in a tweet that also has `#ibminterconnect` is probably talking about cloud computing technologies.

We chose to implement our classifier as a Web Service so that it can be utilized by a variety of applications. It doesn't strive for perfection but gets pretty close. As we said earlier, we take advantage of the facts that tweets are generally short and we know the general theme of the topics. Our classifier is a simple pattern-matching algorithm based on categories and words that represent that category or indicate they are *not* part of that categorization. For example:

> Topic: Cloud Computing
> Matches: cloud, Softlayer, PAAS, SAAS, Bluemix
> Excludes: rain, snow, sleet, storm
>
> Topic: Mobile
> Matches: ipad, ipod, iphone, android, smart phone
> Excludes: music, playlists, store

So if our classifier "sees" a tweet that contains the word *bluemix*, for example, we could return a classification of "Cloud Computing." Of course, if the tweet contains any of the words from the exclude list, we don't classify it as "Cloud Computing" and move on to the next category to be analyzed.

Tweets could discuss a variety of topics, and at times they overlap. So a tweet like the following would return two classifications ("Mobile" and "Cloud Computing") because they have keywords that match both classifications:

`@mattganis building a new iphone app on bluemix is easy!`

So at step 4, the tweet is formatted into a REST service call and sent out for a classification. When the results are returned, they are parsed and put into yet another tuple, which is then sent onto its next step in the stream. In that step, the operator writes the data on the tweets classification into the database to be aggregated with other classifications.

Steps 5 and 6

We've grouped steps 5 and 6 together because they do essentially the same thing (but with different slices of the data). In step 5, the operator receives a tuple that was formed in the JSONtoTuple operator; it contains all of the Twitter handles that were mentioned in the tweet (anything with an @ symbol in front of it). Mentions are useful for determining who is being talked about or referred to in a given tweet (perhaps leading to an influencer). This list of Twitter handles is simply written to the database, so we can quickly determine how many mentions any given Twitter handle received over a given time period. In our example, we save the handle `@mattganis` in the database. Step 6 is similar; here, we receive a tuple that contains just the author of the tweet, which is immediately written out to our database. This step is useful for understanding who is conversing the most in a given stream of Twitter conversations.

Steps 7 and 8

Step 7 is another workhorse operator. Here, the input to the operator is a tuple that contains the tweet payload (`@mattganis loving working with #streams!`). In this step, we parse the tweet and remove all common words (things like *a*, *and*, *with*, and so on) and just keep the relevant words. They are put into a tuple and passed on to step 8, where they are written to the database as well. What this allows us to do is query for the top words (and their frequency) in a stream and form a word cloud (such as the one shown in Figure 8.8), where the larger and darker a word, the more it was used, and the smaller and lighter, the less often it was used.

Figure 8.8 A word cloud generated from tweets around IBM InterConnect.

In the end, our real-time monitor looks something like Figure 8.9. During analysis, if we discover that some categories contain such a large number of tweets that the pie chart is dominated by that category, we are hardly able to get valuable information out of the rest of the categories. For example, in the bottom right of Figure 8.9, the pie chart shows the distribution of tweets based on the language. If English were included, we would not get any readable information about other languages. In cases like these, we record the value of tweets in the English language and then remove or deselect that category to convey more information. As a result, we are able to see the distribution of other languages such as Portuguese and Swedish.

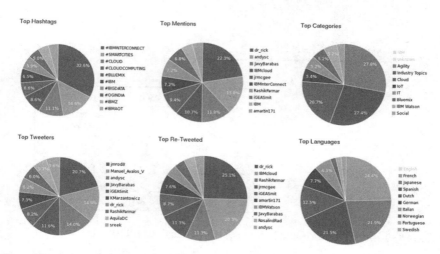

Figure 8.9 Real-time Twitter dashboard around a stream of tweets.

Value Derived from a Conference
Using Real-Time Analytics

Consider a keynote address that needs to be delivered to a large professional conference (or any other large presentation). Consider how much more effective a presentation could be if the speaker refers to topics that he or she knows are of interest to the audience. Sounds obvious, right? But we all know that, as human beings, our priorities, interests, and concerns are always in flux. Even the projects we work on are often moving targets. So how do we prepare to present a topic to an audience and address the topics *currently* on our (collective) minds ?

One way to do this is to monitor social media around the event and look for common themes or topics. Figure 8.10 shows some data from a recent trade show where we monitored the topics of conversation over time.

Popular Topics as of 10:00am	
Category	Percent of Mentions
Security ⇧	40%
Cloud ⇧	26%
IoT ⇧	19%
Mobile Apps ⇩	15%

Popular Topics as of 11:30am (noon)	
Category	Percent of Mentions
Cloud ⇧	48%
IoT ⇧	26%
Mobile Apps ⇩	14%
Security ⇩	15%

Figure 8.10   Topics of conversation from a trade show (10 a.m. versus 11:30 a.m.).

Most conferences today use a Twitter hashtag to promote their event to allow participants to post comments or observations. So imagine you're about to deliver an address to this large crowd. In the morning, the hot topic of conversation at the conference was security (with over 40% of the tweets discussing some aspect of the topic), followed by cloud computing with 26% of the discussion. But by mid-afternoon, the topic of conversation has changed (somewhat drastically) to indicate that almost half of the conversation is centered around the topic of cloud computing (at 48%) with the second topic shifting from security to the Internet of Things (IoT). With this information in hand, you can shift the emphasis of your talk from security to cloud computing given that it is still relevant to your original topic. So if your plan was to focus on security (or even mobile applications), it's clear (at least from a social media discussion) that these topics may not be the uppermost in your audience's minds. A slight tweak to your presentation to highlight areas around the Internet of Things focusing on cloud technologies would, it appears, be much more appealing.

Another application of this technique could be in the context of panel discussions, talk shows, or any live event. If, indeed, you monitor the conversation in social media and aggregate the results (as we did in the previous example), questions to panelists or topics of discussion become much more relevant (and useful) to those listening, thereby increasing the value of your participation. One key point to remember is that you need to understand your audience and determine if what is happening in social venues is truly a representation of their views.

Summary

There are a number of reasons we might want to capture and analyze data in real time. In this chapter, we focused on two:

- Sense and respond
- Early warning

In most cases, early warning systems entail the timely collection and analysis of data, which, when understood, trigger prompt interventions on the part of those watching. In the case of social media, this means getting in front of a potential public relations issue, company-related scandal, or a competitor's breaking news. Sometimes how we respond in the early minutes or hours can have a lasting effect on the impact on the public's perception of an issue.

While early warning is more like "sense and react," "sense and respond" is slightly different in that we want to sense a condition and respond in such a way as to change that condition. In today's world, competition is based on nonstop strategic maneuvering among competitors, product or service positioning, and competition to protect an existing product or market. Agile teams understand this concept of iterations quite well. They iterate through many options, responding to change while discovering the best solution through continuous experimentation or change. In the world of mining social media, a real-time analysis gives us that view into what needs to be changed and the (instant) feedback and reaction allowing us to continually make course corrections along the way.

Finally, in this chapter, we also explored one specific social analytics system, leveraging the concepts of stream computing, to extract value from real-time and near real-time information.

Endnotes

[1] Maraboli, Steve. *Life, the Truth, & Being Free.* A Better Today, 2009.

[2] Davis, Colin J., Jeffrey S. Bowers, and Amina Memon, "Social Influence in Televised Election Debates: A Potential Distortion of Democracy." *PLoS One*, 6, no. 3. (March 30, 2011): e18154.

[3] The Naked Scientists, "Science Interviews," April 3, 2011. Retrieved from http://www.thenakedscientists.com/HTML/content/interviews/interview/1606/.

[4] TechTarget, "REST (Representational State Transfer) Definition." Retrieved from http://searchsoa.techtarget.com/definition/REST.

[5] "Introducing JSON." Retrieved from http://www.json.org.

9

If You Don't Know
What You Want,
You Just May Find It:
Ad Hoc Analysis

"Not all those who wander are lost."

—J. R. R. Tolkien [1]

Up to this point in our discussions, we've looked at how to find data, where to look for it, how to clean it, and now how to process it. Much of what we have discussed thus far involves the process of building a model (or a definition) of what we want to look for and then running an analysis to see if our model fits or provides relevant results. If the data seems to fit the model, we take the output, calling it information, and build our insights or knowledge from there. If the data doesn't fit our model, perhaps we modify the model and try again, or go look for different sources of data that may be more relevant than what we have already gathered.

In this chapter, we discuss *ad hoc analysis*. We introduced this concept in Chapter 6, where we defined it as an analysis that is produced one time to answer a single specific business question. Specifically, we use this type of analysis when dealing with situations as they occur rather than ones that are repeated on a regular basis. As a result, often we are searching for an answer in dataset.

This ad hoc method assumes we are looking for a number of different insights to emerge from our assembled data and that a model will be able to accurately, or at least somewhat accurately, represent the information contained within the dataset. Sometimes we just want to look at the data we've collected and determine the answer to a specific question or questions and perhaps gain some insightful information. Or perhaps we just want to understand the composition or makeup of the data before we go off and build a more complex model and undertake a deeper analysis.

Ad Hoc Analysis

The word *ad hoc* is originally derived from Latin and is loosely translated as "for this" or "for this situation." We use this term to describe something that has been formed or used for a special and immediate purpose, without previous planning. *Ad hoc analysis* is the discipline of analyzing data on an as-needed or requested basis. This analysis is based on a set of data currently available to the person doing the analysis; thus, the resulting analysis is only as good as the data on which it is based. Generally, we look to this process to answer a specific question.

Consider the diagram in Figure 9.1. As we discussed in previous chapters, the process of analytics is often an iterative model, where we attempt an analysis, determine if we have succeeded or failed, make repairs and adjustments, and then try again. Figure 9.1 presents the iterative set of steps recommended for understanding a dataset in an attempt to answer a question from the data. Obviously, we start at the top by locating what we believe to be our relevant data sources. We attempt a first model or perhaps execute a series of simple queries against the data and analyze our results. If we begin to see a pattern emerge, perhaps we can perform a deeper analysis or simply begin to assemble our derived insights. If, on the other hand, our queries reveal no answers or patterns, we have to ask ourselves if we have a sufficient amount of data to analyze or if the model we've built is incorrect. At this point, we either make adjustments by augmenting the model or by adding additional data to our dataset.

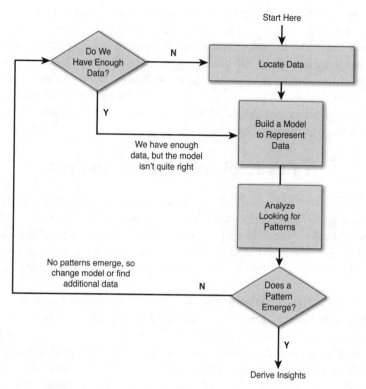

Figure 9.1 Process for deriving insights from data.

The purpose of this type of analysis may be to fill in the blanks left by a larger analysis or perhaps as a precursor to a larger initiative. More importantly, ad hoc reporting allows analysts (or general users) to manipulate and explore the data they have on hand to build reports, often on-the-fly, to answer their questions. Think of dashboards answering the question "What is happening in social media around my topic?" and ad hoc reporting answering the question "Why is it happening?"

As we saw in Chapter 2, collecting large amounts of data is just the first step in a social media analytics campaign. Often we need to cleanse the data we find or perhaps reformat it such that it can become machine-readable.

With smaller collections, the verification of data is often a straightforward process of simply looking at what we have to see if data we are interested in falls into the correct columns or is made up of unreadable characters, thus rendering any analysis useless. Often, what we, as data scientists, want to do is perform some simple queries on the data to ensure that what we are about to analyze is indeed going to give us some meaningful results.

This idea of performing some simple queries is a perfect illustration of what we mean by the ad hoc query of data. In some cases, we want to perform a one-time (or specific) query to build up our knowledge of the information we are uncovering. At times, the simple queries produce just throw-away results, but results that give us an indication about whether we should proceed down our current path.

An Example of Ad Hoc Analysis

As we saw in Chapter 4, we differentiate between two types of analytics: predictive versus descriptive. One looks to describe the contents of the data set under analysis (descriptive), and the other attempts to extract information from existing data sets to determine a pattern of behavior or to predict future outcomes and trends. An ad hoc analysis lies somewhere between these two.

Consider a dataset of tweets that were collected around January 17, 2013. On that date, Lance Armstrong confessed to Oprah Winfrey on national television in the United States that he won all seven of his record Tour de France championships with the help of performance-enhancing drugs and that his attitude was one of "win at all costs." We wanted to understand the public's reaction to this topic, so in this case, we collected data that contained:

- Mentions of Lance Armstrong
- Mentions of Oprah Winfrey

We didn't collect the data for any other purpose than to experiment with some analytics around the event.

With the raw data in hand, we wanted to understand some of the basics about what we had collected before performing some simple descriptive analytics. The first question we wanted to answer was:

Is the data clean (in other words, is it usable)?

For simplicity, we didn't take the full JSON string of data that we got from a typical tweet, since it was not relevant to our analysis. This could actually be an important step for some teams that have concerns about capacity and performance of their analytics environment. A typical tweet can have a large number of name-value pairs that represent all of the various parts of the tweet (when it was posted, the person's name, the Twitter handle, hashtags, and so on). Most of the information that came from Twitter was either redundant or wasn't useful in this exercise. As a result, we took the JSON data and simply converted it to a comma-separated value (CSV) file. This resulted in a data file that contained the following elements:

- Preferred user name
- Display name (what gets displayed in public Twitter)
- The status count (the number of tweets this person has made)
- Language of the tweet
- The number of times the tweet was retweeted
- The posted time
- The text of the tweet

The first thing we wanted to do was just browse the data before we did any kind of analytics on it to see if it was well formed. This was a preliminary but very important step to ensure that all of the data was in its proper columns and was a complete dataset.

This process is best shown with some examples. Up to this point in the book, we've made it a point not to show specific products or dive into how-to descriptions, so here we try to stay as true to that doctrine as possible, but we may have to stray just a bit.

For ad hoc querying, we like to use interactive tools such as IBM's BigSheets, which is part of the Big Insights suite of tools from IBM; custom code that looks over Hadoop clusters; or public domain tools such as R. For this example, we used R.

R is a powerful and widely used analytics tool. It includes virtually every data manipulation, statistical model, and chart that the modern data scientist could ever need. You can easily find, download, and use cutting-edge community-reviewed methods in statistics and predictive modeling from leading researchers in data science, free of charge [2].

Figure 9.2 shows a screen capture of the R session we ran on some of this data. We started off with the trimmed-down version of our dataset as discussed earlier. (Remember, we chose to convert the JSON data into CSV for easier manipulation. The data doesn't change, just the format.)

```
>LAdata<-read.csv("/home/ganis/LA/lance-04-20.csv")  ①
>nrow(LAdata)  ②
[1]366135
>
>unique(LAdata$lang)  ③
[931] DUB
[932] 109344
[933] 1953
[934] 2875
[935] 5049
935 Levels: 27… AI! and Fox and I Bencid Gone. In? JD..zh-tw
>
```

Figure 9.2   Sample R session looking at number of unique languages in our dataset.

Ad hoc analysis essentially is the process of running a number of simple queries against a database to understand more about the data we may want to process with more complex tools.

In section 1 of Figure 9.2, the first step was to bring our data into R. We used the read.csv() function, which reads a comma-separated value file into a variable called LAdata. Note that in this case, the first line of the file contains the headers for each column. For clarity, the first line of the CSV file contains the following (each element representing a name of the column):

```
prefusername,displayname,statuscount,lang,retweetcount,time,body
```

To access a specific column in a table, the syntax is:

```
table_name$column_name
```

To see a specific row, we would use:

```
table_name[index,]
```

Typically, one of our first queries is to look at size—just to understand how big of a dataset we're working with (see section 2 in Figure 9.2). The nrow() function in R simply looks at the number of rows of data read into the table variable (in this case, LAdata) and returns a count. So we can quickly see that this dataset had about 360,000 tweets from the second day of the interview. Not a very useful analytic, but a descriptive feature we may want to have when summarizing our data source.

Because this was our initial look at the data, the first thought was to get a quick overview of what we had collected. From the previous step, we knew we had about 360,000 tweets, but where did they come from? What language were they in?

In section 3 of Figure 9.2, we used the `unique()` function in R to look at a column of data in our table and summarize it for us, showing the individual values (or just the unique values). So if French, for example, was used in a tweet, the column called `lang` would contain `fr`. The `unique()` function lists it only once, so it gives a good representation of the number of unique languages used in the sample.

Interestingly, when we ran the command `unique(LAdata$lang)`, we saw that R believed there were 935 unique values in the `lang` column of our dataset! And the output of the `unique()` command reported that the 933rd unique language was `"1953"`; something didn't seem right.

Obviously, `"1953"` isn't a valid language, so using R's query capabilities, we looked at that offending line of data to see where others may have errors. To do that, we used an R query that looked like this:

```
LAdata[LAdata$lang=="1953",]
```

This simple query says:

"Show the row of data in LAdata where the lang column has the value '1953.'"

What we got back resembled this:

Prefuser-name	Displayname	Status-count	Lang	Retweet-count	Time	Body
mattganis	Matt Ganis	PhD	1953	En	2013-01-18T10:05:57.00Z	(empty)

Notice that the `statuscount` has the value `PhD` and the `lang` field has the value `"1953"`. No doubt what happened was that this person entered his name in a format like this: `Matt Ganis, PhD`.

So when we took the original data and moved it into a CSV format, this name field looked like two separate elements just separated by a comma. Consequently, all of the fields ended up shifting to the right.

Simply cleaning up the original data and re-creating the CSV file fixed the problem. The cleanup was to remove all nonessential characters from the user-created data. In this case, those characters included commas, linefeeds, newlines, and so on. The important thing is the lesson learned:

Don't trust any free-form text data.

By "free-form," we mean any input provided by a user that doesn't have any given structure or format.

Looking at Figure 9.3, we can see that data collected from a web drop-down menu (the example on the left) is an example of what we mean by "well formed." In this case, when the user selects an option, we know exactly what values are possible. However, data collected from an input field, where a user can (and will) type anything he or she wants, is considered "free form." We need to look closer at this data than a well-formed set of data because we have no way of knowing ahead of time what the user may or may not enter. The content in the search query field shown on the right side of Figure 9.3 is an example of free-form input.

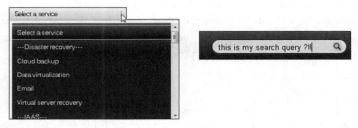

Figure 9.3   Example of free-form input.

When we looked at the data in a comma-separated value format, our cleansing program didn't realize (and neither did we) that someone might use a comma in the name field. Basically, our first ad hoc query helped us uncover an issue with our JSON-to-CSV conversion.

Once we corrected this issue, we were able to see that our data appeared to be more correct (see Figure 9.4). Again, using the `unique()` command from R to determine the number of unique languages represented in this dataset, we can see in Figure 9.4 that the number is now 32. This number is much more reasonable than the previous value of 935, as reported in the initial queries from Figure 9.2.

```
>LAdata<-read.csv("/home/ganis/LA/lance-04-20.csv")
>nrow(LAdata)
[1]365059
>unique(LAdata$lang)
 en  fr  es  nl  it  pt  ar  fi  ca  tr  de  pl
 ja  sv  da  no  ru  id  ko  eu  cs  el zh-cn th hu zh-tw hi  fil
msa  he  uk  ur

32 Levels: ar ca cs da de el en es eu fi fil fr he hi hu id it ja ko msa..zh-tw
>table(LAdata$lang)

  ar    ca    cs    da    de    el    en    es    eu    fi   fil
 125   467    22   253  1611    39 288875 50160   107    65    47

  fr    he    hi    hu    id    it    ja    ko   msa    nl    no
8967     8     5    15   981  1254   513    67     5  5765   320
```

Figure 9.4   Another view of R with data corrected and reloaded.

So now, with the data reloaded, we could look at the various languages represented in our sample. Note that the R command unique() looked at the column of data lang and reported all of the unique values. We can see that there are 32 languages, which seems a much more reasonable number. To get a better idea of how much of our data was represented in specific languages, we again issued a simple R command to represent the data in tabular form (table(LAdata$lang)). Note that, for clarity, we show only the first two lines of this output. What might be more useful is to look at the representation of the data graphically.

So, with a quick query, we can see that the English-speaking population was the most vocal, followed by French (fr), Spanish (es), Dutch (nl), and Portuguese (pt).

For the purpose of this example, we chose to focus on the predominant language used in this sample, English. One of the first things we wanted to understand was the general feeling around this topic and the kinds of things people were saying.

Remember, we view ad hoc analysis as a simple query, or a "peek" at a dataset. Some computation may be involved, but if we were to look at it from a classification perspective, these are the simple, lightweight analytics, whereas the deeper insights and relationships (that is, computationally heavy) come with longer-running processes. Don't misunderstand; we're not saying that these are not valuable pieces of information. The more information we have about a topic, the more accurate our insights or knowledge becomes.

There's another way to think about this scenario. On the far right of the graph in Figure 9.5, where we show "Deep Analysis," we have a rich set of insights and relationships between terms and concepts built up in our analysis. This deep analysis leverages all of the descriptive statistics we collect, and the simple ad hoc queries/analysis we do and is combined with a complex textual analysis. This is why we show the upward graph in the effort needed to derive value. Creating a set of descriptive statistics is relatively low in effort contrasted with the larger effort to derive deeper insights.

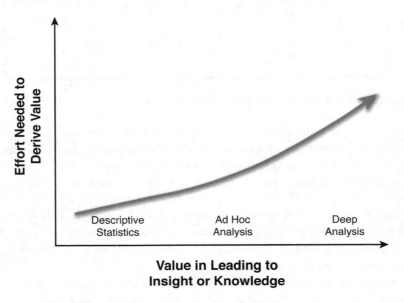

Figure 9.5   Relative value/effort of various insight techniques.

Data Integrity

One of the topics that we want to concern ourselves with is the integrity of the data we use. This is an important topic because many times when performing ad hoc queries or manipulation of data, we could inadvertently change the integrity of the dataset. A simple change to a value could lead to erroneous results. For this reason, we like to say that we "augment" datasets, but we don't change them. That may seem like a subtle difference, but it's meant to draw a distinction between changing data and adding additional data to an existing dataset.

In our case, we wanted to understand the discussion around the topic of Lance Armstrong's confession, but we thought it might be interesting to look at it from a gender perspective, to understand if males reacted differently to his confession than females. For example, if we examined the general sentiment to Mr. Armstrong's confession, we may obtain an overwhelming negative reaction. One hypothesis could be that this makes sense if the audience was predominantly male. Males may view cheating in an athletic competition as outrageous, while perhaps females land more on the sympathetic side and view the confession more ambivalently, or perhaps positively. While perhaps not as relevant in this experiment, the idea of understanding how males and females react to different events could become important for areas such as marketing or public relations.

Unfortunately, Twitter and many of the other social media outlets don't supply that information. Many allow users to enter it into a profile, but often that data is not readily available for analysis. To get around this limitation, we can compute the gender based on some of the fields we have in this sample (see Figure 9.6).

Remember, we currently have the following information:

- Preferred user name
- Display name (what gets displayed in public Twitter)
- The status count (the number of tweets this person has made)
- Language of the tweet
- The number of times the tweet was retweeted
- The posted time
- The text of the tweet

From this, if we take the display name from the tweet, we can look up the name in a dictionary of common names and return a value of "male," "female," or "unknown" (if we can't find the name or if there is ambiguity in the name, such as Kim or Chris).

In the profile in Figure 9.6, the display name is represented in the tweet as Karen Scilla Ganis. So for our ad hoc query, we simply took the first part of the display name (we assumed it's a first name) and looked it up in a dictionary of common names (in this case, a dictionary of common US names). We built a new column in our dataset and inserted the result of our query (in this case, "female") into the dataset and then proceeded to the next name. When we're done, we had an augmented dataset that contains our original data point (if we should need it again), the display name, but we also created a new field (called "gender") that contains our computation of the user's gender.

Karen Scilla Ganis
@kscilla

What lies behind us and what lies before us are tiny matters compared to what lies within us....

𝒮 RideConnectWestchester.org
🕐 Joined August 2010

Figure 9.6 A sample tweet.

With that, a quick query revealed the following new demographic for our sample:

Males	140,852
Females	67,119
Undetermined	80,904

Using our simple calculation, we were able to classify about 72% of our dataset into a male or female category. If we wanted to spend more time, we could probably do additional work on the undetermined users because many of the display names use forms such as "Mr. John Jones" or "Mrs. Kelly Jackson" (clearly, *Mr.* and *Mrs.* aren't proper first names, but we could easily deduce that they would be male or female with a few additional tests). Likewise, we were not naïve enough to think that our numbers were perfect. We knew that there would be (and definitely are) some misclassifications based on gender-neutral or unisex names. But given the fairly large numbers of tweets, we assumed those are in the minority (but it would be useful to look for a measure of uncertainty if we were to make any conclusions based on the derived gender).

The next thing we might want to get a feel for is the general tone of the conversations. What are the hot buttons in the conversations?

One way to do this quickly is to create a word cloud. We discussed them previously, but since we'll be looking at a few here, let's review the concept quickly.

Basically, a *word cloud* takes all of the relevant words in a set of text and displays them in such a way as to indicate use. Words appearing in a larger font indicate that they are used more frequently, and words appearing in smaller fonts are obviously used less frequently. Often, people use color to indicate levels of use or intensity. These conventions are useful, but only to the point of giving you, the analyst, a feeling for areas you may want to explore further in the dataset. Many applications allow the user to remove words or text that may cause confusion. For example, in these word clouds, we removed all of the English "stop" words (*the*, *this*, *is*, *was*, and so on). The theory is this: If we were to count the uses of those stop words, they would far outpace the other words. We also eliminated punctuation and converted everything to lowercase to avoid case as a factor (when somebody uses *IBM* or *ibm*, they still mean the same thing).

The other thing we removed was common words we don't need to show in a word cloud. In this case, since this was an interview done by Oprah Winfrey with Lance Armstrong, we simply removed any references to their names. If a word cloud shows a lot of mentions of these words, it doesn't really tell us any net new information.

For example, Figure 9.7 shows our derived word cloud (showing the top 150 words) used within the 288,875 tweets that were marked as being in English.

Figure 9.7   A word cloud representation of our current data.

Many of the terms are obvious, but the power of the word cloud is that it gives us a great starting point for deeper analysis. If we were starting blind (with just a set of tweets about the topic in front of us), we would probably start building a model with words such as *drugs* and *cheating*, which are shown in this word cloud. We might not have thought of using words like *doping* or *doped*.

One thing we found very interesting was a wide-sweeping reference to Manti Te'o. Many people drew comparisons to the story of how Manti Te'o revealed that his girlfriend, a supposed cancer victim, never existed. In other words, he lied just as Lance Armstrong did. This result was something we never would have predicted, but it could provide some valuable insights into the perception of Mr. Armstrong and his denying allegations about his use of performance-enhancing drugs.

A look at the word clouds broken down by gender (see Figure 9.8) could be useful in revealing different feelings or emotions. In this exercise, we divided all of the content from the tweets in our database into those tweets authored by males and those authored by females. We then took these two subsets of words and converted them into word clouds, as shown in Figure 9.8.

Figure 9.8   Word cloud representation by gender.

In the word cloud on the left, we see that males were focused on what Rick Reilly (a sports writer for ESPN) was saying as well as many references again to Manti Te'o. The female side had similar results, but we can see that the magnitude of the word use in both cases is less. Interestingly, males referenced Sheryl Crow, whereas females used the word *futurecrow*. Both males and females commented on Lance Armstrong's apologies and the stripping of awards. Both groups seemed to give similar emphasis to words such as *lying* and *doping*.

Summary

While it is a technique in and of itself, ad hoc analysis is an important aspect of performing a social media analysis. While simple in nature, these types of queries can help to add a bit of context to a larger analysis, or on their own, they can provide pieces to an even larger puzzle. But more importantly, the ability to explore our datasets, either by counting the number of males and females in our sample or understanding the languages used, provides vital information to analysts about how to proceed or build larger, more complex models for understanding our data.

Endnotes

[1] Tolkien, John Ronald Reuel. *The Fellowship of the Ring: Being the First Part of The Lord of the Rings.* Houghton Mifflin Harcourt, 2012.

[2] Revolution Analytics, "What Is R?" *Blog.* Retrieved from http://www.revolution-analytics.com/what-r.

10

Rivers Run Deep:
Deep Analysis

There is nothing so terrible as activity without insight.

—Johann Wolfgang von Goethe [1]

Discovering themes and patterns from social media content can be a very exciting endeavor. Sometimes the questions to be answered are too complex to be looked at in real time, or they need to establish a relationship between two or more entities, or the analysis involves multiple different phases. We call this a *deep analysis*. In this chapter, we delve into some use cases that require a more complex type of process or analysis, and we explore what we can uncover with a more sophisticated method analysis.

Responding to Leads Identified in Social Media

Many services and products in the marketplace try to facilitate discovering leads in social media. In the following sections, we discuss an experimental project that we are working on in IBM. For the purposes of this discussion, we break it up into three phases:

- Identifying leads
- Qualifying/classifying leads
- Suggested action

Identifying Leads

Our Social Listening team, led by Mila Gessner, began working with an account team within IBM. The goal of this exercise was to see if we could analyze conversations taking place within social media venues, around the topics that were of interest to us or some pilot set of customers, to identify sales leads for our customer-facing marketing representatives. Team members identified 10 accounts across a variety of industries. They also identified lines of businesses within these companies to focus on. A list of key IBM competitors relevant to these accounts and the industries and lines of business were identified. Using the methods already identified in this book, the team completed the data identification phase and determined the type of data, the sources of data, and the duration of data to be included in the analysis. After several iterations, team members were able to settle on a set of keywords to use to search for content for this analysis on a daily basis. Figure 10.1 shows the process that was used in this phase.

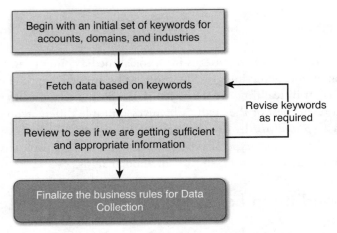

Figure 10.1   Process to finalize business rules for data collection.

The next step was to use an IBM software package called IBM Social Media Analytics (SMA) to develop a model to perform social media analysis of all the content being pulled in through the data identification phase. The sales team and social analysis team worked together iteratively to settle on the keywords that were to be used for the topic areas that we were going to focus on. During the first couple of iterations of the model-building phase, the teams realized that the list of keywords was really missing the mark. A separate effort was taken to identify the appropriate keywords for this project. While this was going on, the teams also developed a model that took in the content being provided by the initial keywords filter and classified into a broad category called "Leads." These are considered potential sales or service opportunities based on the model. The goal was to share this with the sales and sales support teams for further steps of lead qualification and follow-through.

At the end of this phase, the teams had a strong list of keywords covering the following areas:

- **List of selected accounts**—These are the names and aliases of the accounts that the account teams selected for this pilot project.
- **List of industries**—This is a validated list of industries that cover the accounts we are interested in doing the listening for, such as Retail, Banking, and Education.
- **Subject categories**—These are the specific areas of business solutions that we are interested in targeting such as Finance, Operations, Information Technology, and Security.

Figure 10.2 illustrates the process steps utilized in this phase.

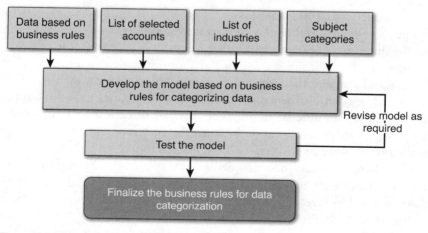

Figure 10.2 Process to finalize business rules for data categorization.

Qualifying/Classifying Leads

As discussed in the previous section, the output of the social listening team was a set of leads that could be analyzed on a daily basis. The team receiving the insights would look at the leads to identify which could be considered as real leads to be pursued.

One challenge encountered immediately was that there were too many potential leads but the actual number of leads to be pursued was very small. The busy salesforce was spending too much time reading through a large amount of social media updated in an attempt to identify which ones required action. In essence, the team had to wade through a number of results to find the most valuable items—sort of like looking for a needle in a pile of needles. One of the major problems was that of duplication; let us illustrate this with an example.

Suppose that the CIO of a bank gives an interview in a trade journal. In this interview, the CIO specifies that his company is about to revamp the technology infrastructure for supporting mobile access. This sounds like a clear opportunity that is worth exploring. The Social Listening Model that we had developed was designed to capture such cases and flag the story for further review and analysis by the sales team. However, what happened in this particular case (and in many other cases like these) is that the article was widely referenced in a variety of other journals, news sources, and social media venues. So, instead of having one lead about this opportunity, our system flagged over 100 references.

The team wrote a utility program to take the raw leads as input and weed out the duplicates. Team members first filtered out articles that had identical titles that brought the number of posts on this topic down to 70. What they noticed was that the same article would appear under a slightly different title. The team broadened the definition of duplicates to include those articles whose title differed in only one, two, or three words. This process also involved active collaboration between the analyst and business teams to ensure that we were filtering enough but not too much!

This phase is typical in social media analysis projects. Even though the software makes a lot of advances in facilitating analysis of text, in certain phases manual intervention is critical to the success of the program. In our experience, this filtering/cleanup is highly specific to each deep analysis project and could require a lot of investment in terms of people time. For the sake of this discussion, we have highlighted this simple example of deduplication. This process is illustrated in Figure 10.3.

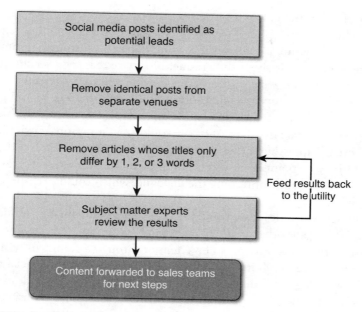

Figure 10.3 Process of eliminating duplicates.

The team would look at these leads and determine which leads to follow up on. After several months of using this approach, the team developed some logic and informal business rules for determining which leads have high potential. As of this writing, the team is looking at further automating these basic "rules of thumb."

Suggested Action

The analytics and sales teams worked together through many situations to identify what the next step was going to be once a lead was identified. This part of the project was very subjective, but we are able to specify some suggested actions to give you an idea of how to incorporate this in your specific project.

The main suggested action in each of these potential leads was to follow through in an attempt to determine if we can nurture the lead into a sale. This follow-through can take on several different forms.

In this first example, let's assume a user expresses an interest in a specific IBM product or service via Twitter. One suggestion is to respond back to the tweet with pointers to a specific white paper or customer testimonial providing more details about the product or service that the user showed an interest in. However, we can also perform some additional research on the Twitter handle to understand what sort of profile information we can gather about the user from the Twitter site. If, for example, we learn that this user is from the San Francisco Bay Area, we could send a personal invitation to an IBM event happening in the Bay Area of California, or wherever the user may be from. The point is, we can begin to establish an interest in providing more information and continuing the dialogue, which could perhaps lead to additional sales.

In another type of lead, we could uncover that a company has announced plans to investigate other markets or expand its product/service lines. We may have learned this through a news item or through a comment posted by the someone placed high in the company (such as the CIO) in social media channels or a blog. We could take this information and pass the lead on to the appropriate sales team in that region or city to explore potential sales opportunities further, perhaps getting the jump on some of our competitors.

In another example, we could stumble upon a person who shows interest in learning about some new technology—say, cognitive computing facilities—being showcased by the IBM Watson division in the health-care industry. We may have learned this from a comment posted on a blog by an IBM subject matter expert. In this case, we would want to create a follow-up by posting a schedule of training events or conferences on the topic of cognitive computing given there seemed to be heightened interest. The hope is that when the person actually enrolls for a session, we can learn more about her specific situation to see if there are any potential sales leads to be explored.

Finally, let's look at a specific example that we encountered on this project. In the preceding section on qualifying leads, we gave an example of a bank. In this particular instance, the CIO of the bank had announced that it was in the process of revamping its entire mobile platform and was looking for solutions in the area of fraud prevention. When this lead was discovered, IBM had recently acquired a company specializing in fraud detection in financial institutions. A number of steps were taken to follow up. First, an invitation was sent to this company for a conference where IBM was showcasing these services. Second, a specific meeting was arranged between the management team of this bank and the appropriate IBM services team, along with the subject matter expert in fraud prevention. As a result of these two simple follow-ups, which originated from a discovery made in social media, our IBM sales teams were able to close on a deal with the bank and our new fraud detection acquisition.

Support for Deep Analysis in Analytics Software

A lot of new development is happening within deep analysis in analytics software. In the following sections, we share a couple of examples of capabilities in IBM Social Media Analytics that can assist analysts in their deep analysis projects. We illustrate these capabilities in the context of another real project that we encountered.

Topic Evolution

According to the SMA product documentation, Evolving Topics is defined as follows:

> Evolving Topics is a unique algorithm that will analyze social media content to discover threads of conversation emerging in social media. This is different than a general word cloud where the focus is on overall re-occurrence in social media. When you are going to analyze social media content, you specify the time frame you want to assess evolving topics. For example, discover topics that are emerging in social media over the last 30 days.

This feature will help analysts identify topics that they may not have known to include in the model. In 2013, for example, there was a massive disruption of activities due to floods. A social media analytics model was developed for understanding the issues and relief plans. When the team prepared the model, team members used some commonsense knowledge to decide on what keywords to search for. For the keywords they selected, a large amount of social media text was pulled into the model for analysis. The Top Evolution view from the SMA Package showed a number of terms that were part of the conversations that were happening around the floods in Calgary, Alberta, Canada. The analyst team did further research on many of the new and unexpected terms and were able to enhance the model with richer and more relevant keywords such as *yycflood* and *wearecalgary*.

Figure 10.4 shows the Topic Evolution view for the Calgary Floods project.

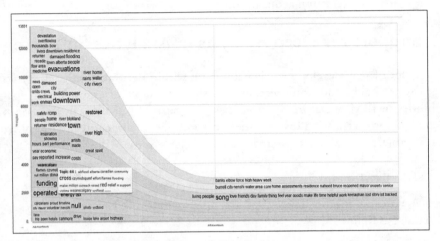

Figure 10.4   Topic Evolution view for the Calgary Floods project.

In our experience, this feature has served us well. For many listening projects, we do not typically get a well-thought-out list of keywords. The listening team starts out with a beginning list of keywords and then uses the Topic Evolution function iteratively to enhance the list of keywords. The typical process followed in "keywords" development using Topic Evolution is illustrated in Figure 10.5.

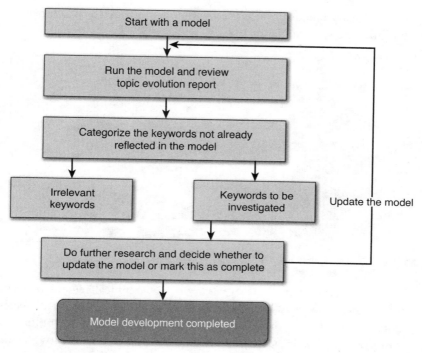

Figure 10.5   Process for taking iterative steps to finalize the model.

Affinity Analysis in Reporting

In IBM Social Media Analytics, the reporting environment offers an Affinity measure for many reports. The Affinity measure analyzes how closely two dimensions (or attributes of a dimension) are related to each other. This helps analysts gain insight about possible strengths, weaknesses, opportunities, or threat areas based on the affinity between the dimensions or attributes.

The Affinities measure is based on a statistical method that is known as the chi-square test of independence. This method estimates how often two dimensions should occur together if they were independent (for example, products and product features). It compares the estimate with the actual count and identifies whether the difference is statistically significant (either higher or lower than expected).

For the Calgary Floods project, the final model included a two-dimensional affinity matrix (see Figure 10.6).

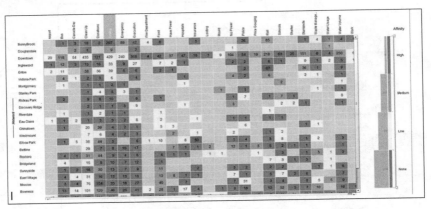

Figure 10.6   Complete affinity matrix for the Calgary Floods project.

The vertical dimension shows a variety of geographical regions or parts affected by the flood. The horizontal dimension shows a number of issues or problem areas. The color of the cell corresponding to each combination of the *Region* and *Issue* indicates how strong the relationship is between the two dimensions. The darker the color, the more statistically significant is the relationship. For example, the matrix shows that the issue about *Donations* is quite strong in the *Mission* region. Similarly, the issues about *insurance* are quite strong in the region called *Elbow Park*. A table such as this can be used to prioritize actions in response to the issues when cities are faced with limited resources and limited time.

Figure 10.7 shows an expanded image of the top-left portion of this affinity matrix.

	Airport	Bus	Canada Day	Clean Up	Donations	Driving
BonnyBrook		1	3	18	2	297
Douglasdale			2	1		9
Downtown	20	118	54	435	121	429
Inglewood	1	12	3	15	16	33
Eriton	2	11		58	36	39
Victoria Park		4	1	2	3	6

Red = High Affinity	Orange = Med Affinity	Yellow = Low Affinity	Gray = No Affinity

Figure 10.7 A small portion of the affinity matrix for the Calgary Floods project.

The color of the cell indicates the level of affinity. The color red indicates a high affinity, orange is indicative of a medium affinity, and yellow indicates low affinity (gray is representative of no affinity or relationship). The number in each cell shows how many times the two dimensions occur together in the given dataset.

This example shows that there is a strong correlation between *driving* issues and the region *BonnyBrook*; this is implied by the strong red color of the cell. The same chart implies that the *driving* related concerns are not that relevant for the Victoria Park region. You might notice that the cell associated with *downtown* and *clean up* has a big number (435); however, based on statistical weight, the affinity between these two dimensions is considered to be low.

Affinity analysis can be a very effective tool in understanding the relationship between different dimensions of a model built for a particular use case. It becomes a critical tool for assisting with prioritization of the follow-up actions resulting from this phase of the analysis.

Summary

This chapter showed that dedicated analysts, with the help of adequate support from social media analytics tools, can perform a wide variety of sophisticated and complex analysis to help address the needs of their individual use cases.

Through a deep or more complex analysis of a dataset, we are able to produce a richer set of analytic mechanisms that provide a view into the data that might not be seen otherwise. Through the use of such tools as affinity matrices or Evolving Topic calculation, analysts can come to see patterns where similar terms or concepts continue to reveal themselves. Previously, we discussed concepts such as descriptive statistics, whose aim is to describe the dataset in an effort to draw conclusions. Here, in what we call deep analysis, we take descriptive statistics one step further by not only looking at how the data is grouped together, but rather how it is grouped together and what else is grouped around it or associated with it; then we look to understand how those two concepts relate to each other.

This type of analysis doesn't come cheap, in either CPU capacity or human deduction/reasoning. However, the results, when discovered, can be highly informative insights that lead analysts from data, to insights, and finally to knowledge.

Endnote

[1] von Goethe, Johann Wolfgang, Frederick Ungar, and Heinz Norden. *Goethe's World View, Presented in His Reflections and Maxims: With New English Translations and the German Original* (New York: F. Ungar Publishing Co., 1963).

11

The Enterprise Social Network

This is the end of business as usual.

—Brian Solis, Principal at Altimeter Group [1]

An enterprise social network (ESN) is an internal, private social network used to assist communication within a business [2]. As the number of companies investing in ESNs grows, employees are discovering more and more ways to conduct business on the ESNs.

IDC expects the worldwide enterprise social networks market revenue to grow from $1.46 billion in 2014 to $3.5 billion by 2019, representing a compound annual growth rate (CAGR) of 19.1%[3].

In Chapter 6, we described *domain of analysis* as an important dimension of social media analytics. We broadly divide this domain into internal and external. A majority of our discussion so far has focused on insights that can be gleaned from content available in external public social media (such as Twitter). In this chapter, we focus on social media content that is generated inside a company's firewall. This, we believe, is a very rich source of information, and a variety of business insights can be generated from it. Here, we discuss the concepts and a few specific examples regarding how companies can take advantage of this ever-growing collection of social data inside their social networks.

Employee privacy is an important consideration when looking at analytics based on enterprise social networks. We discuss how this was addressed for the Personal Social Dashboard use case in IBM. We want to utilize people's individual posts to help create and leverage organization knowledge, but we need to do this without compromising the privacy rights of individual employees. We also describe how this was accomplished for the Personal Social Dashboard project.

Most of the content in this chapter is based on our personal experience with an IBM project called Project Breadcrumb, and its primary use case is the IBM Personal Social Dashboard (or PSD). This project is a collaborative effort involving many people in IBM over the years. We want to specifically highlight the contributions of Marie Wallace (social media strategist), David Robinson (big data architect), Jason Plurad (lead developer), Shiri Kremer-Davidson (chief data scientist), Aroop Pandya (data architect), Santosh Borse (data acquisition), and Hardik Dave (initial CIO project lead). Marie Wallace has written and spoken about this project in a variety of external venues (including TED Talks). Most of her writing on this project can be found on her website at http://allthingsanalytics.com/ [4].

Social Is Much More Than Just Collaboration

Many articles have been written about the benefits that companies are deriving from their investments in ESNs [5].

IBM first deployed an ESN in 2009. ESNs were initially deployed to facilitate collaboration among employees. In our experience, they have turned out to do much more for the companies. Figure 11.1 illustrates some of the significant advantages afforded by ESNs, beyond other traditional means of collaboration and communication as described further in the section that follows.

Social Isn't Just About Collaboration

Transparency of Communication →
- Email vs. micro-blogging
- Meetings vs. Communities
- Forums and Wikis

Frictionless Redistribution of Knowledge →
- Social Bookmarking and Tagging
- Liking and Recommending
- Communities, Files, Forums, Blogs and Wikis

Deconstructing Knowledge Creation →
- Social Content interactively tracking contributors and contributions
- Breaking down knowledge into its contributions and contributors

Serendipitous Discovery and Innovation →
- Facilitating interchange of ideas across geographical and organizational boundaries
- Disruptive Innovation occurs at network edges

Figure 11.1 Social is much more than just collaboration.

Transparency of Communication

When a CEO or a senior leader writes a blog in the ESN about the latest quarterly results and encourages employees to openly respond with their comments, there is a great deal of transparency in communication. This is not possible using traditional means of communication.

NOTE

The concepts we discuss in this section are based on the insight Marie Wallace shares at http://allthingsanalytics.com/about/archives/ [6].

Frictionless Redistribution of Knowledge

When a piece of new information, technique, or finding is shared in an ESN, it reaches many members of the network without any special extra effort on the part of the originator. We (Avinash) recently encountered an IT problem with my Lotus Notes Mail system. I worked with Help Desk and got my issue resolved. I shared this experience on my wall, and this information was available to members of my network immediately. If those people further shared this information with their networks, this timesaving tip would be available to hundreds of employees within a short span of time and without any barriers.

Deconstructing Knowledge Creation

Discussion forums are a common feature of ESNs. These forums are created to elicit comments and ideas from different people on a given topic. Many times the forums are started with a description of a problem, and during the course of the discussion, after several members contribute, a solution emerges. This process not only creates knowledge that the company can leverage in the future but also distinctly identifies knowledge creators.

Serendipitous Discovery and Innovation

By far, the biggest benefit of ESNs in my experience is accidental discovery of useful nuggets of information. In October 2014, I was in the process of preparing a presentation for a talk that I was going to give at IBM's Insight 2014 conference in Las Vegas. As part of our ESN's features, I get a newsfeed of posts from the people I follow. One day I came across a post that referenced a study by MIT and Deloitte directly related to the subject of my talk. I was able to quickly take this information into account and enhance my presentation.

Enterprise Social Network Is the Memory of the Organization

Employee-to-employee interactions in an ESN are obviously quite valuable. When I have a question about a new product or process, somebody else generally responds with an answer. In many ways, then, this transaction is complete.

NOTE

The concepts we discuss in this section are based on the insight Marie Wallace shares at http://allthingsanalytics.com/2013/10/02/is-it-time-to-bin-the-enterprise-social-network/ [7].

Figure 11.2 illustrates a subset of actual transactions that can take place in an ESN. You can see that, over time, various transactions are initiated and completed in the network. As time goes on, the network becomes the memory of the organization. Even though this may not have been the intent or the goal, the ESN ends up leaving breadcrumbs to indicate what people are doing and how they are behaving in different business situations. We contend that this is a very critical but underutilized resource in companies. This information can be mined for valuable insights with the help of analytics.

The Greatest Value Is What It Leaves Behind...

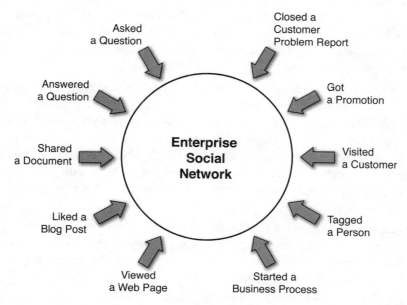

Figure 11.2 Greatest value is what it leaves behind.

Understanding the Enterprise Graph

We have now established the value of the information left behind by social interactions in an ESN. The storage technology that is optimal for this type of information is called graph storage. A specific instance of this type of graph for a specific company is called the Enterprise Graph. In an ideal implementation, the Enterprise Graph combines transactional, social, and business data and also provides a knowledge base to perform analysis such as influence, social proximity, reputation, retention, performance, expertise, and more.

The basic components of an Enterprise Graph, shown in Figure 11.3, are as follows:

- **Data Sources**—This is any source of data or metadata that we are interested in including in the Enterprise Graph. This includes social interaction data from an enterprise social network. For example, consider profile status updates and comments from everybody in a person's social network, including likes and tags.

- **Data Services**—Data Services enable business applications to contribute data to the ESN via data APIs. For example, an application that compensates employees with a reward or recognition will utilize services (APIs) to contribute to profile status updates with the information about awards.

- **Graph Store**—This is the physical storage utilized to store all of the interactional data that we are interested in analyzing. Graph APIs make interactional data easily consumable by analytics and business applications. For example, for an organization of 100 people, the graph contains a node for each person in the organization and an edge for each transaction between two nodes. As a result, the graph contains information about who did with what with whom and when (in the ESN).

- **Analytics**—Analytics algorithms generate graph-centric insights such as influence, expertise, and reputation. For example, the algorithms can compute a rank-ordered list of people with the maximum number of likes on their profiles.

- **Analytics Services**—Analytics services make graph analytics easily consumable by business applications via analytics APIs. For example, an Expertise Locator application can query the graph using analytics services to identify a topic expert who is also very active in the ESN.

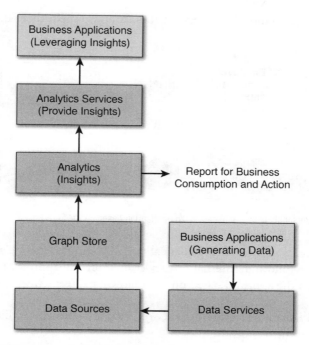

Figure 11.3 Basic components of an Enterprise Graph.

We can implement a number of useful applications that leverage the information from the graph. In the following sections, we describe one such application called the Personal Social Dashboard.

Personal Social Dashboard: Details of Implementation

The Personal Social Dashboard (see Figure 11.4) is based on a project in IBM. Internally, IBM uses an ESN based on IBM Connections, which includes a variety of features such as profiles, communities, forums, blogs, wikis, files, and bookmarks. The ESN is available to all IBMers, and there are varying levels of adoption and use of connections across business units and across geographies. Two groups of stakeholders are served by this application: individual employees and management.

The main objective for the individual employees is to help them understand their social impact and how to effectively activate their network for maximum value. For management, the objective is to help managers and executives understand how teams collaborate and to help them increase collective value.

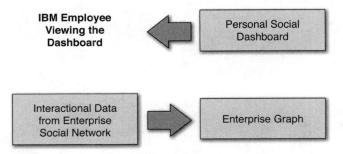

Figure 11.4 Personal Social Dashboard is an application based on the Enterprise Graph.

Before we could process metadata about IBM employees' social activities, we needed to follow an internal privacy evaluation and approval process. We were granted the approval based on the following agreements:

1. We will share the individual scorecard only with the individual who is signed into the system.
2. The overall engagement score or individual component scores will not be made available to anybody else.
3. We can share aggregate reports utilizing overall scores and component scores for groups, divisions, or countries to management teams; however, all such reports will be anonymized.

Some benefits that can be derived from an implementation of an application like the Personal Social Dashboard include the following:

- The scorecard evokes a sense of competition, and people tend to want to improve their scores, which improves adoption of the enterprise social network and thus improves social collaboration.
- The component scores give employees hints about what activities will contribute to their scores (activity versus reaction). This will enable employees to focus more on creating content that is valued by others and thus improve their individual eminence, which in turn adds value to the business unit.

- The Personal Social Dashboard also provides a very detailed (anonymized) view of average scores by country and by business unit. This has already assisted managers and executives in understanding how ESNs are being utilized in their organizations and countries.

Key Performance Indicators (KPIs)

Based on extensive research conducted by the IBM Research team in Haifa, the IBM project team settled on four KPIs to represent or measure employee engagement [8]. The four KPIs represent four social behaviors:

- **Activity Scorecard**—Measures the person's periodic social activity effort; computed based on number of activities.

- **Reaction Scorecard**—Measures how the person's content is perceived by others; focuses on quality of activity based on reactions to it.

- **Eminence Scorecard**—Measures how the *person* is perceived by others; focuses on number of people interacting with the person or his content.

- **Network Scorecard**—Measures the person's network; initially focuses on size—both network and followers.

The main page of the dashboard shows a composite score as well as the score of the four individual subcomponents (see Figure 11.5). To illustrate the capabilities of this application, we utilize Avinash's scores and scorecard. The scorecard shows an overall score of 81. There is also a trend graph that plots Avinash's score over the past six months. The bottom half of the screen shows the four subcomponent scores and a comparison of Avinash's scores against an average of the organizational unit that he belongs to. For instance, his activity score of 76 is higher than the average activity score for his organization, which is 18. Similarly, we are able to compare Avinash's other component scores against his organization's average score.

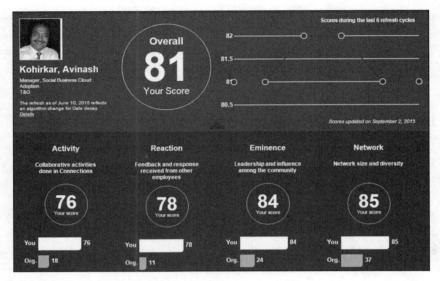

Figure 11.5   Personal Social Dashboard: home page.

How Does This Score Compare Against Others?

Figure 11.6 shows that Avinash's overall score gives him a rank of 410 within IBM, and there are 84 other people who have the same score as he does. Within his organization (T&O), he has a rank of 88, and there are 20 other people in the organization who have the same score.

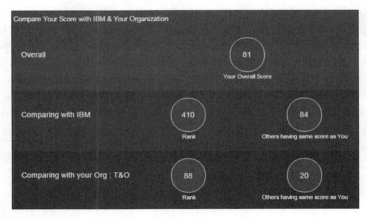

Figure 11.6   Comparison of Avinash's score with others.

Activity Scoreboard

The discussion in this and the following three sections considers the reader as an employee.

Are you, as an employee, actively engaging with people on a regular basis? This measure is calculated by analyzing your various activities in relation to other employees, placing emphasis on more involved contributions (creating content, commenting, and so on) and less emphasis on the lighter-weight ones (reading, liking, and so on). This is illustrated in Figure 11.7.

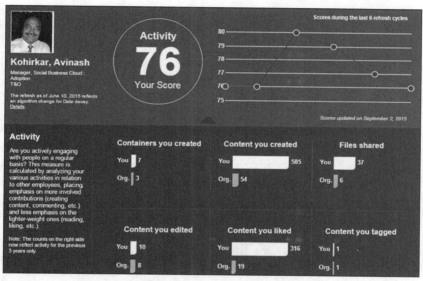

Figure 11.7   Personal Social Dashboard: activity.

This scorecard also shows the counts of the following six additional factors that collectively influence the overall Activity score:

- **Containers You Created**—Are you creating collaboration spaces where people can engage? Are you taking an active leadership in providing an environment for sharing? This drill-down provides the number of blogs, communities, forums, or wikis you have created.

- **Content You Created**—Have you been making an effort to provide content to the social network? This drill-down provides a count of what you have created (files, posts, status updates, and the like).

- **Content You Shared**—Have you been sharing interesting content with your colleagues? This drill-down provides a count of content you have shared (files, posts, status updates, and so on).

- **Content You Edited**—Are you contributing to the content created by your colleagues? This drill-down provides a count of content you have edited (pages, files, and so on).

- **Content You Liked**—Are you generous with your positive feedback? This drill-down provides a count of the content you have liked.

- **Content You Tagged**—Do you like to help the system to better qualify and organize the content? Or do you give your colleagues a thumbs-up by specifically tagging them with an expertise or skill? This drill-down provides a count of the content you have tagged.

Reaction Scorecard

Does your content generate a reaction from your fellow employees? This measure (see Figure 11.8) is calculated by analyzing your colleagues' activities on your content, placing more emphasis on engaged contributions (comments, likes) and less emphasis on the more passive ones (reads, follows).

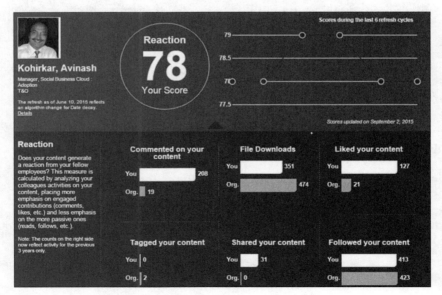

Figure 11.8   Personal Social Dashboard: reaction.

It also shows the counts of the following six additional factors that collectively influence the overall Reaction score:

- **Commented on your content**—Do people like to give you feedback on your content and share their opinions? This drill-down provides the number of comments that your content has received.

- **File downloads**—Do people download and read the content in the files that you uploaded? This drill-down provides the number of file downloads you have received.

- **Liked your content**—Do people like your content? This drill-down provides the number of likes your content has received.

- **Tagged your content**—Do people tag your content? This drill-down provides the number of tags that people have applied to your content.

- **Shared your content**—Do people like to share your content with their colleagues? This drill-down provides the number of times people have shared your content.

- **Followed your content**—Do people like to keep track of your content by following it so they get updates when it is modified? This drill-down provides the number of times that people have followed your content.

Eminence Scorecard

Do people value your opinion? Do they listen when you talk? This measure is calculated by analyzing how your colleagues interact with you (as an individual) and your content (as a reflection of their opinions). This is illustrated in Figure 11.9.

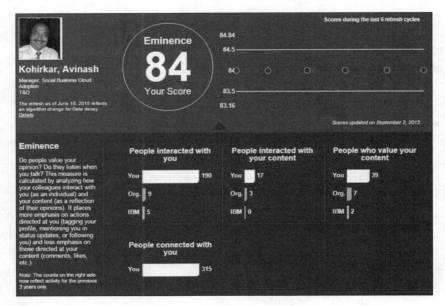

Figure 11.9   Personal Social Dashboard: eminence.

It places more emphasis on actions directed at you (tagging your profile, mentioning you in status updates, or following you) and less emphasis on those directed at your content (comments, likes, and so on).

It also shows the counts of the following four additional factors that collectively influence the overall Eminence score:

- **People interacted with you**—Do people like to regularly engage with you directly? This drill-down provides the number of people who have interacted with you directly (posted to your board, mentioned you in a status update, tagged you, shared something with you).

- **People interacted with your content**—Do people like to regularly engage with your content? This drill-down provides the number of people who commented on your content (shared their opinion).

- **People who value your content**—Do people value your content? This drill-down provides the number of people who liked your content.

- **People connected with you**—Do people like to be part of your network? This drill-down provides the number of people who followed or befriended you.

Network Scorecard

The Network scorecard focuses on the network size and diversity (see Figure 11.10).

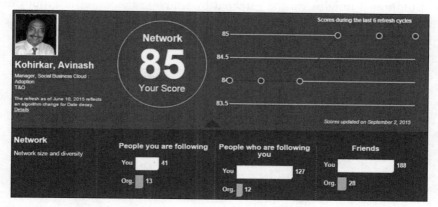

Figure 11.10   Personal Social Dashboard: network.

It also shows the counts of the following three additional factors that collectively influence the overall Network score:

- **People you are following**—How many people do you follow to keep up with what they are doing and saying? This drill-down provides the number of people that you are following.

- **People who are following you**—How many people like to follow what you are doing and saying? Are you speaking into the void? This drill-down provides a count of the people following you.

- **Friends**—Do you have a rich network of colleagues that you are connected to? This drill-down provides a count of the people you are friends with.

Assessing Business Benefits from Social Graph Data

An analytics team in IBM decided to study the impact of social behavior on business outcomes.

Over the first half of 2014, the team analyzed IBM's Enterprise Graph (year 2013 data), IBM patents (about 4,500 patents), and customer advocacy data (for about 4,000 people). They concluded that there is a statistically significant positive correlation between high social engagement scores, as captured in the social graph, and the number of patents. In addition, there is a statistically positive correlation between high social engagement scores and the likelihood of getting selected as a customer advocate.

Additional insights can be gathered by studying the scores of groups of people. Figure 11.11 shows the hypothetical score distribution of a possible department or division in an organization.

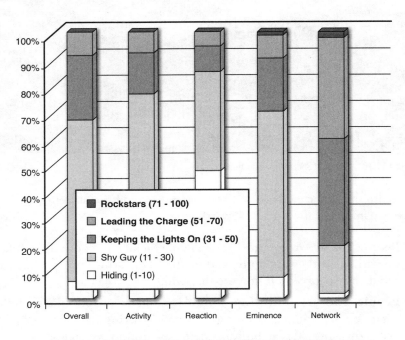

Score/100	Overall	Activity	Reaction	Eminence	Network
Average	27	22	15	27	45
Lowest	1	0	0	2	3
Highest	67	64	64	71	75

Figure 11.11 Score distribution for a hypothetical group.

An analysis of these scores can yield different results and insights. One such insight is that a large number of people seem to have a decent Network score, but only a small number of people are doing well in terms of other scores, as illustrated in Figure 11.12. One interpretation is that people focus on building their networks but forget to engage. By the way, this is a common pattern that we observe when we study different groups.

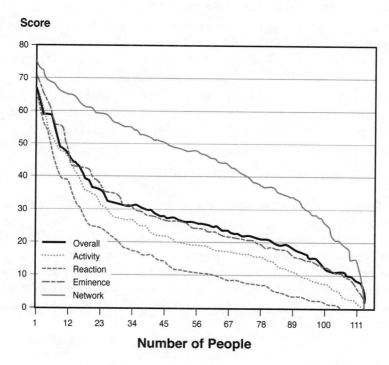

Figure 11.12   Insights from aggregate scores.

What's Next for the Enterprise Graph?

The Personal Social Dashboard has been used extensively to provide platform-level metrics such as the number of social activities of certain types. The team is looking to move beyond this to some metrics related to business outcomes. Can we show that increased social behavior of certain types can result in positive business outcomes at the department, business unit, or company level?

- **Sales outcomes**—If we include sales-related data such as number of leads, number of opportunities, number of proposals completed, and amount of revenue generated, can we attempt to find social behaviors that contribute to positive sales performance?
- **Employee performance outcomes**—If we include data such as promotions, awards, successful project completions, and recognitions, can we attempt to find social behaviors that improve employee performance outcomes?
- **APIs**—Application Programming Interfaces enable other business applications to provide new data that can be added to the Enterprise Graph and to consume and enhance (or report) graph analytics.

Summary

So far in this book, we have primarily focused on the business benefits that can be gained by using social media analytics on external social media data. In this chapter, we discussed the business value that can be gleaned from internal social media or employee contributions in a company's enterprise social network. We illustrated the concepts and benefits using a specific application called the Personal Social Dashboard. We hope you get an idea of how social media analytics can be beneficial for analyzing content in your company's ESN.

Endnotes

[1] Solis, Brian, *The End of Business as Usual: Rewire the Way You Work to Succeed in the Consumer Revolution* (Hoboken, New Jersey: John Wiley and Sons, 2011).

[2] Kitt, Denise, "What Is An Enterprise Social Network?, CRM Switch—CRM," May 24, 2012. Retrieved from http://www.crmswitch.com/social-crm/enterprise-social-network/.

[3] Thompson, Vanessa, IDC Market Analysis "Worldwide Enterprise Social Networks and Online Communities 2015–2019 Forecast and 2014 Vendor Shares," July 2015, IDC #257492.

[4] Wallace, Marie, "People Analytics Is Tricky to Do, But There Is Light at the End of the Tunnel," *All Things Analytics,* August 25, 2015. Retrieved from http://allthingsanalytics.com/.

[5] Working, Russell, "9 Benefits of an Internal Social Network," *Ragan.com*, November 8, 2012. Retrieved from http://www.ragan.com/Main/Articles/9_benefits_of_an_internal_social_network_45790.aspx.

[6] Wallace, Marie. Retrieved from http://allthingsanalytics.com/about/archives/.

[7] Wallace, Marie, "Is It Time to Bin the Enterprise Social Network," *Marie's Ramblings & Ruminations*, October 2, 2013. Retrieved from http://allthingsanalytics.com/2013/10/02/is-it-time-to-bin-the-enterprise-social-network/.

[8] Jacovi, Michal et al., "The Perception of Others: Inferring Reputation from Social Media in the Enterprise," *Proceedings CSCW 2014*, Baltimore, Maryland.

12

Murphy Was Right!
The Art of What Could
Go Wrong

It is an established fact that in nine cases out of ten whatever can go wrong in a magical performance will do so.

—Adam Hull Shirk, as quoted in *Murphy's Law* [1]

From what we can tell, *Murphy's Law* (which in its most famous form states: "If anything can go wrong, it will") was supposedly first coined at Edwards Air Force Base in the United States around 1949. While many seem to claim credit for the concept, it appears that it was named after Capt. Edward A. Murphy, an engineer working on a project for the Air Force to see how much sudden deceleration a pilot could withstand in a crash. As the story goes, one day, after finding that a piece of equipment was wired incorrectly, Captain Murphy cursed the technician responsible and said, "If there is any way to do it wrong, he'll find it." The contractor's project manager kept a list of "laws" and upon hearing this statement added this to his list, which he simply called Murphy's Law.

Sometime afterward, an Air Force doctor, Dr. John Paul Stapp, who participated in the deceleration project, rode a sled on a track to a stop at rate of over 40 Gs (or about 392 meters per second squared). When he gave a press conference, he noted that their good safety record on the project was due to a firm belief in Murphy's Law and in the necessity to try to circumvent it. The rest, as they say, is history.

And so it is with analytics and text analytics in particular. Regardless of the amount of planning or forethought put into a project, something always goes wrong. Sometimes it's something small, perhaps an oversight; other times it could be as large as making some incorrect assumptions and having to start from the beginning. No matter, the objective isn't to remove all possibilities of things going wrong, but rather simply to be prepared for them.

Recap: The Social Analytics Process

Up to this point in this book, we have discussed the various steps we need to take on the journey to analyze social media content. We've tried to focus on the "what's possible" rather than the "how to" because tools and data sources are constantly changing and evolving. But more importantly, we've tried to take a logical step-by-step discussion of what needs to be done in performing an analysis, from posing a question, to gathering and cleaning data, and then on to doing the analysis. Consider the diagram in Figure 12.1. Many of the steps in this diagram have been discussed in previous chapters and should be familiar to you. The thing to consider is that an analysis isn't a single, well-defined set of steps; it tends to be quite iterative in nature. That is, we try something, perhaps searching for a set of data; if it appears we have the correct data sources, we go on to the next step to collect data points. If we then determine we don't have enough data or the correct data, we go back and look for new sources rather than continue with faulty information. Over time, as we iterate through the problem, the answers begin to emerge.

This is the thrust of this chapter: what can (and probably will) go wrong in each of the steps along the way.

While Figure 12.1 represents our view of an iterative approach to an analytic analysis, it's impossible to diagram every step of a process, especially as we make subtle changes to tools or search terms. However, we believe this represents a respectable view of the process and therefore the points where things could go wrong.

Previously, we described the process as the five Ws—Who, What, Where, When, and Why. Having a crisp description of *what* we are looking for may seem obvious to most (step 1 in Figure 12.1), but sometimes we can be stubborn. Often we don't think that the question we are asking is the right one, or perhaps we need to modify it. We see this later in the examples, but for now, we express the first step as "defining the problem" or perhaps simply "posing a question to be answered." For example, "What do teenagers think of the latest movie trailer for an upcoming new release?" or "How is our brand perceived in the European marketplace?"

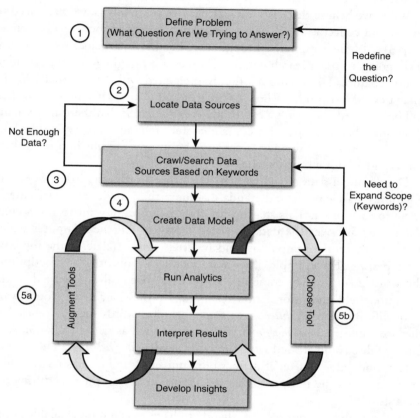

Figure 12.1   The social analytics process.

Obviously, when we know the question we want to answer, our next step (labeled step 2 in Figure 12.1) is to find the data that will help us uncover that answer. This shouldn't be a long, tedious step, but it's important, if nothing else, as a litmus test regarding the analysis. By this, we mean that if we check for data around this topic, and we find sufficient evidence that is enough to produce a meaningful result, we can (and should) proceed for an analysis. How do we know that we have enough data? The real answer is: We don't. At least not until we've done an analysis to see if there is a sufficient number of results to warrant a conclusion. But again, a quick scan of social media sites or search on Twitter can give us a gut feel that we do or do not have enough material to work with. If we don't, perhaps, as the diagram shows, we need to modify the question we are trying to answer.

When we believe there is sufficient data for our analysis, we then need to go out and collect as much as we can from a variety of social media venues (step 3). Although we may ensure that we include a particular set of sites, if we're going to use a search engine or a message board aggregator (we tend to use Boardreader because it's tightly integrated with IBM's Social Media Analytics [SMA] product) but we can't be quite sure what sites or content will be returned. This isn't a bad thing; the problem is that there are so many social sites that could possibly contain content relevant to our question. The work done in step 2 was just a cursory check; now we put in a set of key-words and ask for all the matches.

Developing a data model (step 4) is a process or method that we use to organize data elements and standardize how the individual data elements relate to each other. This step is important because we want to run a com-puter program over the data; we need a way to tell the computer which words or themes are important and if certain words relate to the topic we are exploring. For example, if we were looking at job titles or descriptions, the word *architect* may come up. If we were specifically interested in the computer field and information technology professionals, we would want to qualify the word *architect* with some technical words such as *network* so that we could find *network architect* or terms such as *system* or *computer* to uncover discussion around *system architect* or *computer architect*. This is what a data model does for us: it defines our "universe" and creates relationships between words and phrases so that we can make sense of the data during our analysis.

In the analysis of our data, it's handy to have several tools available at our disposal to gain a different perspective on discussions taking place around the topic. We like to call this "our bag of tricks." In some cases, it may make sense to look at a word cloud of conversation, and in others, it may make sense to watch a word cloud evolve over time (so computing a time series word cloud may make sense). When we talk about step 5a, augment-ing the tools, that's really about configuring them to perform at peak for a particular task. For example, thinking about a word cloud again, if we took a large amount of data around computer professionals, say the IT architect example from the previous step, and built a word cloud, no doubt the largest word in the cloud would be *architect*. (Remember, in word clouds, the more frequent a word is used, the larger it becomes in relation to the other words.) So here, we might create our initial cloud, see that *architect* is overwhelming the cloud, and simply change the configuration to eliminate that word. Think about it: we know the data collected has to do with *IT architects*, so why do we need to show it in our cloud? By eliminating it, we allow other words to stand out and perhaps reveal some insights. This is the iterative process at its best. In the Lance Armstrong example from Chapter 9, we ran several iterations, removing words like *lance*, *lancearmstrong*, *armstong*, and *Oprah* until we had a word cloud without the very obvious terms.

This analysis is also about tool usage. Some tools may do a great job at determining sentiment, whereas others may do a better job at breaking down text into grammatical form (noun, verb, adjective, and so on) that enable us to better understand the meanings and use of various words or phrases.

As we said, it is difficult to enumerate each and every step to take on an analytical journey. It is very much an iterative approach (perhaps we should call it "exploratory analysis") as there is no prescribed way of doing things. But with that said, let's take a look at some of these steps and see where things can (and undoubtedly, will) go wrong.

Finding the Right Data

Torture the data, and it will confess to anything.

—Ronald Coase, Economics, Nobel Prize Laureate [2]

Data is the fundamental building block upon which we build our analysis. As we discussed previously, data is created in a wide variety of blogs, wikis, and microblog sites across the Internet. Every website we visit, every post we make in social media, every picture or video we upload—everything. Because there is so much data available to us across the Internet, sometimes finding the "right" data can be challenging. Often the data we find or gather for an analysis is directly related to the topic we are investigating; however, often the data isn't what it seems.

In 2012, there was a scandal involving Chinese factory workers and the conditions under which they were expected to work. Several US-based firms were "called out" in the press for using these companies in the production of their products.

The question we were trying to answer was:

"Is IBM being associated with potential "bad press" in any of the social media venues?" And if so, where? Also, what is the perception of IBM in relation to its competitors?

A quick manual survey of various wiki and blog sites showed there was indeed conversation happening around this particular event and factory. With that in mind, our plan was to mine the social media space for any occurrence of the particular factory which included mentions of IBM and then build a more comprehensive model to understand the conversations. This model would consist of key terminologies that may (or may not) reflect the public's perception of the factory worker's concerns. Later revisions would then take this analysis and segment it by various competitors to see how IBM was viewed amongst its competitors.

Upon collecting all of the available data and subjecting it to our analytic model, we began to build a set of insights. One of the first metrics we produced was a count of the number of mentions This is the number of times various companies, including IBM, were mentioned in all of the social media content that we were able to collect. We also began to summarize the locations where these conversations were taking place. This is an important piece of information not only for obtaining unsolicited opinions but also for marketing and relationship building. There may be a time when we may want to participate in the conversation.

We plotted this information on a bar graph using two bars for each company (Figure 12.2). The first bar in each grouping (on the left) shows data that we first collected (labeled "no city specified"). At first glance, this looks like a major problem for IBM. The graph is showing that there are a large number of references to IBM in the context of this company and the working conditions in various Chinese factories.

A closer look at our results showed that this particular company operated many different factories across China and Asia in general. Our first interpretation was that people were associating IBM with this event. However, we came to realize that the poor working conditions were limited to a factory in a single city. Once we realized that, we limited our model to that particular city and then any mentions of IBM and its competitors. The result was the second bar (the one on the right in each grouping) in Figure 12.2 (labeled "in the context of a city"). As it turned out, there was no association of IBM and the factory in question.

12: Murphy Was Right! The Art of What Could Go Wrong

195

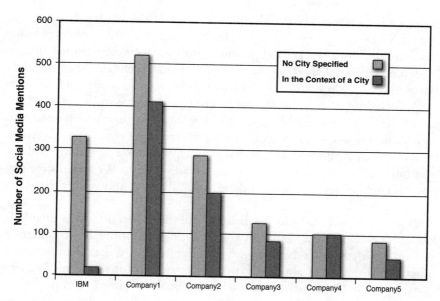

Figure 12.2 Mentions of IBM (and others) in relation to poor working conditions in China.

The reason we received these types of results wasn't so much that our data was flawed; but for this particular analysis, it just wasn't scoped properly. The moral of this story: double-check your findings early and often. Had we continued to build out a full analysis based on this data, it would have been like attempting to ask the crowd at a baseball game what they thought about a movie premiere; that is, data about a topic from a completely unrelated source.

Communicating Clearly

Speak clearly, if you speak at all; carve every word before you let it fall.

—Oliver Wendell Holmes, Sr. [3]

What makes social media analytics, or any kind of text analytics for the matter, difficult is that most of the data we're looking to analyze is unstructured or—maybe better said—not consistent. The problem is that we humans have different ways of saying the same thing. What we say or how we say it may make sense to us, but often it is unclear to others. The English language is funny; many people claim it's one of the hardest languages to master. Consider the case of words that are classified as homonyms (words that have the same spelling and pronunciation but have different meanings).

Remember in Chapter 2 when we discussed the refinement of our data (separating the wheat from the chaff), we showed an example of inadvertently including data that wasn't related to our problem, and we showed the use of the words *Apple* and *sapphire*. These examples involved homonyms, which can be some of the most difficult problems to overcome in this space.

We've seen a number of these issues when we start a new analysis. Let's take our analysis of financial institutions as an example. We were looking at how the public views various banking establishments and what their views on savings were.

One of the banks we tried to gather social discussion on was Citibank. It has a very active Twitter account, and a quick search for viable information showed a fairly high level of activity. In our collection of data, we uncovered other banks that were also generating a fair amount of social media mentions. In Table 12.1, these banks are labeled Bank-1, Bank-2, and Bank-3.

Table 12.1   Preliminary Social Media Search Results Around Customer Satisfaction in Banking

	Rates	Customer Service	Loans	Security	Product*	Misc
Bank-1	3,041	715	4,021	1,405	4,913/320	401
Citibank	4,403	1,107	3,507	1,316	3,121/231	3,109
Bank-2	2,591	1,109	807	641	1,789,102	353
Bank-3	2,787	853	1,781	723	1,832,256	206

What's interesting about this bank is that it has a number of Twitter handles for specific geographies—for example, @citibankau (Australia), @citibankIN (Citibank Indonesia), and @citibankeurope. Consequently, our assumption was that the data we were collecting was for US banks (which was the scope of our experiment). What we forgot about was the fact that Citibank also sponsors a baseball stadium for the New York Mets in New York City. So as we pulled information from Twitter, we used the search term *citi* (as well as a few others like @citibank, and so on). When we did the first pass at our analysis, we had some preliminary statistics, as shown in Table 12.1.

One of the topics we included in our analysis was the public's perception of certificate of deposit (CD) rates and offerings from various banks. In this instance, when we were gathering data, we included reference to home (mortgage) loans, refinancing, lines of credit, and CDs.

Unfortunately, the term *CD* is another homonym:

CD, as in certificate of deposit
CD, as in compact disc

In Table 12.1, notice the large amount of discussion around bank products (CDs were grouped under Products). We had to rework our data model to qualify the word *CD* with the word *bank*. This showed a bit of improvement, and things got a little better, but a quick look at Figure 12.3 shows the kinds of tweets we were still collecting. Clearly, we still had more work to do. The good thing was that the incorrect (and the correct) use of the word *CD* was applied to all the banks. That just means we had less confidence in discussion around that topic.

Figure 12.3   Trying to qualify the word *CD* with *Bank*—close but not perfect.

Our bigger problem was with the references to baseball around Citibank. The odd part of this was the more than 3,000 uncategorized statements for Citibank. We expected a number of comments or tweets to be uncategorizable, but this number was off by a factor of 100× compared to the others. A closer inspection showed a large number of references to baseball and sports. This result wasn't too unusual because we knew that many large corporations (banks included) sponsor sporting events or teams. But then we uncovered tweets such as shown in Figure 12.4.

Figure 12.4   Tweet not directly related to banking with Citibank.

While this was potentially an important message if we were looking only at Citibank (and the positive sentiment surrounding its backing of a baseball team), in this case, such tweets were not at all relevant to our experiment.

We had two choices at this point. Referring back to Figure 12.1, we could:

- Rework the question we were trying to answer (step 1)
- Look to eliminate discussion about citi field (step 4)

NOTE

Because our original project was to understand the public's view of banking services and not their general like or dislike of a particular bank, we chose to rework our data model to eliminate references to baseball and citi field since they are not related to banking services.

Choosing Filter Words Carefully

Part of IBM's Social Media Analytics offering was not only the tools to perform the computations and analysis of unstructured data, but also a service to allow different groups inside IBM to pull data off the Twitter stream for a variety of applications. Because this was a "self-service" application, our group didn't vet any of the search terms used by the various groups. In one case, one of the teams wanted to track the number of times a specific set of users had their tweets "favorited" or, in Facebook terms, "liked." Unfortunately, this team didn't understand the concept of how to collect data with our tools. Instead of detecting a like, they simply watched the Twitter stream for any use of the word *like*! Given the hundreds of millions of messages tweeted in a given day, you can imagine how many would use the word *like* in their tweets. As a result, we were delivering approximately 1 million tweets per hour to their application, 99% of which were irrelevant due to the incorrect collection rules. If left unattended, the analysis of that data would result in a useless set of insights or results.

Understanding That Sometimes Less Is More

Because we are programmatically pulling data into our analytics software, we sometimes have to be careful not only about the mislabeling of data, but in this case the duplication of data.

12: Murphy Was Right! The Art of What Could Go Wrong

199

In one case, we were looking at a number of issues across the information technology industry, and we wanted to see where IBM ranked in the discussion along with several leaders in this space. When we pulled our data and started to group the number of mentions by company, we produced a graph that looked something like Figure 12.5.

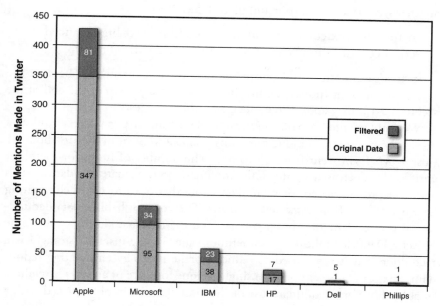

Figure 12.5 Count of mentions for technology companies.

Upon careful inspection, we discovered that many of the items in our data collection were duplicated entries. For example, the mentions around *apple* numbered around 347 specific references; *Microsoft,* about 95; and so on. Our analytics just didn't look right as we continued our analysis, and eventually, we realized that many of the entries in the sample were duplicates.

How could this be?

Consider a URL to a specific story on the http://thecrux.com website. (Note that we are not pointing out any flaws on this site at all; this is just a random example illustrating how two new entries can appear to be two separate entities.)

If we look at a news story about the prediction of the next financial crisis, the Web URL is:

http://thecrux.com/dyncontent/psibookmf_next-big-financial-
crisis-coming-soon/?cid=MKT015071&eid=MKT035893&snaid=
&step=start

So if we pull data from this site (assuming we used the keywords *hedge-fund* and *crisis*), it would be mapped to that URL as the source. But say another web page linked to it and used this URL:

http://thecrux.com/dyncontent/psibookmf_next-big-financial-
crisis-coming-soon/?cid=MKT015071&eid=MKT035893

In this case, both would return the same exact content, but because the URLs are different (notice the missing *&snaid=&step=start* at the end of the second URL), they appear to come from different sites.

We implemented a data duplication algorithm in our process, and as a result, the number of unique mentions of *apple* went from 347 to about 81 (just as *Microsoft* went from 95 to 34). The number of items for the other entities also decreased significantly, forcing us to reevaluate our data sources and keywords to search for more data. Note that our process of eliminating data is different from *data deduplication*. The concept behind data deduplication is essentially to save on storage (and the repeated storing of the same object). Data deduplication (sometimes called single-instance storage) is a technique that is often used to reduce storage needs by eliminating redundant data. In many cases, only a single unique instance of an item is retained in an archive; any redundant use of the same item is simply replaced with a pointer to the single copy.

Think of email as an example. How many times has someone sent a large file to a large distribution list, only to have numerous people "reply with history" and forward a copy of the large file. In the end, everyone's email inbox gets flooded with numerous copies of the same large file. By using a data deduplication technique, only one instance of that large file would be stored, and all subsequent uses would simply point back to the original. In our case, we didn't want that. If the item of text (or discussion) was the same, we simply wanted to remove the redundant entry from our analysis. If someone made reference to the URL pointing to the content, that was fine. But if someone cut and pasted the content from one URL to a unique URL, we would eliminate the second source.

12: Murphy Was Right! The Art of What Could Go Wrong

201

Customizing and Modifying Tools

In many cases, we've found that most of the tools that we use in our work need some kind of additional configuration. Mostly, we find this when we attempt to look at things such as sentiment, where we are trying to understand if people are speaking positively or negatively about a topic. The reason for this is that most tools use a simple dictionary lookup of words to calculate if a statement is expressing a positive or negative thought. To illustrate this, consider the following tweet:

Customer Service for *xyz company* is the worst I've ever seen.

Most applications will scan over the words used in a set of text and simply add up all the positive words and all the negative words. They then subtract the count of positive words from the count of negative words to produce a score:

Positive Score − Negative Score = Sentiment Score

If that score is positive (that is, there were more positive words than negative), the overall sentiment is said to be positive. If the count of negative words is higher than the count of positive words, the subtraction of the positive word count from the negative will produce a negative number, indicating an overall negative sentiment.

In the preceding example, if we were to use this scoring method, we could derive:

A count of zero for the positive terms (there were no clearly positive words in the text)

A count of one for the negative terms (the word *worst*)

And then using the preceding formula, we would derive an overall sentiment score of:

0 (the positive score) − 1 (the negative score) = −1

So in this case, we would obtain a score of −1, indicating that the text is basically presenting a negative sentiment. There can be many variations on this algorithm, which tends to produce several shades of gray in the answer. For example, in the tweet shown here, the word *service* could be considered a positive term, although perhaps not as positive as words such as *good, fantastic,* or *excellent.* So the system may choose to score that word as slightly positive and assign it a score of +0.25 rather simply considering it as being equal to other words that have a stronger connotation of positive.

As an example, consider these two tweets:

Tweet 1: I thought the movie was decent.
Tweet 2: That was a great movie!!!

With both of those tweets, if we were to use the algorithm described here (simply counting the number of positive and negative words), both of these tweets would have a positive sentiment score of +1.0. Tweet 1 would be positive because the word *decent* is considered to have a positive connotation, and no negative words are used. In the case of Tweet 2, no negative words are used, and the word *great* would be viewed as positive, which would generate a score of +1.0.

However, that may not really be representative of the true intent. Tweet 2, while representing a positive sentiment, is less enthusiastic. In this case, it would be good to give the word *decent* (along with phrases like *not bad, passable,* or *acceptable*) scores that differed from words like *excellent, thrilling,* or *stellar*.

In our case, we gave the word *decent* a positive sentiment of +0.25. So it's considered positive in sentiment, but only one-quarter that of other words, such as *great,* which would get a full score of +1.0. So in these examples, Tweet 1 would be of positive sentiment with a score of +0.25, and Tweet 2 would have a positive score of +1.0, indicating the greater sense of positive connotation.

This is where our customizations come in (Step 5a in the flowchart from Figure 12.1).

We may need to add (or subtract) a number of words from a dictionary based on their use. Consider the commonly used words shown in Table 12.2. How should each word be treated? Should it be treated as implying a positive sentiment? Or should it be treated as connoting a negative sentiment? The choice can seem quite arbitrary, but as long as we're consistent in our dictionary augmentations, this can add tremendous value to our analytics.

Table 12.2   Examples of Words That Can Have a Positive or Negative Connotation

English Word	Positive Connotations	Negative Connotations
Chapter 1 Difficult	Can be challenging Ex: *It was difficult to believe how generous he was.*	Someone or something can cause problems or be problematic Ex: *Installing the software patch can be difficult at best.*
Chapter 2 Reservation	A reservation at a restaurant Ex: *Out of all of those restaurants, Chez Paul is the only one where we can ensure we have a reservation.*	The feeling of being hesitant Ex: *John has reservations about the success of that new business venture.*
Chapter 3 Chicken	A food or dinner Ex: *You should have the chicken at Chez Paul!*	A coward Ex: *The software team didn't implement the service calls—those chickens!*
Chapter 4 Childish	Childlike or simplistic Ex: *The childish advertisement made its point quite effectively.*	Can imply silliness Ex: *The overall experience was quite childish.*

Most of the time, when we look at microblogging content (Facebook, Twitter, LinkedIn, and so on), we find that most of the content is fairly neutral—that is, neither positive nor negative in score. Think of a Facebook post that says:

> Attending a session at #IBMAmplify on the use of Social Media Analytics

There may be some interesting information to be gained from this posting, but there is no particular feeling being expressed. We tend to find that a large amount of microblog content is like this (which is fine).

One of the issues we run into when doing a sentiment analysis is considering the use of words such as *disaster*—a word that clearly indicates some kind of negative sentiment. Consider the following LinkedIn update, for example:

> Spending my day reading about disaster recovery products on the market today.

Using the algorithm we outlined previously, the sentiment score of this post would be computed at a −1.0 (since *disaster* would be found in the negative dictionary, and there are no other words found in the positive dictionary).

However, when the word *recovery* is used in conjunction with *disaster,* our sentiment score should be computed as zero (or the expression of no particular feeling) because the phrase *disaster recovery* really isn't positive or negative. We've seen this situation countless numbers of times, where the negative connotation of the word *disaster* essentially cancels out the positive sentiment expressed around it.

Using the Right Tool for the Right Job

As we discussed previously, in our group we maintain a number of different tools to help us with all of our analytics projects. Some of these tools are "homegrown," or tools and utilities that our team wrote for a specific task. Many of these tools are written in Java or R and utilize many of IBM's big data tools such as Hadoop or DB2.

We also employ a number of IBM commercial products such as IBM's Social Media Analytics, SPSS, IBM Content Analytics, and various Watson services now available on Bluemix. Many of these tools specialize in a particular facet of the overall process. For example, SMA does an excellent job of deriving sentiment and summarizing data, whereas SPSS allows for a greater flexibility and deeper statistical analysis. What we've learned over time is to take the best parts of each of these tools to derive a more complete answer to the question we are trying to answer. We've often found ourselves sticking firmly to a specific tool rather than being open to a variety of results.

Analyzing Consumer Reaction During Hurricane Sandy

In 2012, Hurricane Sandy struck a wide area across the Atlantic Ocean from Haiti and Jamaica and then north into the eastern coast of the United States and Canada. According to many records, more than 200 deaths were attributed to the storm, with approximately 146 of those in the United States and around 98 in the Caribbean. Sandy has been labeled as one of the deadliest and most destructive hurricanes from the 2012 Atlantic hurricane season, and recent estimates indicated that it ranks second in terms of dollar

12: Murphy Was Right! The Art of What Could Go Wrong

205

value in destruction in US history. Damage estimates have placed the cost to repair and replace damages at upwards of $68 billion US.

One of the engagements we worked on was the public's perception of various home improvement and appliance stores within the United States during this period. Specifically, we were looking at the public's reaction to updates, news about needed supplies, and the various responses to emergencies from these companies.

In this case, our main source of data was the public microblogs (Facebook and Twitter). Almost immediately the public gravitated toward a number of hashtags, and our first pass was to focus on them as a way to gather data. Our filters included the following (there were many more in the end; this is just a sampling):

#sandy
#sandyhelp
#hurricane
#Hurricanesandy
#Hurricanesandyproblems
#sandyaid
#sandyvolunteer
#NYCSandyNeeds
#HelpStatenIsland
#SandyReports
#frankenstorm
#hoboken
#sandytoday
#hoboken411
#noheat
#nopower

This example raises an important point about both gathering data and promoting trackable events. By using a hashtag, individuals are telling others that the comment they are making or information they are providing is directly related to a specific event. This point is important because it can really help alleviate any problems with data validity. Since it's already tagged by topic, we can be somewhat assured that it is part of the dataset we might be interested in. So, in establishing your own social media campaign, having a unique hashtag makes the job of doing analytics around the campaign that much easier. Please note that if you were to use a common hashtag (say #ff—Follow Friday) because your event happened on a Friday, be prepared to do a lot of data cleansing and filtering, since much of the data will be unrelated to your event. From an analyst's perspective, you would be increasing the amount of noise in your dataset and drowning out the signal (the relevant information). We always want to keep the signal-to-noise ratio as high as possible, or maybe better said, we have to have data about our topic (the signal) than the other nonrelated issues (the noise).

NOTE

Our tool of choice for analyzing the tweets was IBM's Social Media Analytics product (then called Cognos Consumer Insights, or CCI). It seemed a perfect vehicle for analyzing the sentiment and thoughts of individuals, and again, because our question was to explore the reaction around home improvement centers, using this tool seemed to be the best way to proceed. Initially, we were able to achieve a number of insights from our data.

A number of interesting positive as well as negative statements were made about a number of the organizations. Specifically, they were being criticized for not donating plastic bags for some of the relief efforts or closing stores early before the storms hit (claiming they cared more about their employees than the general population that was "in need"). On the positive side, a number of comments were made on the helpfulness of the employees and the fact that some stores brought in extra inventory (such as generators or pumps) early in anticipation of the storm. Overall, there seemed to be an equal amount of positive and negative sentiment.

What we really wanted to understand, however, was what topics or issues the general public was raising during this catastrophe. Using SMA's Evolving Topics tool, we were able to look at terms or phrases that were used over the span of time that we were investigating in an attempt to uncover frequently mentioned topics (see Figure 12.6). The Evolving Topics algorithm identifies word phrases that occur multiple times within the same document and also across multiple documents, so our hope was that this would uncover some interesting insights.

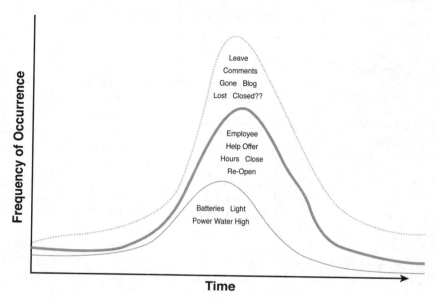

Figure 12.6   Example of an Evolving Topics chart.

While we appreciate how SMA can do an analysis across its dataset, we were having trouble uncovering the main points of the conversations that were happening. Although we had a significant amount of time invested in the creation of our SMA models, we still weren't getting the results we needed to answer our question. Looking back to Figure 12.1, we had all of the data we were ever going to get, so it wasn't a matter of looking for more or different content. It really came down to how we did the analytics and what tools could "tease" those insights out of our data (steps 5a or 5b).

IBM Watson Content Analytics (then called simply IBM Content Analytics, or ICA) is a tool that breaks down content into facets (see an example of an ICA analysis in Figure 12.7). The Content Analytics engine then provides data about the frequency and correlation information for key-words of the specific facets. Facets can be nouns, noun phrases, verbs, adjectives, and so on. What we are showing in Figure 12.7 is from a different analysis, but we wanted to illustrate the power of ICA and its ability to segment text into its grammatical components. From this analysis, we can begin to derive the topics of conversations and the frequency with which they are happening.

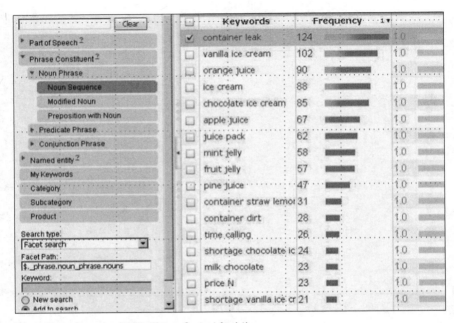

Figure 12.7   Example of IBM's Watson Content Analytics.

Think of what a noun is. It's the subject of a sentence or a comment. The verbs describe the intensity of the topic or how people are feeling.

Exporting our data from SMA and then re-importing into IBM Watson Content Analytics allowed us to create a list of top topics on the minds of people during this event (see Figure 12.8).

This list was exactly what we were looking for: the topics that people were discussing during the storm as they related to various home improvement centers. We were then able to generate increased sets of metrics and insights based on these themes. For example, when the discussion of generators arose, almost 50% of the discussion was around the need and the urgency of the need for them, while 32% complained of out-of-stock issues. This seems to be an interesting (and measurable) metric that store managers may want to have in the future (hopefully, a future catastrophe isn't as severe).

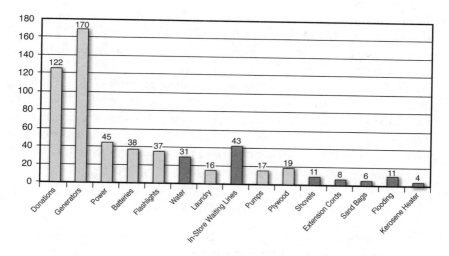

Figure 12.8 Top topics of conversation during Hurricane Sandy.

So while this example might not be a case of something going wrong, it could have been. Things could have gone wrong had we attempted to use just a single tool in our quest to answer the questions posed. Sometimes we need to take a step backward (or perhaps sideways) to make progress forward; such is the life of an analyst.

Through this analysis, we were able to uncover a number of issues raised by consumers about the various home improvement stores in the area. We were able to report that many consumers were actively looking for batteries and generators during the storm; these items were clearly understocked by many of the stores. What was actually an unanticipated finding was a backlash aimed at the employees of some of the stores. It seemed that many of them abandoned the stores as the storms hit, leaving consumers with no place to turn for those batteries or generators. Those comments were teased from the dataset based on the keywords that arose from the evolving topic graph in Figure 12.6.

Summary

In this chapter, we provided some thoughts and ideas about what could go wrong in any analysis. Please don't misunderstand. We're not saying that everything will go wrong, but it's been our experience that not one project we've worked on went from inception to completion without some kind of a hiccup or glitch. These aren't bad; each little roadblock is a learning lesson for the next time. In our case, each time we've hit one of those and produced a tool or workaround, we have found use for that same solution somewhere down the road.

This chapter was *not* about how to avoid these problems. There is no way to predict many of these issues in advance. Our goal in writing this chapter was to alert you to what could possibly go wrong. We're sure there are other issues; in fact, we *know* there are. Victory comes not in the avoidance of these problems, but in the knowledge of how to deal with them *when* they arrive!

Endnotes

[1] Wilton, Dave, *Murphy's Law*, April 29, 2007. Retrieved from http://www.wordorigins.org/index.php/site/comments/murphys_law/.

[2] Coase, Ronald H, "How Should Economists Choose?" American Enterprise Institute for Public Policy Research, Thomas Jefferson Center Foundation, 1982.

[3] Holmes, Oliver Wendell, *The Autocrat of the Breakfast Table*, No. 81 (Boston, MA: Houghton, 1899).

13

Visualization as an Aid to Analytics

Every now and then one paints a picture that seems to have opened a door and serves as a stepping stone to other things.

—Pablo Picasso, as quoted in *Why Greatness Cannot Be Planned* [1]

One of the biggest challenges for nontechnical and business users in producing data visualizations is deciding which visual should be used to represent the data accurately. Maybe it's not so much the accuracy as it is the clarity. But why do it at all? As humans, we tend to think visually (at least a good number of us do). Sometimes concepts or ideas can best be described with pictures rather than just words or verbal discussions. Discussing the differences between 10 different data points is interesting, but if we can convey that thought with a simple picture, why not do that? The idea is that there might be a huge difference between point 1 and point 6 but not so much between point 1 and point 3. In this case, how much easier would it be to just *see* those differences?

Visualizing the information we've gathered allows the consumer of that information to potentially see things in our results that might have otherwise gone unnoticed. Any representation of raw data can convey information, but without a visualization, we could miss out on trends, behavior patterns, or dependencies. Visualizations give us answers faster. Looking at a graph and identifying a trend can take but an instant. However, imagine how much time it would take to scan rows of numbers and pick out that same trend.

A data analytics project isn't complete until the results we've collected are packaged or presented in a way that truly helps the receiver of those insights make decisions or take action based on our work. That means we, as analysts, not only need to know what the data means but also need to be able to represent it in a way that can best convey the information we inferred from it so that our users can derive conclusions, which in turn can drive business outcomes.

The options for data visualization seem to be growing almost by the day. New technologies and techniques can turn number-intensive reports into bright, colorful 3D interactive graphics. But we must be careful. In our zeal to create the prettiest of charts or sexiest rendering, we may lose the message we are trying to convey. Don't get us wrong: Compelling graphics are a wonderful tool in expressing findings, but overuse (or overindulgence) may push the audience from the realm of understanding into the world of confusion. The choice of how to deliver results will depend on clients' needs. Visualization should help tell the story, not drown it out.

In this chapter, we discuss some of the different types of visualizations to consider when presenting the results of an analysis. There isn't a single "right" answer to the question of what kind of a graph provides the clearest insight to a user. There are some best practices when it comes to selecting color or limiting information on a chart to maximize the impact of a message, but it's ultimately about the insights or additional information that was discovered. Many analysts opt for the pretty charts or the snappy presentation, but we must always keep in mind that it's the results that count, often more than the presentation itself.

Common Visualizations

In his *Harvard Business Review* article titled "The Three Elements of Successful Data Visualizations," Jim Stikeleather [2] outlines three areas of concentration that visual designers should consider when creating graphic visualizations. These considerations are

- The design should understand the audience.
- It should set up a clear framework.
- And, probably most important, it should tell a story.

What these considerations really boil down to is this: clarity. Effective visualizations should not confuse the audience but should present a story (or an insight) in a clear, simple-to-understand way that helps the audience understand the conclusions that were drawn from the data. Or better yet, these visualizations should enable them to understand the data in such a way that they can discover new insights or relationships on their own.

Let's look at some of the more simple types of graphics first, many of which we've used throughout this text. The graphs we create should aim to simplify the data in a visually appealing way. The main challenge that many people have with graphs is choosing which chart type to use. We all want a visually appealing chart to present to a customer, but remember, if a chart is visually appealing, we must be careful that we don't spend more time talking about how "cool" the chart looks as compared to the message it is trying to convey.

Let's look at a few chart types.

Pie Charts

Pie charts are best used to illustrate the breakdown of a single dimension as it relates to the whole. Basically, when we want to look at the value of a specific dimension in relation to other values in that same dimension, we could use a pie chart to easily visualize it. Pie charts help us see, with a quick glance, which attribute in series of data is dominant or how any individual attribute or set of attributes relates to each other. Consider the graph in Figure 13.1 that depicts the number of social media posts over a 24-hour period by five specific users.

In other words, it is best to use pie charts when we want to show differences in a specific group based on one variable. In the example in Figure 13.1, we collected the number of times these users used the word *cloud* in their social media postings. It is important to remember that pie charts should be used only with a category or dimension that combines to make up a whole. In this case, we collected 151 tweets, and clearly user 4 was the dominant communicator with a 60% coverage.

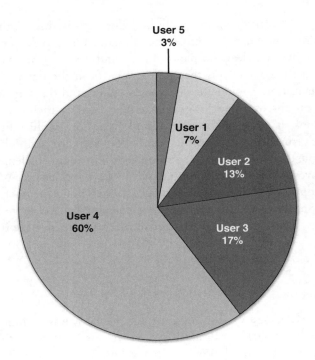

Figure 13.1 Sample pie chart of the number of social media posts by user.

What makes a pie chart useful is the quick visual comparisons that can be done. Again, without the percentages in the graph, we could quickly see that user 4 is more verbal than all of the other users combined. Or we can see that together percentages for users 5 and 1 are close to the amount of conversation initiated by user 2.

Bar Charts

Bar charts, like pie charts, are useful for comparing classes or groups of data. In bar charts, a group can have a single category of data, or it can be broken down further into multiple categories for greater depth of analysis. A bar chart is built in such a way that the heights of the different bars are proportional to the size of the category they represent. Since the x-axis (the horizontal axis) represents the categories that were measured or being represented, it tends to have no scale. The y-axis (the vertical axis) does have a scale, and this indicates the units of measurement. Figure 13.2 looks at the same set of data we used previously.

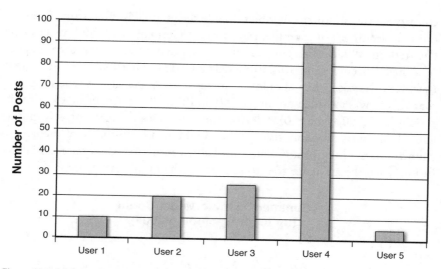

Figure 13.2 Bar graph representing the number of social media posts by user.

With the bar chart, like the pie chart, we are able to easily see that the most prolific social media participant was user 4. What's slightly more difficult is understanding that together all of the other users' posts combined don't equal or compare to those made by user 4. That fact was much easier to see in Figure 13.1. On the other hand, a bar chart does allow us to easily see the user with the smallest number of posts or the user with the biggest number of posts a bit quicker. It must be noted that sometimes the pie slices, because they represent percentages and not actual numbers, make that a bit more difficult to discern. It is a bit easier to compare two bars (consider user 2 and user 3 in Figure 13.2) versus the corresponding pie slices in Figure 13.1. A comparison can be made, but it takes the audience a bit of time to see the difference in a pie chart versus the bar chart.

One danger of using bar charts is the comparison between different graphs or charts. While we didn't have to scale the data in Figure 13.2, sometimes the data points might be so varied that they need to be scaled to be represented on a graph. The bottom line: Watch out for inconsistent scales across multiple graphs. If two charts are put side-by-side, ensure that they are using the same scale. If they don't have the same scale, be aware of the differences and how they might trick the eye.

A perfect example of a scaling problem was discussed by Naomi Robbins in an online article in *Forbes Magazine* [3]. Consider the graphic (which we re-created) in Figure 13.3 showing the relative number of medals won, by country, in the Summer Olympics. While the graphic is interesting, it can be quite misleading. For example, if we look at Germany with 500 medals (the data reports 499, but it's close enough), we might assume that each graphic of a medal is equivalent to 250 medals awarded. That makes sense. But if that were the case, then shouldn't Russia show 4 medals? It would appear that Russia was awarded around 1,250 and the USA number of 1975 really should be 1,500 (250 × 6). Clearly, the scale doesn't work for this graph, and while it was probably trying to show the relative number of medals by country, in the long run, it would probably cause more discussion and confusion when the audience tries to rationalize the numbers.

Figure 13.3   Graphic depicting the number of medals won in the Summer Olympics.

Line Charts

Line charts are similar to bar charts and at times can seem interchangeable; however, a line chart works best for continuous data, whereas bar and column charts work best for data that is categorized. Think of continuous data of the same dimension that is changing over time (the number of posts made over the past 30 days, the number of mentions of a product in a 24-hour period, and so on). Of course, we can use bar charts to show the change of values for a particular entity over time as well; that may come down to style, but generally speaking, a line chart is much more useful in discerning trends and patterns in data.

Let's look at an example of the number of mentions of a particular product over a 24-hour period. The data we use is from Table 13.1, which lists the hour (0–23 hours) and the number of mentions made in that hour. A quick look at the table reveals nothing out of the ordinary. At first glance, this looks like a US-based audience (perhaps the Northeast) because social media posts are made throughout the day and a noticeable drop to zero occurs around 2 a.m. to 6 a.m. (when we assume users are sleeping), but no real trends.

Table 13.1

Sample Data for the Number of Mentions in a 24-Hour Period: Hour	Posts
0	4
1	1
2	0
3	0
4	0
5	0
6	0
7	1
8	2
9	5
10	4
11	7
12	14
13	18
14	6
15	2
16	3
17	3
18	5
19	10
20	15
21	20
22	4
23	2

A line chart, as shown in Figure 13.4, instantly shows an interesting trend.

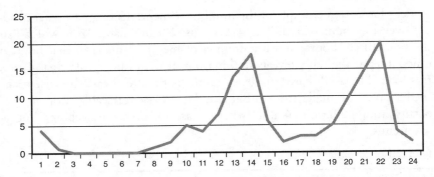

Figure 13.4   Line chart representation of the data in Table 13.1 (number of mentions in a 24-hour period).

It appears that around 13:00 hours and then again at 21:00 hours, discussion about the product or service is at its peak. Clearly, any kind of marketing plan or advertising should take place around these times. But these kinds of trends, while possible to see in Table 13.1, aren't as obvious as when shown as a line chart.

Watching this data over time, perhaps over several of days, could show a repeating, and hopefully predictable, pattern that could be invaluable to those wishing to engage with potential customers or prospects.

Scatter Plots

While line charts provide a way to map independent and dependent variables that are both quantitative (that is, measurements), a scatter plot can be useful to depict a trend or the direction of the data. When both variables are quantitative on a graph, we can interpret a line that spans that data as a slope (or prediction) of future data or trends. Scatter plots are similar to line charts in that they start with mapping quantitative

In the case of Figure 13.5, we can see that the general trend for tweets made over a 24-hour period is on the rise, or generally increasing over time. Obviously, there are peaks and valleys in the data, but the amount of chatter, or conversation, is increasing.

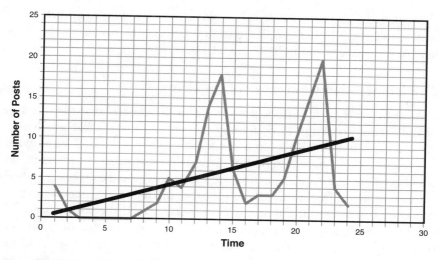

Figure 13.5   Scatter plot and trend for tweets during a 24-hour period.

Common Pitfalls

When creating these graphs, we should consider a few things in an effort to keep messages clear and allow the audience to focus on the story or message being delivered, not on the charts and all the pretty colors.

Information Overload

One of the most common issues we've seen with charts or presentations that attempt to show the results of a study is that they often contain too much information. Consider a simple chart (such as that in Figure 13.2) where the amount of information is kept to a minimum: the label for the data points along the x-axis and the values on the y-axis. There isn't much more needed. Often analysts like to augment their graphs with notes that indicate a peak or valley in the data and perhaps why it might have occurred. Is this information really necessary? Isn't that what a picture is for, to visually show the peak or valley?

Other times we see a pie chart (similar to Figure 13.1) with two or three other graphs that attempt to show a similar concept or provide an alternative way to represent the same concept. If one graph doesn't describe the concept well enough, we need to ask, "Is that graph really providing value?"

While redundancy is one issue, the side effect of adding too much information to a graph is that in order to fit the additional information, font sizes tend to get smaller, approaching unreadable.

The Unintended Consequences of Using 3D

When creating graphs to depict our data, often we feel that they are sort of dull or uninteresting (how interesting can you make a bar graph that depicts users and number of message postings, anyway?). But we all want our results to look visually appealing with the thought that the presentation could keep our audience's attention. Often we're tempted to take a standard graph and turn it into a three-dimensional rendering in an attempt to spice up the message. But this can have at least two unintended consequences.

The representation of the results may be so compelling that the audience misses the message and focuses on the pretty picture. Nothing could be worse! Not only do they not receive the intended message, but in the long run, if this metric is utilized later (say as a descriptive statistic), they may just not understand how it's used. In essence, they may have focused more on the delivery rather than the message.

One of the considerations we mentioned earlier is that the goal in presenting results is to do it in such a way as to avoid confusion. Nothing can derail a discussion about the meaning of an insight or a metric more than a discussion about the validity of the data. Now let's look at the charts in Figure 13.6.

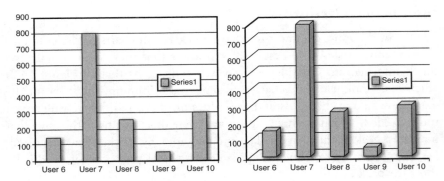

Figure 13.6   Representation of a set of data in both 2D and 3D.

In this figure, the same data is plotted in two dimensions (2D) versus three dimensions (3D). While the chart on the right (the 3D rendering) does look a little prettier, the audience may start to question the values on the chart. Look at user 7. In the 2D graph, the value looks to be 800, yet on the 3D graph, the value appears to be below the 800 line. Upon realizing this, viewers may turn the conversation from the value of seeing user 7 as the most prolific to "why is the value not represented correctly?" Inadvertently, this graph has now raised some doubt in the eyes of the audience to the validity of the data being presented.

Using Too Much Color

Another consideration is color. Often analysts go overboard with the use of colors (and font types for that matter) in their graphs. As with many aspects of visual perception, humans do not all perceive color in the same way. Said another way, every user's perception of an object is influenced by the context (or color) in which it is presented. This doesn't mean we should stay away from color, but it does mean that the use of varied amounts of color should be done sparingly.

Consider the bar chart from Figure 13.2. If each of the bars were drawn in a different color (say blue, red, green, gray, and purple), does that provide any additional value to the chart? Or does it raise the question "What do the colors represent?" and simply add a layer of confusion to the message? Then again, we have to consider that an audience member who sees a bar in a bar chart as red may assume that's a problem or an area to concentrate on (we tend to think of red as indicative of a problem area). Don't use color to decorate the graph. Prettying up a graph might serve a purpose in attracting attention, but from an analytics perspective, it can only distract from what's important—the data and the insights we are attempting to draw from the data.

Alternatively, if our graph were drawn in black and white and one of the bars was coded in a color (say red), it would stand out and perhaps draw attention to that specific point, which may be the intention. In that case, the use of color adds value to the graph in calling out a specific area that merits discussion.

Visually Representing Unstructured Data

Probably the largest problem with social media analytics is figuring out how to compute and then show relationships in the data and also visually represent topics of conversation. One of the more frequently used techniques is that of word frequency.

The frequency with which particular words are used in a set of messages can potentially tell us something meaningful about that set of text. Of course, if all of the messages were produced by a single individual, the frequencies may tell us something about the author because the choice of words an individual uses is often not random but purposeful. In our case, we tend to look at the messages from a wide variety of people in the hopes of detecting common signals or messages in that body of data. A depiction of a word frequency report may be useful if we want to determine whether the most frequently used words of a given text represent a potentially meaningful pattern that may have been overlooked in a casual glance at the data.

The first obvious way to look at the word frequency is to graph the word list and their respective counts in a bar graph. To illustrate this concept, let's use the example of Lance Armstrong's interview with Oprah Winfrey that was described in Chapter 9. As illustrated in Figure 13.7, a bar chart nicely shows the words that are more frequently used compared to words that are less frequently used.

However, when we look more closely at the graph, two things stand out:

- There are far too many words to show along the horizontal axis. After about 10 values, the points get placed too close together, and therefore, it becomes difficult to read. This example shows just the top 60 words in a shortened version of what we've used previously; typically, we like to look at the top 100 to 150 words.

- The scale quickly becomes confusing when there are words that have a very high frequency versus those that are average to low. Remember, average to low in the top 60 words is still significant. The point is that it's difficult to discern the subtle differences between word usage.

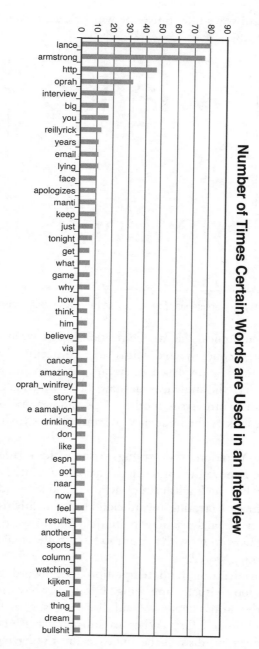

Figure 13.7   Word frequency bar chart of tweets around Lance Armstrong's interview.

For these reasons, we like to use the word cloud version of this analysis (see Figure 13.8).

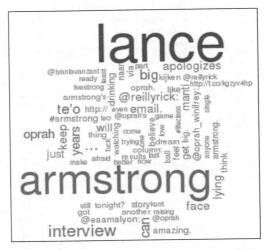

Figure 13.8 Word cloud representation of tweets around Lance Armstrong's interview.

The word cloud quickly shows the relationship between word counts by making the more frequently used words larger. Since these words are larger and more prominently displayed, they quickly catch the audience's eyes. But more than that, the audience can draw their own conclusions about the relative use of one word versus another. This approach becomes even more useful when we look at the frequency of word phrases (two or more words used together).

Another consideration when trying to show the relationship between words used is to remove the clutter in the data. This clutter is often referred to as *stop words*. For the English language, this includes words such as *a*, *the*, *is*, and so on. Imagine creating a word cloud of frequently used words. If we included these in our analysis, more often than not the word cloud would be dominated by the word *the* with a count so high that it would literally drown out any of the other words.

Another consideration (and temptation) with word clouds is trying to make them look visually appealing. Often this has the reverse effect. Remember, early in this chapter we said that the goal of analysts is to report the findings and provide facts. When we introduce fancy charts, say in 3D or with fancy fonts, we distract the audience and risk having them miss the finer points of the insights.

For example, Figure 13.9 shows the same data used in a word cloud that is generated by an online tool.

Figure 13.9   Fancy word cloud generated using an online tool.

We really like this website and often recommend it to users, but with the wrong options selected, the message of the word cloud could get lost in admiration of the graphic that was produced. Remember, the point of creating the graphic is about facts and insights, not sizzle.

Summary

We could spend hundreds of pages talking about presentation styles and formats. Our goal in this chapter was to introduce the importance of visualization—not to just show a relationship between data points or information, but to effectively show it in a way that doesn't confuse the audience or raise more questions than it answers.

Endnotes

[1] Stanley, Kenneth O., and Joel Lehman. "The Art of Breeding Art," in *Why Greatness Cannot Be Planned* (Switzerland: Springer International Publishing, 2015), 21–28.

[2] Stikeleather, Jim. "The Three Elements of Successful Data Visualizations." *Harvard Business Review*, April 19, 2013. Retrieved from https://hbr.org/2013/04/the-three-elements-of-successf.

[3] Robbins, Naomi. "Misleading Graphs: Figures Not Drawn to Scale." *Forbes*, February 16, 2012. Retrieved from http://www.forbes.com/sites/naomirobbins/2012/02/16/misleading-graphs-figures-not-drawn-to-scale.

Case Study

Give a man a fish and you feed him for a day. Teach a man to fish and you feed him for a lifetime.

—Chinese Proverb

In this appendix, we put all of the previous thoughts and discussions to use in a case study format. From May 11–13, 2015, IBM held one of its largest conferences titled "IBMAmplify." This event focusing on marketing, analytics, selling, and fulfillment was designed especially for IBM Commerce clients. Our hope was that with over 3,000 attendees encompassing 20 tracks and more than 200 sessions, the amount of information (and hopefully opinions) shared there would be substantial, and we might be able to derive some interesting insights from this conference. According to the marketing material for this event, "Everyone from thought leaders, product experts, and industry peers will be providing tips and strategies for creating amazing customer experiences across channels, leveraging buyer behaviors and analytics to deliver targeted interactions at every touch point." Consequently, the real question for us is:

What were the key insights or thoughts expressed by the attendees both during and after the event?

If you recall, we divided social media analytics activities into three broad phases:

- Data identification
- Data analysis
- Information interpretation

We approach the discussion of the case study in the context of these phases.

Introduction to the Case Study: IBMAmplify

There were four main themes to the IBMAmplify Conference: eCommerce, Marketing, Customer Analytics, and Merchandising. The eCommerce track focused on the creation of unique brand experiences across all marketing channels for both business-to-business and business-to-consumer. Among the many topics discussed were best practices, trends in eCommerce, and techniques and strategies to help businesses obtain the most from their implementations. Many of the sessions were advertised to include topics such as proven strategies, architectural considerations, case studies, and hands-on skills workshops to help attendees deliver the best customer experience from engagement to fulfillment as well as post sales service.

Customer analytics focused on optimizing the customer experience while understanding the customer journey. The sessions for this track covered best practices and strategies for applying digital, social, and predictive analytics to help users accelerate profitability and improve their business outcomes. The Marketing and Merchandizing tracks focused on business use cases and product demonstrations for generating positive marketing results across a number of areas in the organization.

Data Identification

Early on we examined the concept of data identification when we discussed the need to verify that we could collect enough data to allow us to perform an analysis that could produce meaningful insights or conclusions.

Normally, before undertaking a study such as this, we would perform a number of queries and data collection steps to understand how much data was available for our project. In this case, we were lucky enough to use our real-time analytic engines (discussed in Chapter 8) to watch Twitter for mentions of content around the hashtag #ibmamplify (the identifier used at the conference). Because we did that, we were able to look at some of our descriptive statistics produced by our InfoSphere Streams environment to understand approximately how much data we would have.

A quick look at the number of tweets that we captured and analyzed during the event revealed that we had over 30,000 tweets. This is not an overwhelming amount of data and points to the fact that we will need to bring in more data from other social media venues. However, it is enough to get a feel for what a larger sample may look like. In our experience, it is difficult to create general benchmarks of how much data is sufficient. This really depends on the project at hand. When we are looking for potential security threats in a data stream, even a small amount of data is good enough. On the other hand, when we are looking for which fashion trend is most popular among shoppers, we might need a larger amount of data. For the purpose of this case study, we determined that this data set was sufficient to give us the flexibility we needed to analyze the data in multiple ways.

Part of our real-time analysis included the categorization of tweets into topic areas. We decided to review this to understand what our data sources may look like. Figure A.1 depicts the tweet counts for the various topics over a nine-day period from May 6 through May 14. Even though the conference itself was held from the May 11 through May 15, we chose to collect data several days prior to the event to watch as discussion of topics increased heading into the event.

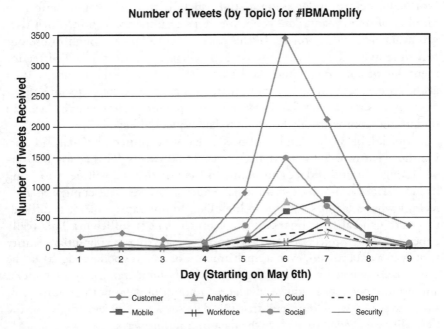

Figure A.1   Number of tweets by topic for IBMAmplify.

Not surprisingly, the number of tweets or discussions that pertained to the concept of "customer" far exceeded all others. We'll come back to the topics of conversation later; at this point, we were more interested in the relative amounts of data and the time frame. The horizontal axis of the graph in Figure A.1 represents data points from days 1 through 9; this represents the nine-day range of our data query with May 6 as day 1 and May 14 as our day 9. Again, not surprisingly, many of the topics peaked at the start of the conference, although topics such as mobile computing and workforce seemed to peak toward the end.

One of the issues we raised early in our discussions on data was the location of people posting content and the language used. Normally, this is an issue when we have an international event or some event is generating reactions worldwide. We understand that people from around the world attend conferences in the United States, but our assumption would be that most of the attendees travel domestically; thus, the predominant language that we would have to analyze would be English.

Using our set of descriptive statistics from InfoSphere Streams (see Figure A.2), we can see that the bulk of the tweets we collected were in English.

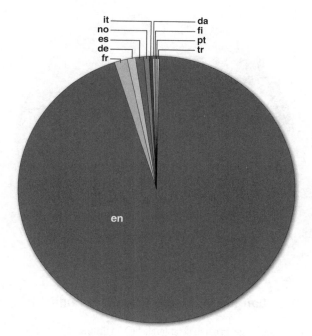

Languages Used (Including English)

Figure A.2 Languages used in tweets over the course of our analysis.

Removing the dominant data point in the graph (English) produced the pie chart shown in Figure A.3, and from that, we can see that the next dominant language used was French, with only 331 tweets over the nine-day period. With our whole dataset containing over 30,000 tweets, that means French language tweets made up approximately 1% of the dataset, and as such, we chose to exclude those tweets from any analysis needing translations (sentiment, and so on). The other languages quickly fell into amounts that were less than 1% and were therefore deemed as negligible. Note that this doesn't mean those tweets or data items were unimportant. We were doing this as a quick study; for a more complete analysis, we would probably look closer at the tweets in French, German, and Spanish (the top three languages after English) simply because together they represent about 3% of the sample. However, due to time constraints, we stuck with just the larger portion of the dataset.

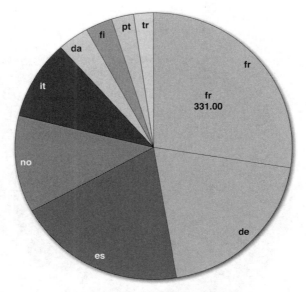

Languages Used (Excluding English)

Figure A.3   Top languages used in our dataset (excluding English).

In Chapter 3, we discussed the potential need to understand who is "talking" in the many analysis projects that we executed. In the case of an IBM-sponsored event, we think this is a critical issue. If we were just to analyze all of the data collected around an event without understanding who was saying it, we might end up with a biased insight. In this case, we wanted to understand if an IBMer or a group closely aligned with IBM was having an impact on the social media conversation. This is just "good" scientific discovery. If we analyzed the tweets and came to the conclusion that the latest IBM product introduced into the marketplace was being perceived as the "greatest thing since sliced bread" (a U.S. colloquialism based on a slogan used by Wonder Bread, indicating a relatively recent invention that is likely to significantly improve people's lives), we might want to be sure IBMers weren't promoting that idea. It's not a "bad" thing if they think their company's products are significantly better than others, but from a business perspective, it's probably much more important to understand IBM's customer's viewpoint instead.

So again, using our descriptive statistics, we looked at the top authors in the sample of data to identify any IBMers who might be promoting their viewpoints. Figure A.4 is a graph of the top authors in Twitter for our datasets. These are essentially the people tweeting the most in our collection of data.

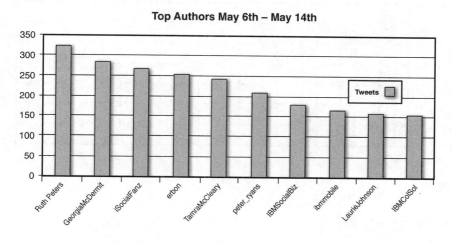

Figure A.4 Top authors May 6–May 14.

Obviously, some of them are IBM-specific Twitter handles (IBMSocialBiz, ibmmobile, IBMColSol). More than likely, the tweets coming from those accounts contained a marketing message of some kind; however, they may indeed contain some social commentary. So for that fact, we didn't exclude them from our analysis just yet, but they became data points in our collection that we marked as "sympathetic to IBM" (or related to IBM) if we detected an overly positive or negative viewpoint in our analysis.

We may also want to look at the other top tweeters to see if they are IBMers as well. Sometimes this task is easy, other times it's difficult, and sometimes it's impossible. For the sake of an unbiased analysis (or the best you can do), it could be worth the effort to understand if those "talking" about you or your brand are potentially biased.

With Twitter, this task is pretty easy. For this case study, we just took our top tweeters and looked at their profiles. In our case, if they identified themselves with IBM or a business partner of IBM, we simply marked them (as we did the others). If they revealed themselves as overly relevant in a conversation, we could make an informed decision about the analysis. See Figure A.5.

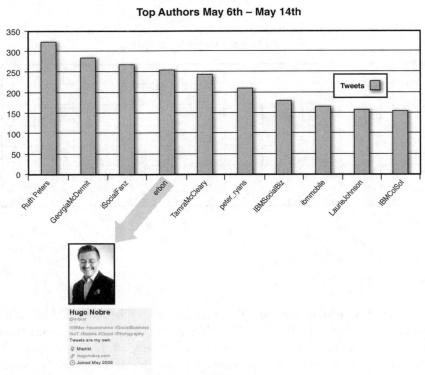

Figure A.5   Identifying users of a company or one closely related to it

Taking a First Pass at the Analysis

Rarely do we define a data model for an analysis and not make changes to it. Our case study is no exception. For our first pass at the data, we decided to look closely at the conversations surrounding the Cloud-Analytics-Mobile-Social-Security (CAMSS) themes because those seem to be hot topics in and around IBM today. Also, since we had created our real-time analysis of conversation themes based on InfoSphere Streams, we knew that a good portion of the dataset included those topics.

The first step in analyzing the data is to define the data model, or the organization of text and keywords, into meaningful buckets. Using IBM's Social Media Analytics (SMA) offering, we defined about eight themes that we believed were being discussed at the conference. As we said, all models will evolve over time, and we fully expected this one to as well. We had to start somewhere, and as Lao Tzu said: "The journey of a thousand miles begins with one step."

For our model, the "buckets" (or themes, as they are referred to in SMA) consisted of the following topics:

- **Analytics**—This includes discussions around Cognos or any of the IBM Watson analytics tools. Any mentions of *insights* or *analysis* would indicate discussions in and around this theme.

- **Customers**—The IBMAmplify conference was centered around the customer experience, so we thought creating this theme might be interesting to create to see if there was any discussion around customer use of IBM tools or services.

- **Mobile**—This is a fairly self-explanatory topic; it involves any discussion around the use of mobile technologies or applications.

- **Cloud**—This includes discussion around moving applications to the cloud as well as comments made around SoftLayer or cloud suppliers such as Amazon Web Services (AWS).

- **Security**—Obviously, anything around the topic of security or breeches in security is included.

- **Social**—Interestingly, we monitored social media for discussions centered around the use or exploitation of social media (for advertising, communication, or brand awareness).

- **Workforce**—Before we started our analysis, a quick look at the Twitter data showed some mentions of the *millennial* workforce, so we added a theme to determine if there was anything of interest around that topic.

- **Design**—IBM has recently published its design thinking language. IBM Design Thinking is a collection of design practices that identify and ideate on the aspects that make a solution desirable to its users. Because the use of Design Thinking from IBM is relatively new, we decided to see if there was any reaction in the marketplace (and specifically at this conference).

In IBM's SMA product, a concept is a topic area that is specific to a particular use case (or in our case, a topic under study). A theme is composed of a group of concepts that describe the theme and are typically analyzed together. In SMA, concepts determine the parts of a document that are extracted from a larger body of information that then forms snippets. A snippet is the specific part of a document (remember the word *document* is used generically here to refer to a blog, website, or any other source of social media input) that matches one or more concepts within a theme. A snippet consists of the sentence that contains the concept *and* the sentences that surround the sentence that contains the concept.

The configuration of a concept specifies the terms that must be included, additional terms that must also appear (to provide context), and terms that must not be included. IBM's Social Media Analytics uses the theme and concept definitions to retrieve the documents and create the snippets.

The creation of themes can be thought of as creating a number of buckets, or categorizations of topics. So if we create a theme of *mobile*, what we have to do is decide what words, when used, are being used in the context of mobile computing. Some of the first words that come to mind are the following:

- iPhone
- iPad
- Samsung
- Android

This is not an exhaustive list of keywords, but it is a set of words or phrases that, when used, probably refers to the theme we have defined.

Up until now, we've tried to stay away from specific screen shots of products, but at this point we decided it might be more beneficial (or meaningful) to show what we mean. For example, Figure A.6 illustrates our first iteration on the definition for the "Design" theme.

Figure A.6 Sample SMA screen to define a theme called "Design."

In this case, we created the theme *Design* (labeled 1 in Figure A.6), and in that theme, two concepts that represent conversations around that theme are defined. As an example, in Figure A.6, we show the concept *Design Thinking*, which captures any social media that's gathered containing terms or phrases related to *design thinking*, which is included in the theme of *design*. Later, we use this to understand the relationships between concepts. (For example, is there a strong relationship between the theme *cloud* and the theme *design thinking*? In other words, when people talk about *cloud*, how much of that conversation is around the use of design thinking to build and support applications in the cloud?)

The section labeled 1 in Figure A.6 shows the text elements that match the keywords specified in section 2. In this case, we were looking for any text that contained the phrase *design thinking*. We also included additional terms such as *UCD* and phrases such as *user centered design* in this grouping. If you recall the value pyramid we introduced in Chapter 2, the idea is to gather as much relevant data as possible to enable the analysis to be more complete. To help with the relevancy, SMA attempts to "look ahead" and provide an example of the type and quantity of text that would match this configuration (section 3 of Figure A.6). Again, in the case of IBM's SMA product, there is a close tie with Boardreader, a third-party social media aggregator, that will source the data for our analysis.

As you can see, we are able to be fairly specific about the phrases and what they do and do *not* contain within the string of text under analysis. For example, consider the tweets in Figure A.7 that are around the word *cloud*. It's clear that they refer to weather or climate, so the use of the "exclude" clause in the example in section 2 of Figure A.6 would be helpful (that is, it must not include any reference to the word *weather*).

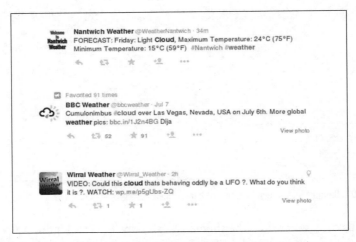

Figure A.7   Sample tweets around *cloud* that refer to weather, not cloud computing.

In our case, we didn't have to worry about this issue too much. Remember, we started with a set of captured data that included the words *IBMAmplify* or *IBM Amplify*, so the assumption we made going into our analysis was that any theme we identified by concept matching would be correct and unambiguous. To put it another way, since the data set refers to IBM and one of its conferences, if the word *cloud* was used, we assumed it referred to cloud computing, or as in the case of Figure A.6, if the phrase was *design thinking*, it was just that—IBM's latest use of the Design Thinking methodology. This relationship between SMA themes/concepts and the keywords is illustrated in Figure A.8.

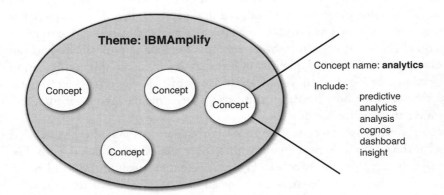

Figure A.8   Relationship between SMA themes/concepts and keywords.

When we build a data model, we start with high-level *themes*, or topics of conversations. Those topics are composed of the ideas or specifics of the conversation—something we call *concepts*. Consider a discussion about cloud computing. While discussing cloud computing, we could focus on the merits of moving or migrating applications to the cloud versus applications that are "born on the cloud." Each of those topics would be considered a *concept* that may be discussed in conversations involving *cloud: migration* or *born on the cloud*.

How people discuss those concepts and what words they use when talking about those concepts are the key words we want to configure into our model. So for a concept like migration, we might look for keywords such as *existing application*, *legacy code*, or *standalone program*, terms that, when used in the context of cloud computing, would imply a migration or movement to the cloud.

Our first model ended up looking something like Table A.1.

Table A.1   First Iteration of IBMAmplify Model

Theme	Concepts
Analytics	#r
	Analysis
	Analyze
	Cognos
	Dashboard
	Insight
	predictive
Cloud	Aws
	Cloud
	softlayer
Customer	B2b
	B2c
	Business to business
	C2b
	Client to business
	Customer

Design	Design Thinking
	Designthinking
Mobile	Android
	Iphone
	Mobile
	Samsung
	Smartphone
	Ipad
Security	Audit
	Hack
	Patch
	Penetrate
	Privacy
	Secure
	Security
	threat
Workforce	Employee
	Millennials
	Millennial
	Training
	Workforce
Social	Collaboration
	Facebook
	Linkedin
	Social
	twitter

Data Analysis

In our data analysis phase, our first inclination was to look at the discussion around CAMSS topics. So after our first analysis was done, we attempted to assess which was the most talked-about topic of the five disciplines (see Figure A.9).

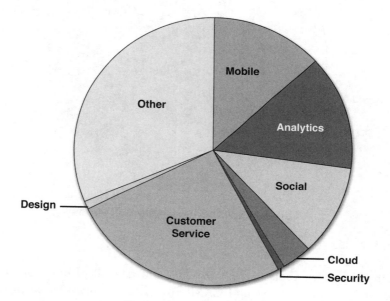

Share of Voice for All Themes

Figure A.9   Share of voice among our themes.

The graph in Figure A.10 shows that *analytics* was the most talked-about topic followed by discussion of *social media* and *mobile solutions*.

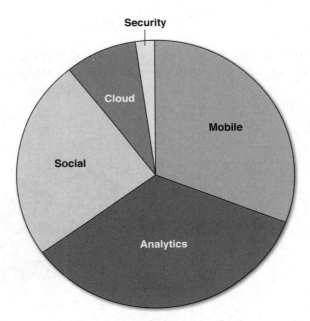

Share of Voice for CAMMS Themes

Figure A.10   Share of voice for CAMSS topics.

However, if we look at the same data and take all of our themes into account, the discussion around CAMSS resulted in only 42% of the total conversations (refer to Figure A.10). Themes around customers and the "other" category (those that didn't fit within our defined themes) accounted for about 58% of our dataset.

We also looked closely for relationships between some of our defined themes (for example, between *mobile* and *analytics*), but we didn't find much in the way of relationships or common discussions. A quick look at the data did seem to show, for example, that at times there was discussion around *Apple* and *mobile* or *Apple* and other topics, so perhaps some of the defined themes and concepts we created were too specific.

One of the more informative tools in IBM's SMA product is the Evolving Topic analysis. An evolving topic is a set of words of phrases that appear in many samples of a dataset and appear to be an active area of conversation (simply due to the number of times the words or phrases are mentioned).

Using the evolving topics graph (see Figure A.11) from our analysis, we can discover new themes or concepts in our dataset that we may not have considered in the creation of our themes/concepts. Looking closely at Figure A.11, we can see there were discussions around *companies* and *commerce* that we hadn't considered, as well as phrases such as *online sales* and *tools* and very little mention of the CAMSS topics we were so actively looking for.

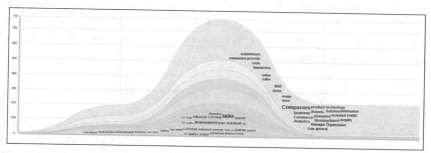

Figure A.11   Evolving topics in the IBM Amplify analysis.

Clearly, we needed to revisit the model.

A Second Attempt at Analyzing the Data

A closer look at the website that announced the conference revealed a number of new areas of interest that could be added to the model. The conference had a number of predetermined tracks that we used as the basis for the model expansion. As a result, we enhanced the model with additional themes that included E-Commerce, Merchandising, Marketing, and Customer Analytics. As we said, our initial focus area was CAMSS (Cloud-Analytics-Mobile-Social-Security) because we wanted to understand the "share of voice" around these areas. This iteration of the model, in which we ended up mixing CAMSS topics with themes highlighted by the conference, created overlaps between our themes. As a result, we lowered the signal, or the strength, of the relationships. We asked our analyst to create a view of the model to separate out only CAMSS topics.

At the same time, when revising our model, we realized that we were narrowing our analysis by insisting that only comments that also referenced *IBMAmplify* be included as part of a theme in our concepts. This is partially an artifact of how IBM's SMA produces what it calls snippets of information to be analyzed. Snippets, which are created at the theme level, consist of a small text segment that surrounds a concept match in a document. As mentioned previously, a snippet consists of a sentence or set of phrases that contains the concept *and* the sentences that surround the sentence that contains the concept. As a result, each snippet can contain more than a single concept.

Inside IBM's SMA, snippets are obtained from various online media sources, such as blogs, discussion forums, and message boards, Twitter, news sites, review sites, and video sites. The content of these sources might be detailed and unstructured, and much of it might be unrelated to the topic of interest. Snippets represent the text segments taken from the documents that are relevant to the theme under analysis.

Information Interpretation

Our new model provided a better representation of the conversations being held at the conference. Even though we abandoned the first data model, much of the earlier analysis shown in Figures A.1 and A.2 is still valid; however, now we can look at them in a more appropriate context. We can see from Figure A.12 that most of the CAMSS topics had a good representation in the discussion, which we had initially assumed would be dominant.

While there appears to be a decent distribution around Mobile, Analytics, eCommerce, Marketing, and Customer Service, some of the lesser-discussed topics were surprisingly around themes such as security and merchandising. Not surprisingly, given the theme of the conference, topics around customer and customer service were strongly represented.

While it's interesting to understand what's on the mind of the attendees, we wanted to dig a little deeper and see if we could find interesting insights or topical areas that might be of interest. One great way to do this is to look at an affinity matrix.

An affinity matrix looks at how closely two dimensions (or attributes) are related to each other. This can help us gain some insight into the strengths or weaknesses of the discussions. It's also a way to identify potential opportunities to discover conversations that we hadn't thought were occurring (or just hadn't considered). According to IBM's documentation, the affinity matrix algorithm in its SMA product estimates how often two dimensions occur together or if they were independent (referenced near each other in the conversation).

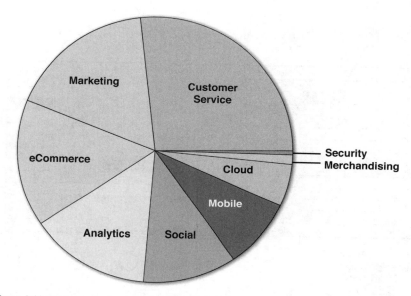

Figure A.12 Breakdown of concepts (discussions) held around IBMAmplify.

In an affinity matrix, we want to look for areas with a high number of references, but areas that also show a high degree of affinity. For example, in Figure A.13, the concepts of *customer* and *customer service* (labeled item 1 in the matrix) have a high number of references (1,210) and a high affinity. That is essentially a false positive, because every time someone uses the term *customer service*, she is by default using the term *customer* as well. Basically, the two words are right next to each other, so the affinity is high.

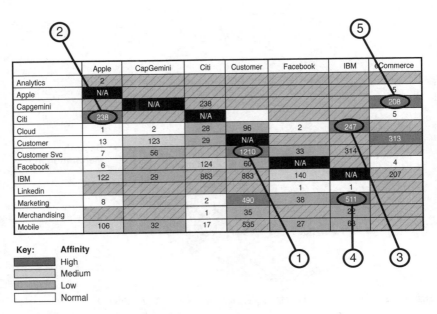

	Apple	CapGemini	Citi	Customer	Facebook	IBM	eCommerce
Analytics	2						
Apple	N/A						5
Capgemini		N/A	238				208
Citi	238		N/A				5
Cloud	1	2	28	96	2	247	
Customer	13	123	29	N/A			313
Customer Svc	7	56		1210	33	314	
Facebook	6		124	60	N/A		4
IBM	122	29	863	883	140	N/A	207
Linkedin					1	1	
Marketing	8		2	490	38	511	
Merchandising			1	35		22	
Mobile	106	32	17	535	27	68	

Key: **Affinity**
High
Medium
Low
Normal

Figure A.13   Affinity matrix for IBMAmplify,

The first thing we noticed was the affinity between *apple* and *citi* (labeled 2 in Figure A.13). We had expected to see *Apple* mentioned more around *mobile* (and indeed there was a higher than normal affinity between *mobile* and *apple,* but not as strong as we expected). While there was a large amount of discussion around IBM and Apple's various partnerships, what stood out in the conversations was how Citibank had created an Apple Watch application, which leveraged IBM's Design Thinking. There were several references to the fact that a number of features were delivered in a relatively short time (crediting design thinking) and pointing to the industry trend of rapid creation of user center applications.

We were not surprised to see the concept (or term) *IBM* used in a high affinity with other terms given this was an IBM-sponsored event. As we said previously, we wanted to be sure to take any trends we uncovered and give more weight to those being discussed by non-IBM employees rather than IBMers.

Right away, we saw *IBM* being referenced with a high affinity to both *cloud* and *marketing* (labeled 3 and 4 in Figure A.13). Again, with the hype around cloud computing and IBM's rich portfolio in this space, this outcome was not surprising. Looking at the data, however, we found a very large set of discussions happening around IBM's latest entry into this market. IBM is moving toward a combination of SaaS/On-Premise offerings, what some would call a "cloud hybrid." Interestingly, many of the attendees were referring to this as *IBM Marketing Cloud.* So again, we saw a high affinity between the terms *IBM* and *Cloud* and *IBM* and *Marketing* (areas 3 and 4 in the affinity matrix in Figure A.13). Clearly, IBM was getting some good coverage of this offering as the data surrounding the topic was fairly overwhelming. As a matter of fact, one of the findings we came up with was to do yet another pass at this model (or perhaps a separate model) looking at just *cloud* and the applications/services around it. We saw references to a wide variety of products and services (products such as Tealeaf or services such analytics and engagement all used in and around the conversations of *cloud*).

Finally, one of the other interesting insights we were able to observe was the frequent association between a company called CapGemini and the topic of *eCommerce* (notice section 5 in Figure A.13). While there were a number of vendors at the conference, it's clear that CapGemini was referenced more than others. This may be an artifact of the company's popularity or its knowledge and use of social media. In any event, most of the discussion around eCommerce was centered around (or had a high affinity) with CapGemini. There was a relatively high affinity between *customer service* and *eCommerce* as well. A quick set of searches revealed deep discussions around CapGemini and comments about presenting flexible presentation layers to customers and intelligent commerce applications. These were all positive comments by or about CapGemini, so clearly this company was standing out in the drive for customer service and eCommerce—a message it made loud and clear !

Conclusions

Like most of the analysis we do, we tend to end up with more questions than answers as we dig deeper into the results. This isn't a bad thing, but you have to remember that at some point, the analysis has to end. For example, as we said earlier, there was interesting discussion around *cloud,* and perhaps a deeper dive into the topic would reveal richer insights into the use and needs of cloud adopters. However, once we find that, will we find there is a whole subconversation around *cloud* and some other topic? The permutations can go on forever.

With this simple analysis, we chose to get an overall understanding of the various themes of conversation. We're happy with the results. In summary, we saw that many of the CAMSS themes are still alive and well in the hearts and minds of many. What was surprising about those conversations was the noted lack of discussion around security. Again, we want to be cautious about drawing far-reaching conclusions about lack of concern because perhaps this audience wasn't focused on security but rather engagement with customers. However, given the strong affinity around Apple/Citi and the latest mobile banking application, there may be cause for caution or additional investigation.

If we had to sum up the major theme of discussion, we would say it was discussion around customer engagement (service) for the mobile space as well as what seems like a strong desire on the part of many of the attendees to investigate the hybrid cloud model (as opposed to a public cloud). Note that we said "investigate" because there was quite a bit of discussion and excitement around the topic, but no definitive talk about moving to it.

Index